MEATPACKING AMERICA

MEATPACKING AMERICA

HOW MIGRATION, WORK, AND FAITH UNITE AND DIVIDE THE HEARTLAND

Kristy Nabhan-Warren

The University of North Carolina Press
Chapel Hill

Designed by April Leidig
Set in Arno by Copperline Book Services, Inc.
Manufactured in the United States of America

The University of North Carolina Press has been a
member of the Green Press Initiative since 2003.

Cover photograph by Kristy Nabhan-Warren

Library of Congress Cataloging-in-Publication Data
Names: Nabhan-Warren, Kristy, author.
Title: Meatpacking America : how migration, work, and faith unite and
    divide the heartland / Kristy Nabhan-Warren.
Description: Chapel Hill : The University of North Carolina Press, 2021. |
    Includes bibliographical references and index.
Identifiers: LCCN 2021003645 | ISBN 9781469663487 (cloth ; alk. paper) |
    ISBN 9781469663494 (paperback ; alk. paper) | ISBN 9781469663500 (ebook)
Subjects: LCSH: Immigrants—Religious life—West North Central States. |
    Americans—Religious life—West North Central States. | West North
    Central States—Social life and customs—21st century. | West North Central
    States—Religious life and customs—21st century. | West North Central
    States—Economic conditions—21st century. | West North Central States—
    Race relations.
Classification: LCC F355 .N33 2021 | DDC 305.800977—dc23
LC record available at https://lccn.loc.gov/2021003645

For Steve

CONTENTS

List of Illustrations ix

Preface xi

Introduction.
Rosa: Journeying to the Dream 1

1 Homemaking 11

2 Rural Faith Encounters 47

3 Snapshots of Rural Priests 73

4 The Work of God and Hogs 89

5 Cattle: Steered by Faith 135

6 In the Belly of the Beast 171

7 Fulfilling Dreams 195

8 Reyna: Staying for the Dream 209

Acknowledgments 219

Notes 225

Index 243

ILLUSTRATIONS

Corinne and Urban Hargrafen, 1947. 16

Urban and Jean Hargrafen, 1949. 18

Lois and Tim Mincks, 1983. 42

Alternative to the traditional "Just Married" sign. 42

Hargrafen family birthday celebration, 1957. 44

Father Joseph Sia, 2017. 49

Rural Iowa CAFO, 2020. 59

Downtown Columbus Junction. 91

Tyson, Columbus Junction. 96

Maurice Batubenga, Tyson employee, 2017. 119

Virgin of Guadalupe celebration at St. Joseph parish,
Columbus Junction, 2017. 126

Iowa Premium Beef, Tama, Iowa, 2020. 139

PREFACE

THE PLACE WHERE I LIVE AND WORK—and where thousands of refugees have journeyed to since the early 1970s—is the Corn Belt state of Iowa.[1] Word has spread among women and men fleeing violence and instability in their home countries that this midwestern state is a beautiful, safe, and affordable place to live where jobs in meatpacking and agriculture are plentiful. As a person born and raised in the Midwest whose livelihood is based on studying and teaching about American religion and culture, I have had the privilege and pleasure of diving into the realities of the newest waves of migration in this part of the country. I have conducted research in my backyard, so to speak, and have spent a lot of time talking with refugees and white Iowans alike in order to see what we can learn about America and its place in the world by centering the nation's Corn Belt. The result of the research is this book, *Meatpacking America*, which aims to tell a complicated and dynamic story of native-born Iowans and more recent arrivals to Iowa and the larger Corn Belt.[2] The elements that drive this story of disparate native-born Iowans and newer arrivals, I argue, are the conjoined passions of religious faith and desire to work hard for one's children and grandchildren in order to achieve a slice of heaven on earth.

What I have discovered complicates many of the stories we tell each other and that the news typically reports. Certainly, the United States, like many nations today, is deeply divided in regard to how migrants—asylum seekers/asylees, refugees, and economic migrants alike—are viewed and treated. U.S. immigration law is complicated and confusing, and it confers a certain legal status and privileges to "refugees" not given to "asylum seekers" and "economic migrants." Yet the reality is that there is a lot of overlap in the experiences of the women and men who are fleeing their home countries. Legally designated refugees receive preferred treatment, and in accordance with U.S. immigration law, they are granted a special immigration status as a group. Refugees must apply for lawful permanent resident status—or their green card—one year after being admitted to the United States and are eligible for U.S. citizenship within five years. Asylum-seekers/asylees—people who do not technically fit the U.S. definition of "refugee status" but who are fleeing violence and instability in their home countries—become eligible to adjust to lawful permanent resident status after one year of residence.

While the list of designated refugee nations is ever-shifting, the countries with the highest number of refugees in the United States include the Democratic Republic of the Congo (DRC), Burma, Ukraine, Bhutan, Eritrea, Afghanistan, Pakistan, Russia, and Ethiopia. In the state of Iowa, where about 1 percent of official U.S. refugees settle, refugees hail from Burma, the DRC, Bhutan, Syria, Somalia, and Sudan. In recent years, Iowa, like many states, has increasingly become home for hundreds if not thousands of asylum seekers from the countries of Central America's Northern Triangle—Guatemala, El Salvador, and Honduras—considered one of the most dangerous areas to live in the world but not officially designated by the United States as refugee nations. Asylum seekers from the Northern Triangle are currently sent back to Guatemala, to the dangerous, unstable conditions that forced them to flee in the first place.[3]

Since the passage of the Refugee Act of 1980, the numbers of legally sanctioned refugees admitted into the United States has dropped precipitously—from 200,000 to 22,500 in 2018.[4] Yet the number of asylum seekers and economic migrants fleeing violence and the related political and economic instability continues to rise; the United States sees in particular women and children from Central America's Northern Triangle.[5] In the United States and Corn Belt states, Sudanese and Congolese, officially granted refugee status, and Central Americans, officially considered economic migrants and asylum seekers, all want better lives for their children. All of these women, men, and children are refugees and are seeking refuge in the United States from the economic, political, and physical violence that harmed them in their countries. They find their way to midwestern states like Iowa, where expansive land, jobs, and safety for their children beckon.

In *Meatpacking America,* I refer to *all* of the brown and Black women and men who come to America for a better life as refugees, whether or not they have officially been granted the status of refugee by the U.S. government. The reality is that all of these women and men—all of them—are fleeing violence of some sort and yearn to live, work, and raise their families in peace. The parsing of their experiences and circumstances by U.S. immigration law operates at the whims of those in charge of government and as such is a flawed, inadequate system. The women and men whose stories fill the pages of this book have suffered greatly and are victims of every sort of violence imaginable. These are women who have been raped by authority figures in their homes and abused by their husbands who have threatened to kill them.

These are children who are stalked and recruited by violent gangs and families who are starving because there are no jobs available. These are men who cannot find work and who refuse to work for gangs. I want to make it crystal clear for the reader that the women, men, and children I have spent time with for the research and writing of this book did not simply want to leave their home countries—they had to or they would die. All of the migrants in this book have sought safety from persecution based on their religion, race, gender, nationality, politics, or social group, whether they meet the official U.S. designation as a refugee or not. They are all de facto, if not de jure, refugees.

The Corn Belt state of Iowa has a unique history of welcoming refugees. Republican governor Robert Ray advocated for group resettlement and refugee status for the Vietnamese Tai Dam "Boat People" in the mid-1970s, the only U.S. governor to take such action.[6] Executive approval from President Gerald Ford for Tai Dam resettlement in Iowa paved the way for an increased cap in the number of refugees to the United States and for the President Carter–penned Refugee Act of 1980. Ray, with the support of hundreds of Iowans, established the humanitarian Iowa SHARES program (standing for Iowa Sends Help to Aid Refugees and End Starvation) and during his five-term governorship put Iowa on the map as a state where politicians, residents, and religious organizations could come together to support asylum seekers and refugees.

When we fast-forward to today's U.S. political climate, it is difficult to imagine politicians and regular citizens coming together to support broad, migration-related initiatives. A cursory glance at social media sites seems to unearth more discord than accord. Yet what I have discovered in the course of researching small towns that dot the rural Iowa landscape is a more nuanced story. Towns like Columbus Junction, which has one school and a meatpacking plant that employs the majority of working adults in the area, and West Liberty, the first Latino-majority town in the state, show that proximity to new neighbors, shared social spaces, and small-town pride bring people together. Meta-level political anti-migrant/refugee sentiments are more difficult to maintain when the best friend of one's child is a refugee. Resentments against "immigrants" soften when residents see how hard their neighbors work and how loving they are toward their children and grandchildren. Spending time in the Corn Belt challenges easy "hot takes" assumptions about white-refugee relations that we find in the media, and to make our way to a more measured perspective, we must dive into rural communities in states like Iowa.

When we take the time to dig beneath what is trending on the news and social media, we can discover what is really going on—and find that it is more layered and far more interesting than what we typically see and hear. Without meaning to sound trite, the story is complicated—and in a nuanced and gripping way that belies social media rancor and discord. As the midwestern author Sarah Smarsh has recently claimed, "Something special is happening in rural America."[7] My research supports Smarsh's claim, and this book will show that the Midwest, in particular the Corn Belt, is a much more interesting, edgy, and forward-looking space than we have been led to believe. This book aims to explain the realities found in Iowa and the American Corn Belt, and perhaps even in the United States at large, and where we stand on issues of migration, work, and faith. The overarching goal of this book is to complicate narratives and tropes of people and places that we have taken for granted as truths.

One of the best places to see and experience what is really happening on the ground regarding migration, work, and religion today is in the Corn Belt. It is in this expansive geography, a vast and mostly rural swath of the larger Midwest dotted with farms, confined animal feeding operations (CAFOs), and meatpacking plants, that we are able to get a better understanding of how religious culture works in America. The quotidian realities of life in the Corn Belt involve intercultural, inter-linguistic, and interreligious exchanges. And many native-born Iowans, I have found, are willing to do the work of investing in a more open and diverse state and nation. Religion interacts dynamically with work and migrant status among both migrants themselves and the native-born Iowans who are their neighbors, fellow worshippers, and employers.

Like Governor Ray and many Iowans in the late 1970s, many native-born Americans in today's midwestern Corn Belt are drawing on their religious faith, wrestling with their privilege, and doing the hard work of introspection and self-examination. This is not to say that anti-immigrant sentiment is nonexistent but that the story of race relations in the Midwest and Corn Belt is more complex than we oftentimes portray it. In her book *Heartland*, Sarah Smarsh writes of the demographic shift from white to Latino in the Midwest: "That's a demographic shift not without tensions, but one that has been embraced by some small-town whites, who knew their home must change to survive. As Europeans who moved west and built sod houses on the prairie learned, you either work together or starve alone."[8] What Smarsh points to here is the necessity of crossing political, cultural, and even religious lines to work toward a common cause: maintaining a viable community. My research for *Meatpacking America* corroborates this assertion that necessity can overwhelm feelings and thus complicates easy tropes we have created about white rural, midwestern Americans.

This book tells a "but-and" story—that is, ethnocentrism and anti-immigrant sentiments are deeply engrained in the warp and weft of life in America, yet how people act and what they do belie the entanglements of racism and its twin, ethnocentrism. What I saw in my seven years' worth of fieldwork in rural Iowa and small towns is that people are complicated and can act in contradictory ways. The reality is that it is much more difficult to hate and dismiss women and men with whom you work and worship and whose children attend the same school as your own children and grandchildren. For native-born and recent arrivals to Iowa, their houses of worship are sanctuaries in a world that is unpredictable and hard. For native-born Iowans, churches became sanctuaries during and after the farm crisis of the 1980s, and for newer arrivals, church becomes a safe harbor, a home where community and safety are possible.[9]

And so in this book, I put the spotlight on two groups of people who are dealing with profound transformations in American society. One group is made up of the refugee women, men, and their children who have migrated and settled and who persist, despite many odds, in making lives for themselves in the midwestern Corn Belt. They have generously shared with me, in firsthand conversations, the stories of their lives. The reader will learn from them why they came to the United States and why they endure against incredible odds. The other group whose stories are vital to the telling of a narrative of the Corn Belt and the intersections of religion, work, and migration include people who have been overlooked and stereotyped by mainline media: white Iowans. In the pages that follow, I aim to portray them as I experienced them—American citizens who for the most part want to be open and welcoming to recent refugees but who struggle with how to best show support for these newcomers in the midst of a climate of fear that has overtaken wide swaths of their communities and nation.

The specter in all of this is white racism, whites' vexed understandings of white privilege and race in America. What I encountered in my ethnographic fieldwork was the sticky wicket of whiteness. The whites I interviewed struggle with their towns' changed and changing demographics. They know intellectually and from experience that their towns were once crumbling and that they are now doing much better, thanks to refugees' substantial economic contributions. They tolerate, and even accept, the presence of refugees in their communities because refugees' labor has kept them alive. Yet they struggle with this major change and the "browning" of their towns and state. They miss their downtowns being all-white, and it is discomforting for them to think about this. Many rural whites are sorting through their complex feelings about refugees. They experience the thriving downtowns and smell the delicious foods that weren't there before, and they see how hard refugees work, which reminds them of their own families' work ethic. They pass by the carefully maintained yards, cars, and homes. But at the same time, many white rural Americans wish things could be what they imagine as "the way they were before"—white and predictable. The complication of white rural America is a longing for whiteness/sameness mixed with an appreciation of the increased diversity in their towns and the new friendships they have made. Yes, the problem of whiteness is racism, a belief that whiteness is superior. It is a racism that points to the cognitive dissonance most white Americans live with and within. Yet what I have discovered in the course of my research is that many white rural Americans have varying degrees of awareness of their racism and complicity in structures that have privileged them since birth. *Meatpacking America* is a book that tries to understand where these Americans are coming from, to paint a more complete portrait of them. It does not privilege their experiences or perspectives, but it does attempt to provide a more in-depth look at them.

To be clear, the majority of white Iowans I interviewed and spent time with supported Donald Trump in the 2016 election, and as of this writing, many still do. Many midwesterners have voted for politicians who espouse hateful rhetoric, but on the ground, these same men and women, I have found, are not the angry white racists that their votes would suggest. Many lean more toward the centrist governor Robert Ray of the past—what some might call "Bob Dole Republicanism" of the late twentieth century—than the current non-centrist Republican Party and its policies. What many of them are struggling with is how to reconcile the anti-immigrant vitriol associated with the Trump White House with the families they attend church with and whom they see working hard to raise their families—families whose values certainly seem to be in sync with their own. We find barriers to forming relationships as much as we find friendships that are forged, however tentatively. What I have discovered is that while a lot of whites may want to work on their prejudices, they are hard to let go of and hamper their progress. Other whites, particularly those who work and pray alongside refugees, can find common ground with their coworkers and parishioners and are able to break down the cultural barriers they have been raised to observe.

What Trump did very well before his 2016 election was to tap into white Americans' fears and also their hopes for a more robust farm economy. Since the farm crisis of the 1980s, these individuals and communities have endured hardship and struggles and have been let down by U.S. policies that have continued to offer their elusive support but have largely failed rural America. As Market to Market researchers explain, "Though barely remembered by much of the urban population, painful recollections of the worst economic downturn since the Great Depression are seared into the memories of many rural Americans, as the combination of too much debt, slumping commodity prices and ill-advised government policies created a perfect storm that came to be known as the farm crisis of the 1980s."[10] Disillusioned with Carter and devastated by executive orders and federal policies, midwesterners moved toward Reagan Republicanism and have stayed mostly Republican since the 1980s.

Fast-forward to today. Optimism still beckons, as many of the farmers and rural white Americans who voted for Trump in 2016 had earlier voted for President Barack Obama, believing that he would do something about their economic hardships and challenges. Their seemingly radical shift in voting pattern is typical of a "purple" state like Iowa. Yet unfortunately, Trump's policies for farmers have actually made their lives worse as trade wars with China gutted hog prices and demanded and levied tariffs on rural American commodities like corn, hogs, and cattle.[11]

These are the very commodities that Corn Belt refugees and economic migrants have come to depend upon for their own livelihoods. And indeed, refugees and migrants themselves are treated as commodities by employers and white native-born Americans—as bodies that can be used for work and production. And these same workers are employed by the Big Agriculture industries, the ones that have benefitted most recently from the Market Facilitation Program, which has favored Big Agriculture and the related protein industries and has hurt small farmers and producers.[12]

When we examine what is happening on the ground, white employers and immigrant/refugee workers alike are trapped within a system of neoliberal exchanges that leaves them mutually dependent yet unequal in status. Yet I have seen firsthand ways that whites attempt to level the playing field and provide opportunities for nonwhite workers to advance in the workplace. While the system may not be set up to the workers' advantage, workplaces are dynamic sites for cultural exchanges and are spaces where religion is invoked by employers and employees alike to provide strength and courage. My research uncovered that there are white employers who feel morally obligated to care for their mostly refugee workers, and the workers themselves turn to faith to give them strength to persevere through difficult and dangerous jobs as well as to provide deep meaning to the work that they do. For both groups, work takes on sacred meanings.

Small-town, rural people in the Midwest have a more nuanced understanding of immigrants and refugees than coastal and urban Americans give them credit for. In small towns and rural hamlets, people interact daily in profound ways. If there is one school, one factory, one church, then the reality of intercultural existence is a deeply felt and lived experience with the "other." What I have also found is that small-town living is anything but small—it is big, big in the sense that these small-town and rural women and men work with and live among refugees and migrants in ways that urbanites cannot comprehend, given the segregated realities of urban living. In Iowa, towns like West Liberty, Columbus Junction, Washington, Ottumwa, Marshalltown, and Tama are places where white Americans interact daily with refugees from around the globe—at the local school, at Walmart, and at church. And it is in the pulpits of the many Corn Belt churches that pastors and preachers encourage their flocks to reach out to their neighbors to welcome them. The CEOs and CFOs of Iowa companies and businesses like Tyson and Iowa Premium Beef draw upon their Christian beliefs and the language of faith and morals, believing that they have a duty to watch over their workers. Some even consider the work and production sacred rituals.

We find religion at work in fascinating ways in the packing plants that dot the rural landscape of Iowa and provide jobs for small-town inhabitants. Religion appears in the workplace language of the CEOs, CFOs, and human resource management. It is visible on the line, worn on workers' bodies, discussed during breaks, and experienced in the locker rooms. It gives the women and men who work on the line the belief that the gritty, difficult work they are doing has a deeper meaning and purpose. Working in the plants pushes one's faith to the limits. It is in the sacred blood of the sacrificed animals. The intensive process of intake, slaughter, and dissection of animals' bodies is itself a ritual process. The places where refugees work are dynamic sites of intercultural, religious, and linguistic exchanges and are key sites of religion in the United States today. This is a book about the work of faith in the heartland, and while faith is nurtured in houses of worship, it is put to the test in visceral ways in the sanctified, bloody packing plants in the Corn Belt.

If we want to truly grasp the dynamics and the complex lives of migrants and refugees in America today, if we want to understand the days that they experience, then we must look inside the meatpacking industry. We must walk in their shoes—in this case, steel-toed, company-issued rubber boots. We need to get a little bloody. As part of the research for this book, I did get bloody and will take the reader through a day in the life of a packing plant worker. If we want to understand rural America and the lives of middle-class Americans, then we must study the meatpacking industry. The larger "protein industry," as it is called by insiders, is a business that employees thousands of women and men across the United States, folks who work incredibly hard to pay the bills, save up for their kids' and grandkids' college, and perhaps even buy a few small luxury items for themselves, like cigarettes, Coca-Cola, or colorful bandannas to wear under their helmet.

As an ethnographer of religion, I am drawn to people's stories of faith and place. Ethnographers embrace being and feeling uncomfortable and seek to make sense of it all. My academic work has always been inspired by and situated within the communities in which I live. I am a white woman of Lebanese, Swedish, and Polish ancestry, and my roots are in working-class, urban northwest Indiana. No doubt my whiteness has aided my research and has granted me access to people and places that I might not have seen or had access to if I were not white. And because I am from a family of blue-collar workers, the children and grandchildren of immigrants who worked hard for the necessities and who were lucky when they had funds for the extras, I could draw on my own familial experiences with my interlocutors when we talked. Work and faith were nodes of connectivity. Like my white and refugee interviewees' faith, my family's faith—Catholic and Lutheran—helped get them through the hard times. Churches were sanctuaries and beacons of hope. Like the women and men I spent time with for this book—white, brown, and Black—members of my nuclear and extended family have worried about how all of the bills would get paid. The research process for this book was difficult; it unearthed feelings of white privilege as well as the specter of economic precarity that dogged my childhood. I was inspired by many of these individuals and their stories of perseverance and endurance, and I hope that my admiration for the individuals I encountered comes through in the following. Yet this admiration does not mean that I am letting folks off the hook, so to speak. I call attention to the entangled problematics of Big Agriculture in the post-NAFTA era, migration policies, and the limitations of religion in the workplace.

As my cousin Gary Paul Nabhan, an ethnobotanist, has often said to me, it is important to do ethnography in our own backyards, because there is always a story there to tell. Gary was one of the first to convince me that there was something important happening right here in Iowa—right next door. And what I discovered, with the encouragement of my friend and key interlocutor Father Joseph Sia, was that the story I set out to tell—initially one focused exclusively on Catholicism in Iowa—became a much bigger project as I met and interviewed Latino refugees and later African refugees from Eastern and Central Africa who talked a lot about their work and their pride in it. It was Father Joseph who encouraged me to go to the places where the majority of his parishioners were employed—the Tyson hog processing plant in Columbus Junction, Iowa. I followed Father Joseph's advice and conducted research at Tyson and later at another packing plant in Iowa that employs African and Latino refugees, Iowa Premium Beef, in order to understand more fully the lives of the women and men who took precious time out of their busy lives to talk to me.

This is a book that started out as focused on white Catholics and Latino Catholics and became a more layered and complex story of women and men seeking refuge in Iowa and for whom their workplaces and houses of worship became the central places in their lives. While the majority of my interlocutors identify as Catholic Christians, some identify with nondenominational Christian churches, some as Kingdom Hall Jehovah's Witnesses, and some as Methodist, and a small number are nonreligious/nonaffiliated families.

Between 2013 and 2019, I interviewed over one hundred women and men for this book: white American-born citizens (40) as well as people from Central America (Guatemala, El Salvador, Honduras, and Mexico) (45), the Democratic Republic of the Congo (15), the Republic of South Africa (3), the Philippines (2), Vietnam (4), Cambodia, and Burma/Myanmar (2). I told all individuals formally interviewed and with whom I had more casual conversations that I was working on a book on work, immigration, and faith in the Corn Belt region. I also let the interviewees know that the research was officially approved by the University of Iowa's Institutional Research Board. Some of the interviews were formal and prearranged conversations, mediated by one of the priests with whom I was working or by a friend of the interviewee. I met many of the women and men whom I interviewed and spent time with through the "snowball method," where one interview leads to the next via word-of-mouth or by being recommended by one individual or family to another. Some of the interviews and conversations lasted just a half hour, while others lasted several hours. Some of the interviews were with small groups of refugees.

The majority of the interviews and conversations were one-on-one; others were small group interviews and conversations. With the latter, small groups of women and men met with me in church basements and coffeehouses to talk. The interviews and more casual conversations occurred in a variety of places throughout the state of Iowa, including Catholic churches, street festivals, grocery stores, coffeehouses, restaurants, private homes, and parks. The interviews and conversations with white native-born American women and men were conducted in English. The interviews and conversations with Latinos were conducted in Spanish, English, and "Spanglish," according to the interviewee's preference. All of the individuals quoted and paraphrased in this book have given oral or written consent to be quoted. I have changed the names of undocumented and asylum-seeking women and men to safeguard their identities. These are vulnerable individuals who are at risk of being deported and whose families have been and may be torn apart yet again. Documented citizens and refugees gave me permission to use their names and want their stories told to draw attention to their experiences and challenges.

Finally, as a scholar who has written about Catholicism for much of my career and who holds a Catholic studies position at my university, I am committed to bringing forward American Catholic stories with broader themes in American life and culture—because U.S. Catholicism, as with all faiths and traditions, does not exist in a cultural, linguistic, or national vacuum. The research I conducted for this book shows how for white Americans and more recent arrivals alike, religion and religious places can provide sanctuary from a world that is unpredictable and frightening. And other spaces, like workplaces, can become sacralized as part of individuals' profound need to make profane places meaningful and sacred. Slaughterhouses are such places. And for the most vulnerable people of all, refugees fleeing political, religious, sexual, and economic violence, the workplace can indeed become a place of predictability, safety, and meaning. Work—even the most dangerous work—can become a haven of meaning-making and even sacredness. Work in dangerous places like slaughterhouses puts faith to the test, and religion is lived in packinghouses. For many of the women and men who work in the line, God/Virgin Mary/Jesus/Jehovah/Allah watches over them. And as work can become a hub of myths, rituals, and symbols that provide meaning to individuals and their families' lives, the dreams that refugees came to discover seem like they just might be possible to achieve.

This is a book about making a life and building community and about how no one feels completely at home in rural America. For whites, the state has changed so much: demographics, closed churches, new industries. For the

MEATPACKING AMERICA

Rosa

JOURNEYING TO THE DREAM

I T HAD BEEN A LONG, arduous journey from her village in central Mexico. As Rosa crossed the Rio Grande with her baby girl on her back, sleepily cocooned in the rebozo—the brightly colored shawl—given to her by her mother, she reflexively clutched the tarnished silver medallion she wore around her neck of the Virgin of Guadalupe her mother had also given to her years earlier to keep her safe. "La Virgen, I promise to provide a safe home for my child and future children if you help me cross over to be with my husband, who is working in the fields of *el medio-oeste*," she prayed. Aided by a coyote who led her and a small group of migrants to Ciudad Juárez and then across the border to the United States, Rosa was worried, as she knew that without papers, *la migra* could stop her at any time. And although the coyote was highly recommended, one couldn't be sure of a successful or safe journey. But life, Rosa thought as she walked, was about taking risks—risks to make a better life for herself and her baby. Poverty and lack of opportunities for herself and her child, coupled with increasingly erratic local gangs, propelled her to leave her native land. Her husband Juan had crossed over a year before and had secured good work and a new casa for them in which to live in a place called Iowa, a land of green fields and wide-open skies. Rosa missed her beloved and prayed to the Virgen María, the Blessed Mother of Jesús, Queen of Heaven and most perfect of women, to stay by her side and to watch over her and baby Catalina, "Cati."

Rosa's petitions and prayers were answered by her beloved María. She and Cati made it to the designated safe house somewhere on the U.S.-Mexico border. It was impossible to tell where they were, as it was dark and no one talked. The smell of fear, mixed with hesitant relief, was palpable. You could just taste it, a *mezcla* of desert mesquite, sweat from the journey, the sun, and a hint of sweetness from agave nectar. Just enough to make you think that life was going to get better. She felt as though her body was a cocktail of emotions, bottled up and ready to explode. The next morning Rosa was given a plate of beans and rice and a stale tortilla, and she and her baby, along with a small huddle of about a dozen other waiting migrants, were picked up by a hot, windowless van that transported them to a place Rosa had only dreamed about. For the past year she had imagined being reunited with her husband to make a home, *el hogar*, in los Estados Unidos. Juan had crossed over a year and a half earlier and had been working as a farmhand to earn money to bring his wife and child over.

The drive in the van was long, but it was difficult to tell exactly how long. They stopped a few times to relieve themselves on the side of the road, the driver supplying them with tissue paper and a garbage bag and a squirt of hand sanitizer that had an alcohol-y smell to it. As she nursed and rocked her baby, trying to stay cool and drinking water from her canteen sparingly, Rosa prayed again. The inside of the van was hot, and she gently fanned her baby. She tried to stay strong for her little girl and kept thinking of why she was taking this dangerous journey to El Norte: it was to give Cati a better life. She repeated it as a mantra in her mind, over and over, "Es para Cati, es para Cati . . ." As fear mixed with hope flooded her mind, Rosa made another *promesa* to the Virgin. Rosa prayed to her Blessed Mother that if she continued to watch over her and Cati, she would build a small shrine in her yard with her husband in Iowa where she believed . . . she hoped . . . she was traveling. Rosa thought of the flowers she would plant and the candles she would light in honor of the Virgin Mary. She felt more at peace, but as she looked down at Cati's sweat-dotted brow, she worried.

Finally, after many hours, they arrived. When they tumbled out of the van in rural eastern Iowa, the first thing that Rosa did before embracing Juan was to kiss the ground. It was green like her home village in the state of Guerrero, Mexico. When she smelled the air around her, it smelled like corn and beans—like home. Her chest heaved with relief, and she wept out of relief and gratitude. She knew, with every fiber of her being, that it was la Virgen de Guadalupe, María, who had watched over her and Cati. And as she ran to Juan's open arms, sobbing and exhaling, she knew she was home. Home was where Juan and Cati were, and home was here in the U.S. Midwest. And María, well, she would be with her wherever she went. Rosa decided right there and then that she would never take off her medallion of María, her lucky, holy amulet. María had watched over her and Cati and had brought them to their home.

Migration, Work, and Faith / *Migración, Trabajo, y Fé*

This is Rosa's story. Rosa is one of the many refugees I talked with over a period of six years.[1] While the name I've given her here is a pseudonym because of her undocumented status, Rosa is a real person, and her arduous journey was real too. Rosa's exhausting trek to her husband and new home had a happy outcome. Yet as the anthropologist Shannon Speed has shown, women from Central America and Mexico seeking refuge tend to not have happy endings. Their stories are full of devastation and heartbreak. Physical, emotional, and sexual violence abounds in the stories of asylum-seeking Central American and Mexican refugees, and women are especially vulnerable.[2] Vulnerability, as Speed writes, is not an "inherent characteristic" of these women but rather "one imposed in multiple, intersecting ways as power is deployed in the world."[3] This book amplifies those who have been made vulnerable by the settler-capitalist state, women and men who are, in Speed's words, "vulneradas."[4]

A goal of mine for this book is to amplify the voices of the women and men I have spent time with and whose personal stories shed light on big issues for our nation and the world. Rural Iowa, Rosa's final destination, is a global hub of food production, and Rosa and her husband perform labor that feeds not only U.S. women and men but people around the world. The Central American migrants, African and Asian refugees, economic migrants, religious leaders, and white CEOs of meatpacking plants whose stories fill the pages of this book all have something important to teach us. Collectively and individually, their lived experiences offer insights into the complexities of immigration, the deep-seated desire to work, and the role of faith and provide a wellspring of hope in the midst of struggle. Like Rosa, the women and men in this book are trying to live their lives to the fullest.[5]

As the native Iowan and Pulitzer Prize–winning journalist Art Cullen has shown in his careful and nuanced reporting, rural and small-town midwestern America is an ideal place to go to understand the complexities of migration, work, and faith in the United States.[6] Why? Because rural America is home to an ever-widening diversity of peoples and cultures from all over the globe who come for jobs, a low cost of living, and family. And rural America is home to Big Agriculture and meatpacking, the primary employers of immigrant labor in today's America. Immigrants in Iowa, Kansas, Nebraska, and

Illinois are literally feeding the world. It is only by conducting on-the-ground fieldwork in rural states such as Iowa and the broader Corn Belt that we can get a handle on the ever-shifting ethnic, racial, religious, and work dynamics in the United States.

Meatpacking America has national and global resonance. By revealing how residents of Iowa, and of the region interchangeably called the "Midwest" and the "heartland," live out the challenges and opportunities of everyday life, this book clearly illuminates the broader trends that link the United States transnationally with the Americas. The patterns that connect Iowa, the Corn Belt, and the United States to Central and South America include migration, relocation, and settlement. As I wrapped up this book, the coronavirus, COVID-19, was exposing our interconnectedness as global citizens and consumers. Here in Iowa, a key player in the protein industry, corporations like Tyson have been closely monitoring the health of their workers, extending medical benefits, and making sure consumers know the meat is safe for consumption.[7] Some of the individuals who are most vulnerable to the virus and its effects are the working poor, wage laborers who kill, process, and package the meat that is consumed by the rest of us.

In shining a light on those who have come to Iowa, I saw up close how the Corn Belt can be both an alienating and inhospitable place and a welcoming place. I spent more than six years in what the anthropologist Renato Rosaldo has called "deep hanging out" with Iowans in places that matter to them. I had many cups of coffee and home-baked pastries in white native-born Iowans' homes and talked with them at coffeehouses, churches, and community centers. I visited Iowa meatpacking plants and Iowa farms where Latino and African refugees from around the world work. I spent time at Iowa Catholic parishes, in agricultural fields, and at a host of community organizations. I interviewed and talked more informally with over a hundred native-born Iowa citizens and refugees from many global locales. The women and men whose stories fill the pages of this book all care deeply about their families and communities, and they draw on their religious faith and spirituality for strength to get through the hard times.

What we are seeing and hearing right now in Iowa, the Midwest, and the United States more broadly is a debate about migration and who "belongs" in our country and more locally in our cities and towns. In rural America, residents see themselves, as the sociologist of religion Robert Wuthnow has eloquently pointed out, as living in moral communities, places where they feel a deep sense of belonging: "a specialized sense of place to which and in which people feel an obligation to one another and to support their feelings of being at home and doing the right things."[8]

In rural and small-town America, we see Latino and African refugees working jobs that few white Iowans would want or even could perform, given the intensely physical and bloody nature of the work. We see firsthand how religious leaders and activists are reaching out to assist newcomers to their parishes, churches, and communities. And we also see how sometimes these newcomers are shunned and rejected. I have come away from these intense, oftentimes deeply emotional ethnographic encounters in cafés, church basements, farm fields, and packing plants across the Hawkeye State absolutely convinced that if we want to understand the immigration debates going on in America today, then we must travel to places where folks are working things out—making missteps, but trying nonetheless. And what I have discovered in the course of doing research for this book is that religion plays an important role in how white Iowans and Latino and African refugees alike manage the shifting dynamics of life in America. The moral compass that women and men derive from their involvement in their churches carries over to the workplace and to places where they encounter each other.

Latinos and other refugees tend to work for white Americans and draw upon their religious convictions to successfully navigate and sacralize work. How do they get through a grueling and bloody shift of cutting, packaging, and cleaning up after slaughtered animals? By turning to their faith in God and in the idea that a divine power has a plan for them and their family. That a divine power is watching over them when they are hard at work and when they are driving home after a long shift, exhausted, to be with their family. And for white Iowans, they are challenged to abide by the tenets of their religious faith and to demonstrate it with more recent newcomers to America who are chasing dreams that are similar to their own.

Places of worship are important sites, as we know, for demonstrating beliefs and for reaffirming religious identities. But average people spend a small fraction of their weekly time in houses of worship compared with the forty, fifty, even sixty hours a week they spend at their workplace. What I have discovered in the course of this research is that workplaces such as pork and beef slaughterhouses and processing plants are important sites for relaying religiosity—what matters on a deep level—for women and men. While churches, mosques, and temples tend to be considered the primary places where people practice their faith in the United States, they are not the only places. Indeed, many studies show that their status as the center of religiosity in the United States is one place among many, rather than the central place of religious and spiritual gathering, and there is a growing interest in the study of religion at work and the religiosity of workplaces. Recent years have seen several excellent studies on the Christianization of workplaces and capitalism. American historian Bethany Moreton, in her *To Serve God and Wal-Mart: The Making of Christian Free Enterprise*, critically examines the global megacorporation and its touted and copied Christian corporate culture of capitalistic service. Nicole Kirk's *Wannamaker's Temple: The Business of Religion in an Iconic Department Store* shows how Christian morality was cultivated in a premier place of consumption and American identity.[9] And Darren E. Grem's *The Blessings of Business: How Corporations Shaped Conservative Christianity* helps us understand how evangelical Protestant Christian theologies buffeted workplace values and beliefs and consecrated success as God-inspired and divine.[10] *Meatpacking America* joins this ever-growing literature on workplace religion and seeks to understand the role of religion at packinghouses in small-town and rural America. I join Moreton, Kirk, and Grem in their commitment to researching and understanding the complexities and challenges of being religious and practicing religion in the United States. Like these scholars, my research has taken me to workplaces where people spend the majority of their waking moments.

When we consider religion in the contemporary United States specifically, then we must turn our focus to work and places of employment. Work is a necessity to live, and it is at workplaces that we can see the unfolding of religious expressions and the "work" of religion. In this book I take a "lived religion" approach and look at how religion functions in people's everyday lives and how their faith makes it possible for them to survive and even thrive in difficult situations. How do white native-born Americans, like the Iowans featured in this book, deal with a rapidly changing workforce and honor cultural and religious needs of recent refugees? How do refugees manage to adapt to a new culture and workplace demands? For native-born citizens and refugees alike, a deep and abiding faith keeps everything together and makes it possible to keep going.

To understand how religion and faith interact dynamically with migration and work, we must travel to those spaces where people live their faith. We must enter the fields, sit at kitchen tables, don white jackets at the nations' packing plants and get a little bloody, visit entry points and places on the U.S.-Mexico borderland, and spend time over coffee and pie at restaurants and while enjoying tacos, tortas, and *horchata* at taquerias. These are the places where people talk about, live, and practice their faith. And for many people—native-born Americans and more recent immigrants and refugees alike—religious faith is the glue that holds it all together. Religion lives at home, in religious places like churches and mosques, and at work. Religion lives in the fields, factories, 4-H gatherings, church basements, and county fairs, too.

It is jobs that draw refugees to places like Iowa, to rural and small-town communities that feature poultry, pork, and beef packing plants, the major Corn Belt employment magnets. The towns, cities, churches, and workplaces that surround the plants have embraced this new reality and are places of growth. Today, the Midwest and broader rural America are multiethnic, multilingual places and provide an excellent indicator of the present and future of our nation.

This book offers some concrete ideas and examples of how individuals and local communities are working hard to move forward by embracing, rather than resisting, refugees. What I have found in the course of my research is that communities that do the hard work of welcoming change and accepting new arrivals to their communities are those that flourish. Some of what we see on the news and read and view on social media about rural America and the Midwest is certainly true and confirms that racism is alive and well in the nation. And undoubtedly, the systems that have privileged whites and disenfranchised Black and brown people still prevail in the United States and the Corn Belt. Yet my fieldwork has shown me the nuances of relationships in rural America. Average midwesterners, like average Americans, want to make a decent living, put food on the table, and make sure their kids are all right. The majority of rural Americans are not the angry white racists we often see in the all-too-easy tropes and characterizations on social media and the news. Most midwesterners and those living in the Corn Belt want to get along and coexist with their new neighbors. From what I discovered in my research, they respect their work ethic, their love for their families, and their demonstration of faith. White native-born Iowans see themselves and their own values in their Latino and refugee neighbors, fellow churchgoers, and coworkers.

If we want to understand the complicated realities of religion, migration, and work in the United States today, then we must journey to the Corn Belt, a place that has experienced major shifts in population over the past decade. According to Ayumi Takenaka of the Migration Policy Institute, "Population movements today are not only circular and transnational, but are increasingly sequential, involving more than one destination. This general trend is known variously as two-step, remigration, or secondary migration," and the United States is one of the "primary destinations" of secondary migrants.[11]

Iowa is a secondary migration state within the United States, meaning that it is usually not the first destination point in the country but the second, final destination. The safety of the state—with its small towns, cities, and rural spaces—is seen as ideal by refugees. The physical geography reminds refugees of home. Immigrants and refugees from around the world come to places like Iowa because the rent is affordable, the jobs are plentiful, and the schools are good. And we find that recent migrants' goals and dreams are similar to those of European farmers and entrepreneurs who came to the Corn Belt at the turn of the twentieth century. What links migrants of today to those of previous centuries is the deep-seated desire to have a better life than they had in their homelands.

For today's migrants, religion matters in a most urgent way, because it provides a respite from what Alicia Schmidt Camacho calls "migrant melancholia."[12] And while this book documents the sadness of leaving one's homeland and coming to a new place that is foreign, it also chronicles the overwhelming sense of anticipation in realizing a better life that migrants, refugees, and white ethnics share. As the University of Iowa public health scholar and activist Nicole Novak has pointed out, Iowans—those born here and those who have chosen this state as their home—have shown a path forward in the way they have responded to the May 2018 ICE (Immigration and Customs Enforcement) raids at a concrete factory in Mount Pleasant, Iowa. Novak writes, "Many Iowans, including immigrant families, know how to pull together and stand alongside their neighbor when the time calls for it."[13] In this book I will focus on the many women and men who pool their resources and pull together to work toward better futures. They work hard, form meaningful communities, and pray for better lives, and rural America is the place where it happens.

There is a lot of soul-searching going on in America, and we see this clearly in the rural Corn Belt, a hotspot for the new immigration. White non-Latinos work and attend church with Latino, South Asian, and Congolese refugees and see how hard these women and men work to provide for their families. These same parents and grandparents have children and grandchildren who are best friends with María, José, Josephine, Mohammed, and Ismail. These cross-cultural and interfaith encounters are happening all across the Midwest—not just on the coasts—yet they continue to go unreported and underreported as perceptions of the Midwest as "backward," a "fly-over zone," and a monocultural white region persist. What I have discovered is that while the struggle is real for white native-born Iowans to engage in cross-cultural and interfaith dialogue and cooperation, much constructive work is being done.[14]

Midwesterners tend to be portrayed as backwards, simplistic, hayseeds, and so on. Yet my research and lived experience reveals a much more complicated story. My research joins that of a growing number of journalists like Art Cullen and scholars who point out the significance of the Midwest and rural America and correlates with the historian Kristin L. Hoganson, who asserts that "such simplistic caricatures not only belittle an entire region, they also explain behavioral patterns in terms of site-specific ethnic depravity, thereby hiding their true origins and extent. To write such stereotypes into the past creates further distortions, because rural communities have never been static."[15]

Plainly put, if we are to truly understand the present-day realities and future of our nation, we must turn our attention to those places we have considered "fly-over" areas—like the small towns and rural places in Iowa. Why? Because more and more migrants and refugees are choosing to live in these places in the Midwest—and in the South and Southeast—because such non-urban settings are known to be good places to live, areas where these migrant and refugee families can experience a chance at the American Dream. At the very least, these slower-paced communities offer an improved quality of life from what they had known before. And joining these women and men are white native-born Americans who are choosing to retire and resettle in more rural locales.[16] They, too, dream of a better, safer, and happier life.

The places I have visited, lived, and worked have shown me that where we find meatpacking plants and Big Agriculture, we find cosmopolitan, multilingual, and pluralistic America. We find diversity and interreligious exchanges. We find women and men from multiple countries and nations talking and forming friendships. We find inclusivity here in the Corn Belt. And yes, we also find racism rearing its ugly head in overt ways, as we do throughout the country.[17]

I am not arguing that the Midwest is a racial-ethnic utopia. Clearly, there is much work to be done, as there is all over the world. But I do argue that there are many individuals in middle American states like Iowa who are working to make their communities inclusive and more welcoming. I have met these individuals and have shared meals and coffee with them. I have prayed alongside them in the pews, in church basements, and at outdoor festivals. I have laughed and cried with them when they receive news of deportations, the loss of a loved one, and other hardships. Like the Iowa journalist Art Cullen, I have found that most individuals are works in progress and see shared humanity in newer arrivals to the United States who are working hard for their communities.

In middle American places like Iowa, we find hardworking women and men who dream of a better life for their daughters and sons and for their future grandchildren. In many ways, the future of America is seen in the meatpacking and processing plants, in houses of worship, and at kitchen tables where cups of coffee have rested for decades. If we are to understand contemporary America, then we must journey to these places where white Americans, immigrants, and refugees come together.[18]

Faith, work, family, and food are common denominators that unite so many Americans, and I hope that this book manages to capture the dynamism of these elements and how they animate daily life. Here in the midwestern Corn Belt, religion lives in the fields, farms, and packing plants as much as in the churches.

CHAPTER 1

Homemaking

WHEN SHE SMILES her entire face lights up, and she smiles a lot. Corinne Hargrafen, a blue-eyed, white-haired, and impeccably dressed beauty of ninety-five (she was born in 1925), has lived in rural Iowa her entire life. Of Irish and German heritage, Catholic through and through, Corinne understands the values of hard work and sacrifice. Her father, an O'Toole, and her mother, an O'Connor, were among the first settlers in Ardon, a hamlet in rural eastern Iowa. They were farmers, raising cattle, pigs, corn, beans, hay, and soybeans for personal use and for profit, and they went to church each and every Sunday.

Corinne and her four sisters were the only Catholic kids to go to public school in Letts, Iowa, at the time; the other kids, she recalled in our interview, "went to the country school and later to Muscatine High School." Corinne remembered some anti-Catholic remarks from other schoolmates on the playground during recess. "Mostly," she said, it was harmless, but she did feel the sting of being an outsider. "You see, folks drew lines back then." Corinne recalled feeling shunned and even a little embarrassed about her Catholic faith and was eager to get home each day, where she was surrounded by love and safety. For a young Corinne, home and parish were safe and affirming places she could always count on.

For the O'Tooles, like most Catholic and Protestant families of the time, home and church were sanctuaries. Yet in the 1920s, for Catholic families like Corinne's, home and parish were also refuge from what the historian Linda Gordon terms the "second coming" of the KKK: the vitriolic, anti–African American, and increasingly anti-immigrant and mainstream social movement that was seen as "ordinary and respectable" by the majority of

Americans.[1] Corinne was uncomfortable talking too much about this time in her life, when she felt "other" on the playground and in class, surrounded by Protestant peers. As a young girl, Corinne was not aware that her lingering sense of feeling different was rooted in the area's anti-Catholic past and present, as with the Iowan American Protective Association from nearby Clinton and the presence of the KKK in rural Iowa.[2] In Clinton, Irish Catholic Democrats were particularly suspect for their economic and political successes. Yet as the Iowa historian Jo Ann Manfra has asserted, "The worldwide machinations of the Pope, not the grip of a conservative political coalition in a provincial Iowa river town," was the impetus for the creation of the American Protective Association in 1887 in Clinton.[3] Corinne and her Irish Catholic family were still viewed with suspicion by their non-Catholic eastern Iowa neighbors in the 1920s and 1930s as fears of Catholic immigrants making the United States a country for the pope still lingered.

For families like Corinne's, pictures of the Holy Family—Mary, Jesus, and Joseph—hung on the walls, as well as a Catholic calendar, sacralizing their home as Catholic. Statues of the Blessed Virgin Mary and Jesus stood proudly in the living room, among the first to greet visitors and to mark the home as Catholic. She has fond memories of the new dress and shoes she and her sisters received each summer for church. Church clothes were special items, and after Mass the girls would return home and hang up their Sunday best to be washed, starched, and ironed for the next Sunday. Corinne has vivid memories of the gas-motor-powered washing machine the family acquired when she was a preteen, and she recalled the detailed process of caring for church clothing. Careful sudsing, rinsing, and wringing the wet clothes through the press took a lot of care and time before the clothes were hung outside to dry during three of the seasons and in the basement during the winter. Housework, including washing clothes, cooking food, canning, and cleaning, was an important part of her youth as a farm girl.

Working hard, making homes, and finding solace in faith was a thread that connected Catholic and non-Catholic farm families then and now. Iowa author Carol Bodensteiner, a generation younger than Corinne and from a German Lutheran farming family and culture, has recounted her childhood and the intensive preparation girls underwent to be wives and mothers. The training started early:

> Shortly after my 10th birthday, about the same time I got to start carrying milk, Mom got it in her head I was also old enough to take on responsibility of cooking breakfast. Through some logic of her own, Mom

decided that planning and preparing breakfasts for a week at a stretch would be good training. But making breakfasts on top of carrying milk would slow mornings down too much, particularly when we kids had to get to school by 8 o'clock. The trade-off was that she took over most of my barn chores when I made breakfast. This was the latest step in Mom's plan to secure our futures as competent housewives.[4]

Work, food, and faith were at the center of Corinne's and Carol's farm families' lives. Sundays meant church and chicken suppers for both families. Carol's family took their church attendance in the eastern Iowa town of Spragueville as seriously as did Corinne's Catholic family in Ardon, roughly an hour and a half apart by auto. And the families had to represent and show up in their Sunday best. Supper preparation always began as early as Saturday night, when chickens would be set out to thaw in sinks for the Sunday feast. For Corinne's and Carol's families, faith and farming went together like a hand in a glove. In her memoir, Carol reminisced about her church, Salem Lutheran, which literally "backed up to a field, and whether planted to corn or hay or oats, the field was a reminder of our connection to the land." Carol recalled singing "Bringing in the Sheaves" with passion, feeling "a particular connection to God and those fields."[5] For her part, Corinne's memories of the St. Malachy Catholic parish are replete with descriptions of the land: corn stalks swaying in the wind, the lush greenness in the humid spring and in the damp heat of summer, the sweet smell of warm corn being nurtured by the Iowa sun. The images of Jesus, the saints, and the Virgin Mary blend with the sights, sounds, and smells of the fields that surrounded her rural community and its beloved parish.

76 Township and Irish Catholics

When Corinne thinks back to her youth and her Catholic faith, she remembers the rosary that Grandma O'Toole gave her for her confirmation, as well as the winter coat that marked sacred and seasonal times of "church" and "winter." She also has distinct memories of the hat that she, like all Catholic girls and women, had to wear to Mass. During our conversation she lowered her baby blues, and the fine lines around them crinkled as she giggled, thinking about the mandatory covering of heads and hair for Catholic women at the time. She exclaimed, "Oh, we didn't dare to go to church without a hat. It didn't matter what kind of hat, as long as we covered our heads." When she and other girls and ladies cleaned St. Malachy's, they would cover their heads with cotton "hankies." And for their part, the men had to always wear suit jackets. Corinne remembered one summer that "it was so hot, I mean *so hot* that you'd stick to your pew. So hot that the windows and doors were opened. That day the priest told the men that when it was that hot, they did not have to wear suits and slacks to church. While I understood this, I sure wish that he had told us ladies that we did not have to wear hats!"

Corinne's experiences with gendered expectations and norms were part of a broad pre–Vatican II American Catholic culture wherein women were subjected to certain forms of bodily comportment and discipline, from which men were exempted. Scholars of American Catholic culture have long pointed out the distinctive gendered expectations of young men and young women and how women, and their bodies in particular, bore the burden of a tradition and patriarchy. Catholic girls were raised to be good daughters, sisters, and brides to and for the male Christ. Women were always to be in relation to men, and mandatory head coverings were meant to show their deference to and respect for a male deity as much as to the men in the parish. While Corinne talked about wearing her veil on a blistering hot day as a minor annoyance and can now laugh it off, as a young girl she also felt the unwelcome warmth of a gendered slight and how irritating it was. She remembers how it felt—literally and figuratively—to this day. Paula Kane, a historian of American Catholicism, provides historical context for early twentieth-century American Catholic patriarchy and manhood, contextualizing it with the anti-Catholic nativism of the time. Kane asserts that American Catholicism responded to outside forces by "providing an all-encompassing Catholic subculture" wherein male and female gendered roles, materiality, and affects were heightened so that there arose a cult of "Catholic manliness" as much as a "Catholic womanhood."[6] Veil-covered heads of rural Iowa Catholic girls and women were one manifestation of a broader U.S. Catholic movement to make sure its women were feminine enough and even more so than their Protestant counterparts.

The rural Iowa Catholic Mass of Corinne's youth and into her middle age was in Latin, as it was throughout the United States, for this was before the mid-1960s church council that, among many other things, put an end to the Latin-only Mass. Corinne recalled following along as best as she could, as she did not understand the language. As with the thousands of young Catholics across the United States in the 1930s and 1940s, her Catholicism was one of comportment and knowing when to follow cues from her parents and other adults in the parish. "We'd sit there and listen, and we caught on, you know; we would know when to sit, when to stand, and when to go home. Our parish was mostly older folks, and we were the only family with young children at the time. When Urban [Corinne's husband] and I brought our own children to Mass after we were married, well, there were other children by that time."

As Corinne thought about her children's and grandchildren's Catholic education, she could see a stark difference from her own. "Because we were a little country church, we really didn't have much religious education. We had no Bible school per se. We were out in the country, you know." What stood out for Corinne were the Christmas celebrations at St. Malachy's, the annual festivities and rituals that she and her family looked forward to all year, when her "little country church" was bedecked for the holidays. One of Corinne's most cherished memories of her parish was the midnight Christmas Mass. Kerosene lamps were lit along the pathway to the front doors, and boughs of fir trees lined the walkways. "We were a church of only about forty or so people, but at Christmastime the numbers tripled. A lot of people came to see the beautiful country church all dressed up for Christmas."

As far as church decorum went, "we had to be quiet, *real quiet*, in church." Once they were home, she and her sisters could let loose and play. One of their favorite pastimes was playing in a cardboard box "store" that their father had made for them. Corinne smiled when she recalled those fun times with her sisters: "We would take our store outside and put the dolls and buggies all around it. We would drag the dogs and cats outside, too, you see, to join in the fun. Then we'd get eggs from the chickens for our 'store' and we'd make sure to feed the chickens too." The girls would listen to a battery-powered radio on Sunday afternoons as they played store together.

Following in her mother's footsteps, Corinne earned her associate's degree from the Iowa State Teachers College at the age of eighteen and became a primary schoolteacher. She taught in the rural town of Delhi for two years. During one of her visits home to Ardon, she attended a Friday evening dance with some girlfriends and was spotted by a handsome young German Catholic named Urban Hargrafen. He had watched Corinne that night, a bit too nervous to ask her to dance, but he managed to muster up the courage to call her a few days later to invite her to the next week's Friday dance. Soon the two were inseparable and attended every Friday night dance "in whichever little town hosted it," said Corinne. After a short courtship, they married in 1947, two years after the end of the Second World War and on the cusp of transitioning from the Great Depression to postwar economic prosperity. Like many other newly married white ethnic women of her time, Corinne took an early retirement from teaching to become a full-time wife and mother. She remembered life as "good . . . but hard too."

Corinne and Urban
Hargrafen wedding photo,
June 17, 1947. Photo by
Lois Mincks.

In the early years of their marriage, Corinne and Urban were renters and saved up to buy their own farmhouse. But the young couple, like many other Corn Belt farmers, were short on cash and assets. There was the time early in their marriage that the young family had to move, as the "lady who owned the farm had rented the farmhouse to another family who could pay a higher rent." So they picked up their belongings and moved to another farm and farmhouse. Corinne emphasized that they were "poor" and bought their next home on contract. "Mind you, the home lacked running water, an indoor toilet, and a telephone. But we did not have a landlord, and that was nice." The road leading up to their home was dirt and was often "a muddy mess" due to frequent rains. And it was "pretty tough" having to go to the outhouse during the cold and windy Iowa winters. Yet it was "their" outhouse and "their" muddy road, not a landlord's, and this was consolation to Corinne, who was working on making her home with Urban and their expanding household. Her attitude was one born of necessity, "because you had to do what you had to do." It was hard, yes, but despite the poverty, sacrifice, and hardships that she and her family of six endured, life, Corinne insisted, was good. She and Urban always had food on the table. She made sure their children—Jean, William, Lois, and Roger—had clean clothes and shoes to wear to school. Their hair was always combed and wetted down. Their shoes were shined. And they all bathed regularly in a galvanized tub in the bathroom, which they filled with water heated on the wood-fired stove. When she was deemed old enough, Lois was in charge of heating the water on the stove, carrying it ever so carefully across the room, and pouring it in the tub. After each bather, she would scoop out the cooled water, pour it outside on the grass, and add more hot water.

Like the majority of Iowa's white ethnic farmers of the 1940s and 1950s, Corinne and Urban farmed what is called a "general farm," one that is a mix of crops and animals, horse and tractor power, and a family and hired labor. As historian Lisa Lynn Ossian writes, "General farming also represented a philosophical approach to agriculture with Iowa farmers priding themselves on the independence of their farms as family units" and embodied a "small business approach with an emphasis on cash crops and animals and a dependence on family labor. Its ideals were continuity, flexibility, and independence, along with modest growth and endurance."[7]

The couple raised their four children in the Catholic Church, in the small rural Irish Catholic parish of St. Malachy, which had welcomed the German Catholic Urban and Irish Catholic Corinne as a mixed ethnic couple. Old ethnic tensions were downplayed in favor of a pan-ethnic "American" Catholic identity. Farming and Catholicism were the bookends of their family's life, and weekly Mass was a welcome respite from the demanding physical work of the week. Sunday was a time to wear their best clothes and to sit and enjoy the meal that Corinne had prepared. It was also a day for the kids to play and for their parents to enjoy them. Corinne smiled when she thought back to the carefully sewed and ironed dresses she'd made for her girls and the suits her sons and husband had donned. The church was always a sanctuary for her, a place she had volunteered to keep clean since she was young. She recalled the colored stained-glass windows that she would look up at during Mass. The colors, which shifted in intensity depending on the angle of the sun, always made her happy, she said. And the carved walnut pews of St. Malachy's felt

Urban Hargrafen and baby Jean, first day in the field in Letts, Iowa, April 6, 1949. Photo by Corinne Hargrafen.

smooth and cool to the touch, making her feel like she was "at home," in a special and sacred place. The little country church in Ardon was truly home to Corinne.

One thing this Catholic Iowan teacher, mother, and wife knew well was housekeeping, and taking care of her church was second nature. She had been raised to do all of this. And bringing up her children drew on many of her teaching skills, too. Above all else, church was the center of her family's social life and a sanctuary in what was then a heavily Protestant region.

As Catholics, Corinne and her family were, at the time, religious minorities in eastern Iowa. While they were white ethnics and benefited from social privileges their whiteness afforded them, their religion hindered certain aspects of their lives. Corinne remembered being teased about her religion and being called a "papist" in her grade school, and her children reported that the Protestant kids at school were mean. Corinne did her best to teach her kids tolerance and understanding, but she said that sometimes the anti-Catholic rebuffs and remarks "just made me mad—I am part Irish, you know, and we Irish have a bit of a temper!"

Corinne was born and bred Irish Catholic in a district of eastern Iowa known as the 76 Township, containing the "original" Irish Catholic families the O'Tooles, the O'Connors, the O'Shaughnesseys, the Cashmans, the Burnses, and the Furlongs. During the years of the Irish potato famine, a number of Irish Catholic families were drawn to America with hopes of a more stable life and made their way to this section of Iowa, where land was available and where some relatives and acquaintances had already put down roots in the 76 Township and Muscatine County.[8] It was a small slice of Irish Catholic Americana. The original brick St. Malachy Church was built in 1856 to serve the needs of the 76 Township Irish Catholic families. It was designated by Bishop Loras of the Archdiocese of Dubuque as an "out-mission," which meant that it would be served by priests whenever they were traveling through, given the shortage of priests at the time. According to the St. Malachy Preservation Society records, the first priest assigned to the parish was Father William Purcell from Washington, Iowa's St. James parish. Once a month, Father Purcell rode his horse the thirty-five miles from Washington and stayed at parishioner Bartholomew Cashman's log cabin for the weekend. During his time at St. Malachy's, he performed baptisms, weddings, and Sunday Mass.

The number of parishioners soon outgrew the small brick church, and a new one was built in 1902, right up the road from St. Malachy's cemetery, on land donated by a local non-Catholic, Isaac Lee. Despite vestiges of anti-Catholicism that dated to the late nineteenth century, there were instances of interfaith friendships and cooperation. In small towns and rural hamlets like Ardon, cooperation was necessary for survival. The building was, as Corinne put it, "a plain but also a beautiful country church." It was a wooden frame church, painted white, "very pretty and very simple," the central hub for 76 Township Catholic families. For Corinne's friend Agnes O'Connor, it was a beautiful and special holy place where she felt love and community. Agnes remembered well the day in 1991 that the parishioners were told that their beloved church would be decommissioned. "It was just terrible, just terrible. We all loved the parish so much, and it was more than a church for us; it was our home. It was a place where all of us—Irish Catholics who all farmed—could be together and worship."

When the bishop announced that the parish would be closed and decommissioned, or "suppressed," in June 1991, it was "just devastating" to Corinne, Agnes, and the other Irish Catholics whose lives for two generations revolved around the parish. Indicative of the trauma the decommissioning caused in the lives of the 76 Township families, all of the Catholics I interviewed and spent time with who had grown up in the parish became emotional when we talked. During our conversation in her living room, Corinne stopped for a few moments as her eyes welled up with tears, trying to gain her composure. Her voice cracked, and she repeated how "hard" it was when her beloved parish church closed. St. Malachy's closure was part of a wave of rural parish closings in the 1990s and into the next decade, reflecting a widespread rural decline, and current discussions of closures and consolidations are not abating. An aging population, fewer children taking up farming and instead moving to cities within and outside of Iowa, and declining church attendance has led to several stages of parish closures. Moreover, a persistent shortage of priests has necessitated closures and the consolidation of parishes across the rural state, paralleling urban parish closures caused by priest shortages, declining attendance, and financial challenges from priest sex abuse scandals. Notably, the Diocese of Davenport, which included the parish of St. Malachy, filed for bankruptcy in 2006 in the wake of a sexual abuse scandal that rocked the diocese. Six years after the Chapter 11 filing, the diocese reached a $37 million settlement with creditors.[9] Parish closures and consolidations into clusters continue across the rural state, most recently seen in the Diocese of Sioux City, where the number of parishes went from 108 to 61 by 2017.[10]

St. Malachy's closure was hard on Corinne and her friend Agnes, and it continues to be difficult. Agnes wept each time she talked with me about her Catholic childhood. And to make things even harder, the Wapello, Iowa, rural parish she joined after St. Malachy's closed, St. Mary's, was decommissioned several years later without any warning. Agnes, her hand shaking on her coffee cup, exclaimed, "This was just so terrible. We were told a week before it was officially closed. At least with St. Malachy, as sad as it was, we had time to mourn and to grieve. But this, this was just awful. You know, some families were so upset by the suddenness of it that they just stopped going to church altogether. They were just done with it, you know? Done with the church." Although she was "devastated" by these closings, Agnes found her way to a third rural parish, St. Joseph the Worker in Columbus Junction, where we met. She joined the parish in the early part of the new century and has been an active member since. Agnes hopes that the "third time is the charm" and that this is the parish where she will end her days. She has grown to love her new parish, as it is "all about the community, and I love my community here."

The women and men who made their way to St. Joseph's from St. Malachy's and St. Mary's all say they prefer a smaller, intimate parish setting where you can "really get to know" the fellow parishioners, according to Ann, for whom St. Joseph's is her second parish. Carol, one of the post-Mass coffee ladies' group I had the pleasure of hanging out with, joined St. Joseph's after St. Malachy's closed and has been the organist ever since.

I got to know Ann, Agnes, Corinne, and the other St. Malachy 76-er transplants over the course of a year, drinking coffee and eating doughnuts after Mass at St. Joseph the Worker, which has become their new parish home. The ladies are great friends and banter with the familiarity that old friends have with one another. Agnes usually saves a plate of food and a carafe of coffee for Ann, who typically stays upstairs talking after Mass. The ladies tease her when she finally arrives, telling her that they almost ate her food and drank her coffee. The women talk about the day, the weather, and their grandchildren. On this particular day, Carol shared her concerns for her daughter, who is finishing up nursing school and has three young children. "I just worry that she is taking on so much, and I worry about her health," Carol shared. Her friends commiserated, patting her hand and pouring her coffee.

As many other scholars have shown, for American Catholics, place matters, and the parish has been the center of ethnic, cultural, and religious identity for countless Catholic migrants since the earliest waves of immigrants in the early to mid-nineteenth century. For Carol, Agnes, and Julie, who regularly take the Eucharist, Christ's body, to St. Joseph parishioners who are no longer able to physically be at Mass, the coffee and doughnuts and social bonding are an important part of their week.

While the ladies I met and interviewed have made St. Joseph's in Columbus Junction their new home parish, the transition wasn't easy, as they had so many emotions, experiences, and memories tied up in their former parish of St. Malachy. They are all religious refugees in the sense that they have experienced displacement, loss, and the bewilderment that accompanies forced migration and movement. The ladies are all involved in the preservation of their former decommissioned parish and assist the St. Malachy Preservation Society, which hosts a 4.6-mile run and walk each June to raise funds for the society. Hardbound copies of the St. Malachy photo book are for sale as well, and all proceeds go to the preservation of St. Malachy's. Former parishioners volunteer to mark the course and hand out water and fruit to race participants. The run gives everyone an opportunity to come together to celebrate community and Irish heritage and to share their memories of St. Malachy's.

I was given a tour of the church building by Mike Furlong, president of the Preservation Society. It was cool inside, despite the heat of the day. Even though St. Malachy's was decommissioned in 1991, it still smelled like church: wooden pews, dust, and candle wax. The statues of Jesus, Mary, and other saints were kept in the room behind the front altar, in storage. Mike pointed out the statue of Jesus, whose toes had been chewed off by mice that had taken residence in the old church's walls. "It's a little sad, isn't it?" he said to me, looking at Jesus's nibbled-on toes. I nodded in agreement. The church is kept clean and tidy, and each year the Preservation Society hosts "A Country Christmas" at the old parish in mid-December. The church space is decorated for the holiday, and volunteers serve hot chocolate and cookies as members of a local community choir sing traditional Christmas carols. The old parish Nativity set is put on display, and the pews are waxed and shined for the big event. The 76 Township St. Malachy families remain dedicated to keeping their church beautiful, a physical as well as aesthetic testimony of their faith. The remaining statues of Jesus and the saints at St. Malachy's are more than statues; they are what religious studies scholar Hillary Kaell has called "ambient objects," material items that "act" on human beings."[11] The statue of Jesus, while missing some toes, remains an important reminder to former parishioners that they remain connected to the divine and to this place with all of its smells, objects, and sounds.

The summer fundraising race, established to maintain the church, the land, and the cemetery, tends to bring out as many volunteers as runners, and the former, all 76-ers, look forward to the annual event as a time to reconnect. Some of the attendees at the race I was present for are relative newcomers to the 76 Township. Gary is a lifelong Iowan but new to Ardon. Along with his son, Gary currently rents and farms over 200 acres of land that is owned by Agnes, the former St. Malachy and current St. Joseph the Worker parishioner. The men grow, cultivate, and harvest corn, soybeans, and hay and have been doing so for the past fourteen-plus years. For Gary, being able to farm is a lifelong dream. As a young boy he grew up on a farm roughly ten miles from Ardon and always hoped to be able to go back to farming. Like many young farm-raised Iowans, Gary entered a career not connected to his farming roots after college. In the post–farm crisis economy of Iowa, it was difficult for young farmers to enter the profession, so many went into more lucrative, dependable lines of work. Gary worked for PepsiCo for over twenty-six years, making his way up from driver to operations manager with the company. As Gary pondered his career and his new connection with St. Malachy's through Agnes, the owner of the land he farms, he chuckled and said, "I guess I needed to work to be able to afford to farm." I have heard this sentiment from many other white men I interviewed. They were raised to farm but were kept from entering the profession because of the farm crisis and the crushing debt their families had incurred. Gary hopes to one day complete the farming family circle and purchase some land to farm. But for now, he rents and farms and said that farming is his "happy place."

In the years after the farm crisis, many small family farms like Gary's had to foreclose. The children and grandchildren of those former farmers grew up dreaming, as did Gary, of one day being able to farm again. While Gary does not own the land as his father and grandfather did before him, he said that "just being able to get my hands in the dirt is such a great feeling." Digging in and working the soil takes him back to his childhood. "It's just in your blood, that's the only way I can explain it," he said as we chatted in front of St. Malachy's that hot Iowa summer day. "You just want to farm. I worked hard for many years so that I could go back to my roots as a farmer."

Like Ardon and its St. Malachy parish, the tiny eastern Iowa town of Parnell, or "Little Ireland," as it is fondly called by locals, is another small community whose history is dominated by Irish Catholic families. Parnell's St. Joseph Catholic Church was built in 1889 and was the only church in town until the mid-twentieth century, when German Mennonite families built the second church. The church building and the red brick of St. Joseph Catholic School were Parnell's architectural focal points, and the Sisters of Humility from Ottumwa, Iowa, taught at both the parish school and the public school, which opened in 1915. Making their parish a place that was aesthetically beautiful was important to the Irish Catholic families who built St. Malachy's and to the Parnell families who built St. Joseph's. Members of both communities were determined to create visually pleasing holy places. In Parnell, Catholic families pooled their resources to make sure that St. Joseph's was replete with twenty-foot-high engraved green tin ceilings, a wooden main altar centerpiece that featured baroque-style tin plating, and two side altars trimmed in gold leaf. The walls were inset with stained glass windows, depicting St. Patrick and other patron saints like Mary and Joseph. Indeed, parish families spared no expense in adorning their beloved church.

Three resident priests were brought in from Ireland, solidifying the link between the Emerald Isle and America. For 120 years, generations of O'Briens, Donahues, O'Roarkes, Sullivans, and other communicants received the sacraments of baptism, the Eucharist, confirmation, and marriage at St. Joseph Catholic Church in Parnell. Pastoral Associate Ann Lillis recalled that "the people [of St. Joseph's] were just down-to-earth, pretty middle-class people."

She remembered families of "eight or ten children walking to church, each dressed in their finest; girls were required to wear a circle [on their heads] of lace."

Longtime St. Joseph parishioner Jean O'Brien said that St. Joseph's "felt like a holy place." It was "a beautiful, safe place that felt like home, and a place where you went to pray." O'Brien recalled the "cool, peace-instilling quietness" of the church, which helped her get her "mind in a good place." Yet another longtime parishioner emphasized that "the church held the community together." Father Michael Colonnese involved the congregation in planting a garden behind the church in order to grow food for needy families in nearby Davenport, Iowa. He involved more Spanish-speaking Catholics, apparently, in the venture. Yet, like Ardon's St. Malachy's, St. Joseph's in Parnell was deemed "not viable" as a parish due to the declining membership, extensive repairs needed, and lack of priests. The parish was decommissioned in June 2009, and a memorial was built in the town's sole cemetery, St. Joseph's Cemetery. As with St. Malachy, Parnell's St. Joseph parishioners found new parishes to join, but for some, finding a new parish was far too painful, and they stopped going to church altogether. For St. Joseph cantor Bill McDonald, "I lost my family when the church closed." For Bill and others, finding a new family was neither a desire not an option they considered.

Parish closings, as historian of U.S. Catholicism John Seitz has shown in his moving book *No Closure*, can have devastating emotional, psychological, and psychic effects on parishioners, for whom the parish structure was home and hub. Throughout the mid to late twentieth century, U.S. Catholic bishops focused on consolidating parishes. While the economics of the decisions to close parishes may make sense on paper, they do not make sense to many parishioners. While some St. Malachy parishioners moved to other nearby parishes in Columbus Junction, Nichols, Wapello, and Lone Tree, others stopped going to church. For these Catholics, it was inconceivable that they could ever replicate the holy place and community they had experienced at St. Malachy's. It was easier to maintain a Catholic identity with memories of happier times than it was to locate a new parish.

Corinne and fellow former St. Malachy parishioner Agnes, as we have seen, craved the kind of community they had experienced for so long at their beloved St. Malachy's. While Corinne moved to Columbus Junction's parish of St. Joseph the Worker with a handful of St. Malachy parishioners, Agnes, along with several St. Malachy refugees, moved to the nearby (and now former) Wapello's St. Mary's Catholic parish. While it wasn't the same as her former worship community, it was a "good parish," and Agnes experienced a strong sense of belonging. So it was "just devastating" when the bishop made the sudden announcement that this parish was also being decommissioned, not long after she had made the move there. Agnes and several other former St. Malachy and St. Mary's parishioners emphasized how they were "blindsided" by the announcement of this parish closing. While the St. Malachy closing was deeply upsetting to them, parishioners felt that they had some time to prepare themselves emotionally for it. But with this announcement, Agnes said, "it was the final straw for some Catholic families, and they just stopped attending church. They were done. Just done with church." Agnes got angry and sad when she talked about St. Malachy's—her face became red, her eyes welled with tears, and her words became choked with emotion. I held her hand as she related memories of her parishes closing or, in her words, "shutting down." Agnes felt—and still does in a way—shut out of the Catholic Church because of how the closings made her feel about places that meant so much to her.

Agnes lives about a quarter mile up the road from St. Malachy's, and it is bittersweet for her. She enjoys being so close—it makes her "soul feel good," as she put it to me once. Agnes is the designated parish's master gardener for the property and loves to keep the grounds looking beautiful, but it is tough to see her beloved, shuttered church each day. She consoles her grief by lovingly maintaining the grounds and is proud of the landscaped flowers and tidy front of the old church. She weeds, waters, trims, and plants annuals each spring and mows the lawn too. Gardening is a testament to her deep Catholic faith, her Irish Catholic ethnic heritage and identity, and faith in place. Gardening has become a primary way for Agnes to feel connected to her memories and experiences here. While Agnes has made St. Joseph's in Columbus Junction her third and, she hopes, last parish, it is "not the same" as her beloved St. Malachy's.

Most of the 76-ers I talked with at the fundraiser said they are still feeling a sense of loss and disappointment, but they are pragmatic and have "moved on" because they have had to. They funnel their energies into organizing and holding the run each year, as well as the Christmas concert, but they cannot afford to dwell on their sadness, as their lives are full. Since they knew the bishop was not changing his mind about decommissioning their parish— "What was done was done and there was no going back," one former parishioner told me at the run—the small band of St. Malachy parishioners focused on what they could accomplish and rallied around preserving their church for future generations and for Catholic Iowans. They maintain a sense of their Irish ethnic identity and Catholic faith, and the annual events like the run and Christmas gathering ensure that their sense of community is remembered and maintained.

"This Is My Crazy Horse, My Legacy"

I had the opportunity to spend an afternoon with Mike Furlong, who had given me a tour of St. Malachy's and who offered to share more of his knowledge of eastern Iowa's Irish Catholic culture. It was a gorgeous spring afternoon in rural Iowa, the kind of day where the breeze blows and the scent of ripe flower buds permeate the air. We sat at a picnic table and looked out at his vineyard—four acres of grapevines—and the eighty acres of corn that Mike and his wife Denise own and rent out for farming. Mike lit a cigarette, took a swig of Diet Pepsi, and began talking about how much this land means to him. I sat there, looking at the gorgeous vista and wishing I could have a glass of the wine I had purchased from the winery store, but it was a long drive home and that glass of chilled white Irish Curtain wine (indeed, that was the name) would have to wait until later. As we took in the sun and natural beauty of place, I followed Mike's pointer finger as he indicated several landmarks on the 160-year-old Irish family farm: the family home that has gone through several renovations; the red painted barn that used to house corn and animals and now hosts equipment for the family winery; the cistern that holds water from the well; and the crumbled brick outline of the original St. Malachy Irish Catholic church built in 1856 on the Furlong family property. The church was small and made of clay-fired bricks, which "were soft," but "people could write their initials on [them]." According to Mike, horses and buggies would park across the street from the church, and once a month Father William Purcell would pay a visit from Washington, Iowa, on horseback to deliver the Mass.

Mike laughed a bit as he remembered the intransigence and sharper edges of Irish Catholic families on Sundays, who were by then attending the second St. Malachy parish that was built in 1902, a small church across from the Furlongs' corn acreage. It was larger than the original and could accommodate the growing Irish Catholic community of the 76 Township. Regulars would always allow for some "fudge room," as he called it, for newcomers who were not accustomed to families claiming certain pews. But the "fudge room" lasted only a little while, and newcomers needed to catch on to which families sat where and then avoid those pews and find and claim their own places.

His world, like Corinne's and Agnes's, was a tightly knit, rural ethnic enclave. Mike remembers smells, sounds, and how he felt as a child growing up in a religious and ethnic culture that was rooted in the land and community. These memories have proved so powerful and persuasive that Mike was compelled to become one of the founding members and president of the St. Malachy Preservation Society that was established in 1991, when the parish was suppressed by the Diocese of Davenport. "I have a lot of memories of being an altar boy. There was a lot of pressure on kids to kneel, stand up, stand up straight, you know. In the summers it was so hot, and we wore those cassocks. I remember people fainting in the pews because it was so hot. There was the heat, and then there was the noise. The train would go through during the homily, and the priest would have to stop until the train had passed through. And then the wooden planks would rumble on the bridges. It was hot and loud."

Everything Mike, his parents, and his brother and sister did revolved around the parish. As Mike shared his experiences with his Irish Catholic community, a recent event brought to his mind memories of fun times:

> So we were taking Christmas lights down from St. Malachy just last week, and a memory of sixty years ago came back to me. In the summer the nuns would come teach us summer school, and during breaks we kids would hang out in the fields and come in for a cool drink of Kool-Aid. Who made the Kool-Aid rotated, and a different mom, grandmother, or aunt would make it and bring it out for us in the afternoon. Well, I remember how we just *hated* it when Aunt Katherine made the Kool-Aid. See, she was diabetic and made it without sugar. It was just *awful*, and we dreaded the day Aunt Katherine was in charge of making us Kool-Aid.

Mike laughed, then looked out at his acreage, sighed, and said, "This is a good life. I love it here and am connected to this land. I just never want to leave this." Mike's life these days revolves around the life cycle of his vineyard and caring for the vines: pruning in March, applying fungicide, controlling weeds, working winery-related events, and harvesting in late summer to early fall. In the early years of the vineyard and the winery, Mike, Denise, and some family members did most of the work themselves, but as he has gotten older, Mike has had to hire help. He works with an agency in Muscatine that hires laborers to tend his vast vineyard, and it is primarily Latinos who work his land.

Hiring Latino—specifically Mexican-descent—workers is part of the Furlong family farm history. For close to a decade, Mike's father and mother were contract farmers with the Heinz Company, which had a base in Muscatine.

The family farmed twenty acres of tomatoes and six acres of pickles for Heinz and hired Mexican workers to harvest the crops. Mike pointed toward his home and the two smaller buildings on the property and said that Mexican families lived there during harvesttime. "Several families would go to the Dakotas to hoe the sugar beet fields and then would come back out to Iowa and work for my parents. We had a family living in our basement and a few other families in the small buildings on the property. They picked the tomatoes and pickles by hand and would haul the crops to Muscatine in wagons." Mike remembered the extra cash infusion as a boon to his family's income and has good memories of those years: "The place was really alive during that time, you know. And I now realize that it was pretty neat that I was exposed to another culture at a young age."

While Mike has happy, even idyllic, memories of the time, the reality for the more than 2,000 Mexicans working for Heinz was not idyllic. As Janet Weaver, historian of the Latino Midwest, notes, the majority of these Heinz employees were mostly internal migrants from Texas and were living in poverty. Local organizations such as the Muscatine Migrant Council provided medical and educational services for the migrants and their families and, along with the League of United Latin American Citizens, raised awareness of their poor working and living conditions. The council's goals were fourfold: "first, to improve working conditions for migrant workers and their families; second, to improve the relationship between the workers and the community; third, to provide recreational facilities; and fourth, to provide a day school program with educational and medical services for the children of migrant workers."[12] Historians W. K. Barger and Ernesto M. Reza provide further details on Mexican American labor history in the midwestern Corn Belt, writing that Mexican-descent farmworkers were brought in to work midwestern farm fields as part of the post–World War II bracero movement. Permanent jobs in canneries, like the Heinz factory in Muscatine, "provided many families with the opportunity to settle out of the migrant stream in small towns in the region."[13] As we work to untangle the complexities of migration, race, and policy, it is important for us to understand that even good intentions and actions, like those of the Furlong family, were not panaceas for the deeply entrenched racialized U.S. labor policies that have favored and rewarded corporations like Heinz over Mexican-descent Latino workers. The disconnect between brown and white worlds was maintained and persists today.

For Mike's part, he remembered the farm and the land "being really alive" during his youth. There were lots of workers and extended families, and it was a multicultural, multilingual place to grow up.[14] Today he hires "Mexican

American workers," as he referred to them, to help with the planting and harvesting, but on a smaller scale than in his youth. Yet what remains constant from his youth is a dependence on Latino labor for his success and fortunes. Mike said he recognized his family's reliance on Latino labor. Like many white Americans, Mike wrestles with his whiteness and the privileges that have come with it. Yet at the same time, he has a difficult time remembering the names of the Latinos who worked for his family or even those who now work for him. This inability to remember is part of a wide-scale struggle on the part of white Americans to move beyond seeing Latinos and other refugees and economic migrants as more than fungible commodities. Latino workers, in this instance, are bodies who work to maintain a company's and a farming family's status quo and fortunes.

Mike recalled Latinos as part of his life but mostly in the way they were valued and seen for their labor, not as part of his educational experience and life outside the farm. He has "fond memories" of his school days at a one-room Iowa schoolhouse, which was common for the state before the school consolidations of the 1970s and 1980s. He is grateful to his parents for sending him to Catholic school in Muscatine and for the financial and personal sacrifices that they made, yet this gratitude is tinged with some painful memories for Mike of his mother going to work outside of the home. According to Mike, having a mother who worked outside of the home was seen as a social stigma by other white Catholic farming families of the area. It was especially hard for his sister during high school that her mom worked, for the mothers of her girlfriends were at-home moms whose work was home-based and domestic. That Mike's mother was employed outside of the home to help provide for her family was seen by some as being in violation of gender, racial, and religious norms. Her employment, in some ways, linked her and the Furlong family to the Latinos they hired, who worked out of necessity. Both worked hard and did what they had to do to provide for their families.

On the day of our interview, as Mike looked out over his acreage, he reflected on the life he wants to live. "I really just want to stay in Ardon, drink wine, and farm my grapes. I want to sit in our Adirondack chairs at dusk and look out at nature's beauty with my wife. It is a simple life, really. I don't need to make a lot of money and just want to be happy." Like Gary, who worked for years to afford to farm, Mike is grateful for his former career at the HON Company. "I worked my way up in the company, and at the time of my retirement I had a great salary and very good benefits. I cashed in my 401K, and with the help of my wife, I was able to establish the winery on our family heritage farm."

The family's centuries-old farm is still bearing fruit. As Mike reflected on the ways his Irish Catholic farming heritage has impacted his life, he recounted "more ways than I can say." Since he was a boy, he has thought about what he would leave as his legacy. A trip out west with his aunt and uncle when he was twelve years old cemented his desire to "do something meaningful with my life, do something big." The peak experience of the trip, and in many ways his life, was visiting the Crazy Horse Memorial in the Black Hills of South Dakota. Mike remembered how impressed he was at the imposing sculpture and the story of both Crazy Horse and the artist. He was "blown away" by the sacrifice and grit of the Oglala Lakota leader and how he fought for and worked for his people's way of life. Seeing the huge memorial etched in stone caused Mike to reflect on his own life and what he would do with it. "You know, that monument was huge and imposing, and so was Crazy Horse. He had an imposing personality. He made a strong statement. I remember thinking as I looked at that awesome monument that one day, I wanted to have something that I could leave as my legacy. Well, I think that the winery is my Crazy Horse; it is my legacy." While Mike acknowledged his winery is not the same as Crazy Horse's fight for his people's literal survival, he understands his winery's ethnic-religious roots as a legacy he will sacrifice and fight for. He hopes his grandchildren will continue once he is gone and that Furlongs will continue to cultivate and care for the land.[15]

Working Hard

The land, their Catholic faith, and an ethic of working hard were at the center of the O'Toole, Furlong, and Hargrafen families' lives. The families, like other Irish Catholic farm families, followed the seasons and the cycles. They read the *Farmers' Almanac* religiously, more than any other book, including the Bible. Corinne pointed out that Catholics at that time didn't really open the Bible and were discouraged from reading Scripture. Her memories are supported by ample scholarly data. What linked their livelihoods as farmers and their predilections as Catholics to attend Mass was that both were family-focused activities. Children helped their parents and even grandparents plant, harvest, can, pickle, and dry crops. Family, work, and faith were inseparable—a three-legged stool.

For Mike, Agnes, Corinne, and other Corn Belt farm families of the Depression and World War eras, the cultivation of and preparation of food was a yearlong process. Families had special cellars and cabinets—larders—for canned goods, which would need to last until the next season. Summer berry jams and jellies would need to last until the following year; corn, beans, and squash would have to be canned and also kept cool for use until the next fall harvest. Eggs were procured year-round thanks to hardy hens and the lone and rather fortunate rooster. A successful Sunday chicken supper was dependent on the care of the family's backyard hens—what we today call "free range." And pork and beef were procured from out back or from a neighbor's farm or ranch. Food, faith, and family were deeply intertwined for Corinne's generation and her parents'.

Corinne and her kin worked hard. But work was part of the warp and weft of life—you just did it. As Corinne said, "We didn't see it as work so much, because that is just what you did. You cleaned, cooked, took care of the chickens, bathed the children, did the laundry . . . you name it. That is just what we did." Corinne's country work ethic was put to the test when the new Catholic parish of Columbus Junction was being built. For in addition to making food for her nuclear family, Corinne, like other local Catholic women, made food for the men who completed the new church in the fall of 1958. Unlike the other women, Corinne was pregnant with babies number three and four—twins—but it was certainly *not* uncommon for pregnant farm women to be seen doing all of the chores they regularly did on a daily basis. These women, like their husbands, were the forebears of today's CrossFitters, and their gym was everyday life in the home and the fields.

The summer of 1957 was a hot and humid Iowa summer. The air was heavy, pungent, and moist from the ripening corn—ask any rural midwesterner or farmer about how corn "sweats," and you'll likely get a detailed and experiential response. While the women prepared casseroles, fried chicken, and rolls and mixed up fresh lemonade in metal containers, the men worked to build the newest parish church in rural eastern Iowa.

What became the parish of St. Joseph the Worker was made of what we would today call "recycled" and "upcycled" materials. And the chief architect and builder of the little church was none other than the parish priest himself. Father Clifford A. Egert was, as Corinne recalled, a "man's kind of man." In addition to being a two-parish priest, serving nearby St. Mary's parish in Lone Tree as well as the new St. Joseph's in Columbus Junction—in and of itself not unusual for the rural midwestern Corn Belt—he was a trained carpenter. Father Egert's own father had taught him the skills of the trade, which came in handy when it was time for a new parish in Columbus Junction. Iowa families were expanding in size after the Second World War, in tandem with many families across the nation. The tiny parish of St. Joseph's was bursting at its wooden seams and deemed insufficient to accommodate the town's growing Catholic population. It was time for a larger parish, one that had solid floors, unlike the dirt floors of the original parish building, so it was proposed that a new church be built a few lots over. The problem was that there was almost no money for the new building fund. So, Father Egert did what any stalwart rural priest would do: he acted as chief foreman and laborer of the new church project, quite literally using his body to build the church. According to Corinne, Father's body was "nearly broken by the labor, and his back was never quite the same afterward." But parishioners kept coming to help with the building and stayed to worship once it was built. Aided by St. Joseph's laymen James Helmick, Frank Gabriel, the "Daniels brothers," Elmer Ziskovsky, Raymond Schultz, L. B. Dempsey, Fred Dupuis, and Urban Hargrafen, Father Egert labored hard to build the church out of recycled and upcycled materials from the nearby Washington, Iowa, Catholic parochial school.[16] A fortuitous stroke of good luck occurred, for just when Bishop Ralph L. Hayes of the Diocese of Davenport gave his blessing for a new St. Joseph's parish to be built, Father Thomas Lew of Washington's St. James parish offered the building materials to the good folks of St. Joseph's for their new parish church. But Corinne didn't see this convergence of events as mere "luck"; she saw it as "directed by God Himself." On November 23, 1958, a celebratory "capon supper and bazaar" was hosted in the basement of the newly completed church.

For his part, the postwar priest Father Egert put a new spin on the historic image of the "brick and mortar priest." This designation has been mostly used to describe early to mid-twentieth-century urban American priests who were charged with building parish churches and adjacent schools in a postwar baby boom. Rural country priests were not part of this mostly northern, big city phenomenon. They were operating with smaller budgets and smaller parish communities that were growing modestly by rising birth rates but not by in-migration. Urban parishes, though, were growing by a twin rise in birth rates and in-migrations. Rural midwestern towns such as Columbus Junction did not experience waves of immigrants until the establishment of meatpacking plants in the late 1900s. By the last decades of the twentieth century and into the early twenty-first, the rural Midwest became a destination for refugees from Central America, Africa, and Burma.

Perhaps it is no coincidence that Father Egert and the fictional *Field of Dreams* character Ray Kinsella of Dyersville, Iowa, shared a commitment to the saying "If you build it, they will come." The new St. Joseph's parish in Columbus Junction replaced the old wooden structure parish that had been moved, plank by plank, from nearby Clifton's community center after the town experienced a decline resulting from being too far from the rails. And unlike its namesake, Columbus City, a smidge under two miles away yet not at railway intersections, Columbus Junction sprang up almost overnight, at the intersection of two railroad lines, the Rock Island and the Burlington, Cedar Rapids, and Northern. One town's misfortune was the other's fortune, and Columbus Junction grew quickly after its 1870 platting. Up to the early 1960s, Columbus Junction was mostly a farming community, and the railroad lines provided ready access to ship grain and corn to urban markets. The town came to be known for its meat processing after 1961, when Rath Packing Company established a hog processing plant. Hog processing remains the biggest area employer today at the former Rath plant, now the Tyson plant.

As its name connotes, Columbus Junction has never been a metropolitan or even a micropolitan area but a place where rural meets small town and where industry meets workers. Columbus Junction is, like other meatpacking towns, situated at the confluence of rivers—the Iowa and the Cedar— and next to railroad lines. Small towns like Columbus Junction offer jobs, the amenities that accompany settling in company towns, and affordable living. Like many small towns and rural communities in Iowa and across the Midwest, Columbus Junction's population grew in the 1950s, declining in the 1980s due to the farm crisis and subsequent recessions.[17]

When we examine the spread and movement of Catholicism in the United States, the mid-nineteenth to late nineteenth century was a time of impressive growth and expansion in urban locales and, to a lesser extent, in rural areas as well. Catholicism in Iowa got its start with nineteenth-century missionary Catholic priests who rode their horses all over the Midwest, focusing their efforts on saving souls and planting churches. They were spiritual and material "pickers" who salvaged souls and materials to build what was then frontier parishes and a frontier Catholic Church. Priests like Egert fell in step with their predecessors, men who were wheelers and dealers, pickers, and salvagers.

Midwestern parishes in particular were considered mission churches, spread out geographically in rural and small towns and served by itinerant horseback-riding priests. In the case of St. Joseph's, the Italian Dominican priest Father Samuel Charles Mazzuchelli served the church in Columbus Junction between the years 1835 and 1840. Like Protestant ministers of the same time period, Father rode his horse from mission site to mission site, holding Mass anywhere he could as there were no churches built at this time. Mazzuchelli was known for holding Catholic Mass "in the shelter of the grove, beneath humble cabin roof, in schoolhouse or village hall."[18]

Nineteenth-century and early-to-mid-twentieth-century Iowa Catholics were immersed in an indigenous frontier land. Among white ethnic Christians in Iowa, Roman Catholics were a minority, surrounded by the far more predominant Methodists, Presbyterians, Lutherans, and Reformed Churches. Corinne's experiences of everyday slights and what we today call "microaggressions" are reflected the city's recorded history, where the Catholic presence goes unmentioned.[19] Catholic families stuck to their own and were parochial in geography as well as in spirit. They worked hard, had large families, and mostly thrived as farmers and cattle ranchers.

Corinne had fond memories of Father Egert and had read about his predecessor and pioneer of Catholicism in eastern Iowa, Father Mazzuchelli. She remembered the year 1959, the year the second iteration of St. Joseph's was finished, as one defined by pregnancy, chicken, watermelon, and lemonade. She remembered the checkered tablecloths that were laid out for the men's lunches when they took their breaks from working on the church, and the smells of the freshly made food. "It was a good time, a real good time."

In addition to providing food and cold lemonade for the men, the women's auxiliary group of the church, the Altar and Rosary Society, painted the interior of the church and were tasked with decorating it. Corinne remembered choosing the paint colors with her society friends. They decided on a light shade of willow green, a color that Corinne said reminded her of springtime. It was a fresh, clean color, meant to relax the worshipper as much as it was meant to brighten the small church, she said. The ladies wanted St. Joseph's to be an inviting place and took pride in helping to make it so.

Bob and Lorraine

For East Coast transplant Lorraine Hook (née Gaunya), Iowa and St. Joseph parish in Columbus Junction were welcoming places. Living in Iowa did take some getting used to for this "big city" woman, who moved to her husband Bob's home state. Lorraine met Bob at a USO-sponsored dance in her hometown of New Haven, Connecticut. Bob, a self-described "joker," said during our enjoyable and moving interview in the couple's tidy assisted living home that their marriage was a "casualty of war." "I went to this dance, you see, and met this beautiful French American gal . . . and there it was. Boom. Married her." Lorraine, elegant in a light summer blouse and slacks, smiled and blushed—a bride of sixty-eight years. For her part, Lorraine said her Methodist-raised husband from Wapello, Iowa, was "a very good Catholic husband." Although he never officially "converted," "I may as well have. I took this lovely lady to church every single Sunday." The couple raised their two children in the Catholic Church. Lorraine was active in the Altar and Rosary Society, and Bob always made sure to drop her off and pick her up from her evening church gatherings. He smiled as he looked over at his wife and said, "Basically, I did whatever she told me to do." Meeting with these two was a real pleasure, and they were like one of the couples featured in the 1980s movie *When Harry Went Sally*. The hours I spent in their tidy assisted-living home were deeply moving.

Lorraine grew to love rural Iowa and said that her East Coast urban family "loved" visiting. "They really liked seeing all of the land, the open fields, and the animals. It was so different from what they were used to." The couple raised their daughter and son on the farm that Bob inherited from his father, who had inherited it from his father. Bob's family was of Irish and German descent, and all of the men farmed. Bob and Lorraine's son farmed with his dad, and today he works the family farm and his son lives in the Hook family farmhouse. Bob was raised with a strict Methodist frugality and temperance, he said, and it was because of this ingrained generational ethos that he was successful at farming. "My granddad and dad always said, 'Don't pay high rent for more land and don't buy expensive equipment.'" This lesson was born out of struggle and hardship, for Bob's grandfather lost the family farm when Bob was nine years old. "You see, I didn't grow up on the farm, but my dad did." In his youth, Bob made money by hiring himself out for work on area farms. "I was basically a hired hand. I never had insurance and worked for cheap." Bob harvested corn and beans and learned the value of hard work. To illustrate his frugality, Bob said he has never been able to go into a Baskin-Robbins ice cream shop "or some other fancy ice cream store," because he couldn't fathom spending more than fifty cents for an ice cream cone. And going to a Starbucks? Bob's response: "Forget it!" However, Bob has been known to go to McDonald's for its coffee, which was "real good, real inexpensive." Lorraine gently interrupted her husband's story, saying how generous he was with their children and with her. He may have been "cheap" with himself and his own needs, but she assured me—and wanted to make sure that the reader knows—that Bob would always buy the ice cream cones for the kids. Bob smiled and nodded, clearly still smitten with his wife of almost seven decades.

When the conversation shifted to farming today, Bob said that the problem with the younger generation of midwestern Corn Belt farmers is that they shell out too much money for brand-new equipment and then get into problems with debt. "They like the shiny new tractors and high-end equipment, but you know, all that metal comes at a steep price." Bob and Lorraine's friend

Julie, one of St. Joseph's Eucharistic ministers (and friend of Ann and Agnes, part of the St. Joseph coffee hour trio), joined our conversation and agreed with Bob, noting that her parents had shared equipment with other farmers. Lorraine added that "the down side to this is that you have to work around everyone's schedule, but this frugality is a good thing." Frugality has served Bob and Lorraine well, and they were able to save for their retirement, which they are living off of today. Bob was able to purchase land that his son and grandchildren will inherit. He got a bit choked up when he thought about his grandfather who lost the farm, saying that it made this "Iowa boy" feel good about doing something his grandfather had wanted to do for future generations.

Bob and Lorraine moved to the assisted living facility after Lorraine fell and broke several vertebrae in her back. When we met, she was wearing a back brace and needed help walking. Amazingly spry for his age, Bob moved quickly to help his wife when she needed something—whether it was to go to the restroom, get a drink of water, or to cover herself with a lap throw. He said he "never once" considered living without Lorraine, and they moved into the facility together. This is not to say that living in an apartment has been easy for Bob. It has been difficult for him to be away from the farm and from his home. Ever the joker, he said with a wide grin that the center is his "jail." "But seriously, I have to take care of her, so here I am." After a life of almost seventy years together, he could not imagine being by himself; Bob and Lorraine were so clearly connected.[20]

At the time we met, the couple had not been able to attend Mass as frequently due to Lorraine's medical challenges and were grateful to Julie, who faithfully brought them the Eucharist each Sunday, along with a plate of midwestern food made by and for mere mortals: casseroles, cookies, and sausage, from the post-Mass breakfast served by the Altar and Rosary Society. True to form, Bob joked with Julie, calling her his and Lorraine's "personal priest." On a more serious note, he turned to me and shared how much he appreciated Julie's weekly visits for the friendship as much as for an encounter with Jesus that the bread and wine offered. The affection was mutual, as Julie was happy to provide companionship and holy food for her friends.

A common denominator for all of the white Catholic families I met with in Iowa was that food was of major significance. Everyone talked about food during our meetings: growing food, preparing food, and, yes, eating food. For midwestern families like the O'Tooles and Hargrafens, food, faith, family, and work were at the core of their Corn Belt identity in the early to mid-twentieth century. For an Iowa farm boy who married an East Coast big city gal named Lorraine, a connection to the land and the fruits of the land remained part of his core identity into his old age. And when we look around us at twenty-first-century migrants and refugees, the pull factors remain family, faith, and work.

Gail

Gail Stoller and I met for coffee and lunch before going out to see the movie *Tarzan* at an Iowa City theater. We had become acquainted at her Columbus Junction parish about a year earlier and learned that we both liked to see a movie and go to lunch. And drink coffee. So we made plans for Gail to share her experiences with me over lunch and then we'd go on to the movie, which Gail was very excited about. Let's just say that she was looking forward to seeing Alexander Skarsgård, who played Tarzan, running around the jungle in a loincloth. Though the movie was not exactly critically acclaimed, these two midwestern white women enjoyed the show with a bucket of popcorn.

Gail grew up on a farm in Des Moines County, the far western part of the state. Along with her two brothers, she was raised Methodist in "the same Georgian brick home my daddy was raised in." A youthful woman in her mid-sixties, Gail credits an earlier career selling Mary Kay products with maintaining and protecting her skin. She is the kind of woman who always looks polished: her makeup is perfect, her hair is done just right, and her clothes are pressed. Sensible, shined shoes complete the look. Even her pocketbook is organized. I felt a bit rumpled in my wash-and-wear gear next to this impeccably groomed woman who irons each article of clothing. When we met up for our outing, Gail had recently retired and her husband was to retire from his job selling livestock feed by the end of the year. They are comfortable financially and live "unfussy and simple lives, really."

Gail said that her no-nonsense, practical outlook on life stems from her childhood farm existence.

We didn't have an indoor toilet until I was five, about to start kindergarten. I have vivid memories of having to go out in the middle of the night when nature called, you know, to go to the bathroom. The outhouse was right next to the chicken house, and Daddy kept the outhouse clean and emptied it out twice a year. When I used to tell my sons about how I grew up, which was really typical for farm families, my sons thought—and still do, I think—that I was "just out of the cave," you know? But I am grateful to Mama and Daddy for how they raised me and my brothers. They did right by us.

Gail is a woman who has grit. She grew up having to do chores from a very young age. She and her brothers took their baths in the kitchen sink, and her brothers helped their father chop wood to fuel the wood-burning stove that heated the entire house. "My job, which I was real proud of, was to help Daddy haul in the wood and stack it for our home." She was "one hundred percent" positive that she has never shied away from hard work because she was raised to work and to work hard. "I always worked, whether it was stacking wood or cleaning the chicken coop or helping Mama in the kitchen, and my brothers, they worked too. It is just what you did as farm kids and as a farm family. Work was life, and life was work."

Her mother, "Mama," was and remains her role model in life. "My mama had the most amazing work ethic you could imagine," said Gail. Her mother had polio when she was young and experienced symptoms of what the doctor thought was post-polio syndrome when her children were little; she temporarily lost the use of her left arm as well as her eyesight for three days. "My daddy got her a couple of cows to milk after that so she could have therapy. Her arms grew very strong. She also quilted, kept a large garden, and canned gallons of tomatoes, green beans, and corn each year." Even after she was officially diagnosed with multiple sclerosis, not post-polio syndrome, as the doctor and family had originally thought, her mother kept working and was never wheelchair-bound.

As far as religion went, Gail's mother was raised Southern Baptist and her father was raised Roman Catholic, and they were among the first wave of interfaith marriages, or "mixed marriages," of ethnic whites. As white ethnics became "white," interfaith marriages increased, predominantly among Catholics, Protestants, and Jews. By the time Gail and her husband married, interfaith marriages had become much more common nationwide, a new kind of "civil religion."[21] Gail's parents compromised when their children were born and raised them in the Methodist Church, which to them at the time seemed to be "halfway between the two denominations," said Gail. They attended church regularly, and Gail has fond memories of religion in her youth. When Gail later met and married her husband and converted to Catholicism, she and her mother thought about it as "going home" to her father's religion. "Mama had a strong faith in God, and I know that she is with God now in heaven." Her mother's death in 2007 was a huge blow to Gail, as the two were very close. "I didn't have a sister, and my mom was really my best friend and counsel." Gail's belief in God and her Catholic faith got her through the rough parts of grieving the loss of her mother. Her faith also gave her the strength to take care of her diabetic father after her mother's death. "She had always taken care of him, you know, like women of her generation did for their husbands. Up until her death, really, my mom had cooked all of my daddy's meals. She cleaned the house, cleaned up after him, and took care of him. He was really lost after she died." Gail took it upon herself, as so many daughters of her generation do, to cook for her dad and clean the house when she visited and checked in on him. "I would make his meals and individually package and freeze them so that he would have his lunch and dinners prepared, ready to microwave. He just had no idea how to cook and had never used the stove, even." As she did with her dying mother, Gail cared for her father when he was in hospice after suffering a series of heart attacks. Since he'd never slept in a bed, always in a chair, she made sure that he had a comfortable chair in his room.

Gail remembered worrying that her parents would not approve of her converting to Catholicism when she married Gregory. "But I couldn't have been more wrong, you see, as Mama saw how much Gregory loved me and was completely supportive of my decision." Indeed, the Sunday that Gail made her First Confession, Eucharist, and Confirmation at the same Mass prior to marrying Gregory, "Mama came, and that was a testament to her love and faith. She told me that day that Gregory had so much love in his heart for me, and that's what mattered to her. That I would be loved and treated right." This was the day that her mother told her that her father had been raised Catholic, and for Gail, it "sealed the deal. I knew that this was right. It just *felt* right to become Catholic."

Gail and Gregory raised their two sons in St. Joseph's Catholic Church in Columbus Junction. Before they were born, Gail said it was a little hard easing into the Catholic community, especially since she was new to the faith and did not yet have children. Plus, she worked outside of the home, which was not mainstream at that time for many white women but was becoming more so with the next generation. The birth of her son Eric a few years later, however, "opened everything up for me. The ladies had been a little stiff toward me before, but now, well, they couldn't get enough of my beautiful baby boy, and I felt truly welcomed." It was her seven-pound, twelve-ounce, dark-eyed, olive-skinned, and ringlet-haired baby boy—the "most beautiful baby in the world"—that made church a warm and welcoming place. She was a mother now and was seen as a full-fledged member. Parish members brought gifts and food to her and Gregory's home. Becoming a mother was her entryway into St. Joseph's gendered culture. Her role as a Catholic wife and mother were legitimated by her maternal status. When her second son was born a few years later, the parish support continued. Both boys were raised in the church, and Gail is proud of that. She and Gregory always made the time to "talk to them as individuals, and as their mother I always made sure I spent a lot of time with them." Like other younger mothers at St. Joseph parish, the granddaughters of immigrants, Gail worked outside of the home. While white ethnic immigrant women and their daughters tended to focus on home-making after having children, third-generation Gail worked before and after her marriage and during her childbearing years. Her experience is in tandem with other granddaughters of white ethnic immigrants in that they worked in and outside the home to supplement the family's income as well as for personal pleasure and independence.

Gail was proud of working and earning an income and said she wanted to instill in her sons a strong work ethic "to prepare them for life." During her time as a shift manager at the Columbus Junction Economart grocery store, her sons worked part-time under her supervision when they were in high school. One would clean the floors with a heavy-duty commercial floor cleaner while the other stocked shelves. She later became the accountant for the store and then left Economart to work as the bookkeeper and office manager of the town's funeral home. Always one to advocate for herself, Gail negotiated a company car for work purposes when her boss asked her to also be the head bookkeeper of the Muscatine, Riverside, and Lone Tree funeral homes. When we met for coffee and lunch, Gail had recently retired as the chief accountant. While she was happy to be officially "retired," she was in the process of figuring out what to do with her time, since Gregory was still working.

Lois and Tim

For longtime Columbus Junction resident and St. Joseph parishioner Lois Mincks (née Hargrafen), the farm economy has always been a part of her life. She was raised on a small farm in Letts, Iowa, where she and her three siblings helped their father, Urban, outside in the fields with corn and soybeans and with the cattle that they raised. Lois also assisted her mother, Corinne, in the kitchen and learned to be a skilled baker, seamstress, and cook. Indeed, Lois recently retired as Columbus Junction High School's family consumer science teacher, a job she held for over twenty years. While she no longer farms, she lives on rural acreage where she and her late husband Tim raised their three children. Lois loves looking out her back windows and seeing the fields of corn. "I guess that even though I don't farm, farming is in my blood. I was into 4-H as a girl, and my children were active in 4-H. We have a respect for animals and farm life, and we make our own food, which is important to us." 4-H is a way for many American farm families to ensure that their children maintain a connection with farm life and foodways. And according to Lois, while her own parents were not involved in 4-H, which started as a midwestern-based movement in Ohio and Iowa, "they were living the principles of 4-H every day as farmers." For her part, Lois loved the competitive nature of 4-H. She thrived at sewing in particular and said she is "a pretty good baker, too." I can attest to Lois's baking skills. She had prepared a delicious pecan–brown sugar coffee cake for our meeting that afternoon and set out coffee and water for us to have during our afternoon spent together. Lois most certainly exhibited what Iowa author Carol Bodensteiner calls "country hospitality."

For Lois and the other farm women with whom I spent a lot of time, demonstrating their culinary and homemaking skills was important, as it was a legitimation of their roles as wife and mother. Lois takes pride in fulfilling her gendered roles and talked about feeling empowered by her work in and outside of the home. Her reputation as a formidable baker, cook, and seamstress was well known in Columbus Junction and surrounding rural Iowa. Columbus Junctionites teasingly call her "Betty Crocker," she said, because of her outstanding cakes, pies, and fried chicken. Lois always had the best food at church suppers, at school fundraisers, and in her home for visitors. She "learned from the best," she said: her mother, Corinne.

Lois's skills at the culinary arts were part of her identity, so much so that Tim, her husband of over twenty-five years, surprised her on their wedding day with her car all bedecked with trailing crepe-paper streamers, a pumpkin, and a large sign that read "I found someone better than Betty Crocker!" Lois chuckled when she showed me this photo from their wedding day and said she was "really proud" and "happy" to be identified as a wonderful cook, as she had cultivated this vocation since she was a young girl.

In many ways, Lois and Tim represent a typical midwestern-born white couple. While they did not farm for profit, as their parents did, the couple's livelihood revolved around agriculture and homemaking. And Catholicism was the glue that kept it all together, so much so that Lois "never questioned"

Lois and Tim Mincks's wedding photo, St. Malachy parish, Ardon, Iowa, October 22, 1983. Photo by Corinne Hargrafen.

An alternative to the traditional "Just Married" sign on Tim and Lois Mincks's car, October 22, 1983. Photo by Lois Mincks.

anything about her religion. Now a widow, she said, "I guess I feel the need to believe in God," especially since "he took Tim to save him from pain and suffering," and "that we will be together again someday." She paused before saying ever so softly, "I would really hope that I haven't been misled."

Catholicism was bred in Lois's bones, as it has been with so many white rural midwestern families. After her grandmother Hargrafen, her father's mother, had retired and moved from the farm to town, she insisted on a house across from the town's Catholic church so that she could walk to Mass each day—which she did. Catholic identity and Catholic rituals informed her very being. "When her eleven children were born, it was very important that they be baptized the next Sunday, so some were baptized at just a few days old. She's the one that raised a priest and a nun. Her funeral was something, with all of the priests that attended and all the nuns that sang."

Grandma Hargrafen's Mass-attending, ritual-emphasizing, rule-oriented faith was passed down to her children and their spouses. Son Urban's wife Corinne, who was also raised Catholic, was nonetheless influenced by her mother-in-law's Catholic orientation. For her part, Corinne told Lois and her other children to "marry someone of your religion, as it will be one less problem." Lois followed her advice and passed it down to her own children. Two of her three children are with Catholics, and the third is currently engaged to a Muslim man after a relationship with a Catholic "did not turn out so well," according to Lois. For Lois's part, after seeing how badly the previous relationship ended, she is content that her daughter is with a man who treats her well, and even her mother, Corinne, a pre–Vatican II Catholic, loves to see her granddaughter so happy. While interfaith relationships and marriages have become much more mainstream in Iowa and the larger Midwest since the postwar era among Protestants, Catholics, and Jews, interfaith and ethnoreligious relationships among these groups and Muslims remain rare, as is the case nationwide. The ethnoreligious boundaries that separated Christians denominationally prior to World War II are now shifting into place between Christians and Muslims.

Lois and I spent an entire day together in her beautiful country kitchen, which was filled with the delicious smells of her baking. It had been a difficult year for her as her husband of over twenty-five years had died from cancer that had quickly taken over his body. Much of our time was focused on her identity as an Iowa woman who had married an Iowa man who converted to her Catholic faith because of his deep love for her, which made her love him even more. Lois has spent time this past year typing up her memories of her life

Hargrafen family birthday celebration, 1957. Photo by Lois Mincks.

with Tim, and the exercise has given her moments of happiness in the deep well of grief. Lois was open and candid about her life and faith, and throughout the day she would stop, overcome with a grief that was still so strong, and cry. I held her hand and cried with her as she talked about her deep love for Tim and the emptiness she feels now. Lois was and remains a loving and loyal wife to her beloved spouse.

Lois Hargrafen Mincks's Irish and German Catholic grandparents were among the first wave of immigrants to the state of Iowa. Her mother's parents had fled the poverty and misery that plagued them in the wake of the Irish potato famine. They made their way to the land-rich midwestern state where they would farm, find a church community, and make their mark on the land and its contours. Her father's parents came with their families to farm land and to build a Catholic community. Children of the first wave of migrants, like Lois's mother, Corinne O'Toole Hargrafen, have vivid memories of hard-scrabble times tempered with good memories of parish picnics, family events, and priests who were like family.

Many of these early Irish Catholic migrants became rich in acreage, land that would be farmed by subsequent waves of Latino migrants. When we take a step back and examine continuities and changes with the older and newer waves of migrations, we find that these newer migrants and inhabitants of the Corn Belt came to the fertile region for similar reasons: a chance to remake their lives and to settle and make homes.

CHAPTER 2

Rural Faith Encounters

FOR THE PAST SEVERAL SUMMERS, the Roman Catholic priest Father Joseph Sia has held an outdoor Mass for Mexican farmworkers in rural Conesville, Iowa. This hamlet is seven miles from his Columbus Junction parish. For one evening each hot, humid July, Father Joseph leads this special Mass for the migrant men who travel to rural Iowa each summer on H-2A visas as temporary agricultural workers. The men are bused in to harvest melons in the acreage across the street from where the Mass is held. Delivering the homily in Spanish, this trilingual priest spends several hours after the Mass eating and spending time with the men who have come to rest, pray, and eat. A small makeshift altar is flanked by statues of Santo Niño and la Virgen de Guadalupe.

The large Rodriguez family, who are members of Father Joseph's parish and who live in Conesville, sponsor the Mass and meal each year. They open their home and yard—directly across from the migrant farmworkers' housing facility—to the workers and other guests, serving up fresh tortillas, carne asada, *ensalada*, arroz, and frijoles until after nightfall. Large glass containers of homemade *horchata*, a sweet rice and cinnamon drink, and *agua tamarindo*, a tangy tamarind beverage, along with bottles of Jarritos soda, are offered to the farmworkers and other guests. The host family members spend the entire day preparing the food and setting up tents and chairs in honor of the men who work the fields. They pay for the entire event, as it is something they feel "called to do": "We must give thanks to those who work hard for their families and for us," said the Rodriguez matron. The annual farmworkers' Mass held in a backyard that is adjacent to acres of corn is a celebration of work, Latino heritage, and a deep Catholic faith.

Anyone who drives through the midwestern region of the United States today will be sure to notice one thing: rows upon rows of corn. Whether it is green and stalky in the summer or brown sugar–colored in the fall, corn dominates the Iowa landscape. The plant and its treasured yellow grain are featured in Iowa folklore, art, and midwestern cookouts as well as at local and state fairs, where butter-drenched ears are a featured cuisine. Corn has been the dominant midwestern crop since the mid-nineteenth century, and the states of Illinois, Indiana, Iowa, Minnesota, Nebraska, and South Dakota are collectively known as the Corn Belt.[1] With the rise of commercial agriculture and livestock, most especially hogs and cattle, demand for corn has grown since the mid-twentieth century. And demand for workers has risen as well.

Any nostalgia that we might have for county fairs and Future Farmers of America events, the kind that Lois and Tim Mincks and their children took part in, must be tempered with a new understanding of workers, crops, and animals. Farming is labor-intensive, economically challenging, and difficult work, and the late twentieth-century decline of family farms and the rise of corporate farming and meatpacking has radically altered the landscape of Corn Belt states and impacted family life. The 1980s broad-scale mechanization of farming, animal husbandry, and slaughtering may be more "efficient," but it has proven damaging—even devastating—to the earth and to workers. Indicative of the current state of animal husbandry and welfare and food production today is the confined animal feeding operation, more commonly known as CAFO (pronounced CAH-foh). Such operations might be harder to see from the highway and are certainly not as pleasant to the eye, but these CAFOs are also an increasing presence in the state. Hog, cattle, and chicken CAFOs dot the Corn Belt landscape. Lines of tractor trailer trucks carrying cattle and hogs for slaughter are familiar sights on the I-80 corridor. The smell—pungent, raw—is pervasive as ammonia, hydrogen sulfide, and carbon dioxide form an odoriferous stew.[2]

Iowa is no longer a state known primarily for family farms but is one that is host to the conjoined industries of corporate agriculture and meatpacking. Today it ranks as the top corn-, soybean-, hog-, and egg-producing state in the nation. It ranks second for red meat production, and over 400 million bushels of Iowa-grown corn feeds Iowa livestock. Corn- and meat-related industries have sprung up around the heart of Iowa's economy: from ethanol plants that produce fuel for the car-dependent state (and the rest of the nation) to meatpacking plants where hogs, chicken, and cattle are slaughtered and packaged for human consumption, Iowa is the national and global hub for corn and meat. Iowa is indeed a major "cultivation corridor" of the Midwest.

Father Joseph Sia, Columbus Junction, Iowa, December 12, 2017. Photo by Lois Mincks.

The shift from urban to rural processing plants in the late twentieth century has led to new migration and settlement patterns. Whereas migrants from the late nineteenth to mid-twentieth century migrated primarily to urban areas for work in industry, after the passage of NAFTA, industry work relocated to developing countries, U.S.-Mexico borderlands, and rural America. As eminent sociologist of religion Robert Wuthnow has written, the "huge processing plants in right-to-work states such as Arkansas, Kansas, and South Dakota" attracted Latino immigrant workers for "dirt cheap wages."[3] New Latino migrants settled in small to midsize towns like Garden City, Kansas, and Columbus Junction, Iowa, changing the dynamics of the communities almost overnight.[4]

Latino and African workers not only make up a large percentage of the CAFO workforce that tend hogs, cattle, and chickens but also dominate the workforce at the next phase in food production: the combined slaughterhouses and packing plants that dot the Iowa landscape, including the Columbus Junction Tyson plant that I toured as part of the research for this book.

And more and more, African and Chin Burmese refugees fill the workplaces of meat processing plants. With the legal status of so many Latino workers in question and in flux, refugees are becoming the preferred employee in midwestern Corn Belt meatpacking and Big Ag–related industries. And it is corn that keeps it all running. Corn feeds the animals that provide work for those seeking labor. And it is migrant and refugee labor that has revitalized small towns and rural communities, in addition to creating what Latino scholar Louis Mendoza has called a "cultural paradox" in which "the way of life of elderly whites is often preserved by the labor of new immigrants, who often bring change to their new communities in the form of Spanish language newspapers and radio, Mexican restaurants and tienditas, and a robust presence of Spanish language in the schools and on the soccer fields."[5]

From mid-nineteenth-century Methodist itinerant ministers to Irish and German Catholics who made Iowa their new home, Protestants and Catholics have made their mark on the state's religious and cultural history. Since the 1870s, corn and animal husbandry have defined the contours of the land and the livelihoods of those who inhabit it. But the Corn Belt is more than an agricultural and land-based regional characterization. The Corn Belt can be an evocative conceptual tool to reimagine and rework American religious histories and sociologies. Present-day religion and spirituality in the Corn Belt is part of a complex and emergent Global Midwest. And it is Latinos, the vast majority of whom are Catholic, who are at the center of the Global Midwest. It is Latinos who, joined by even more recent migrants and refugees, including Mayans, Sudanese, Congolese, Vietnamese, and Burmese, cultivate and pick the crops as well as prepare the meat that feeds the world. From the perspective of Corinne Hargrafen, a child of Irish immigrant farmers and the wife of a German Catholic farmer, the rural Corn Belt and parish have changed dramatically in her lifetime. St. Joseph the Worker parish, her second parish after the closing of her childhood-to-early-adulthood-parish of St. Malachy, is aptly named, for it has always been a parish of women and men who have worked hard, from the late nineteenth-century Irish and German Catholic farmer parishioners to today's Latino and Chin Burmese women and men who work at Tyson Fresh Meats down the road. While the ethnic makeup of the parish has changed dramatically in Corinne's lifetime, what has not changed is the reality that working-class people go to St. Joseph's for spiritual nourishment, community, and rest.

St. Joseph's is a moral community where parishioners, like Corinne and daughter Lois, "feel an obligation to one another and uphold local ways of being that govern their expectations about ordinary life and support their feelings of being at home and doing the right things."[6] The moral community of belonging and home is experienced today by the Latino parishioners as well who fill the pews for the Spanish-language Mass each Sunday. White non-Latino parishioners are also drawn to St. Joseph the Worker for the moral community and for what the Latina anthropologist Sujey Vega calls "ethnic belonging."[7]

Rural farmers, mostly white non-Latinos who own the farms and employ Latino and other nonwhite workers, now produce one or two commodities on vast farms that are in effect agribusinesses. While the midwestern family farm of the late nineteenth century and early to mid-twentieth century used to sustain a much wider variety of plants, animals, and the people who cared for them, today's "farms" are monocultural. The concentration of wealth and the decline of diverse farms has led to rapid demographic changes in the rural Midwest.[8] But the mega-farms that remain and the factories that process their commodities depend on Latinos, from those who arrived in the early twentieth century to more recent migrants—undocumented as well as documented. In many Iowa towns and cities, as in many others throughout the United States, Latinos are the fastest-growing group in the state. According to the League of United Latin American Citizens (LULAC), Latinos constituted 6 percent of Iowa's population in 2017, which is a 132.2 percent increase from 2000.[9] By understanding the everyday realities of whites and Latino and African refugees in the Corn Belt, ground zero for the new migrations, we can better grasp the intersectionalities of economics and religion not only in this region of the country but across the United States.

Latinos are now the majority nonwhite ethnic group in a growing number of midwestern towns. By all accounts, Latinos are the major force behind the changing demographics of Iowa and the larger Midwest. Formerly declining, even dying small towns are experiencing a revival. Drive through any small town with a sizable Latino population in Iowa (or anywhere in the United States) and you'll find a *panadería* and *tortillería*, restaurants and small businesses owned by Latinos. As Wuthnow asserts, "Rural America is also profoundly indebted to immigrant laborers working at low-wage jobs in towns, at construction sites, and on farms."[10]

When we focus on the economics of the Corn Belt states, we see that meatpacking has historically been Iowa's largest manufacturing industry. As anthropologist of rural America Deborah Fink has written, in Iowa, the meatpacking and farming industries were separate but mutually supporting and reinforcing; meatpacking was based on wage labor and farming on self-employment.[11] According to Fink, Iowa farms have always hired workers, and these wage laborers "built and maintained the infrastructure that under-girded Iowa's farm and small-town society."[12]

Yet the 1960s–1980s downturn in U.S. manufacturing contributed to the global spread of factories and cheap labor and shuttered U.S. urban meatpacking giants in cities like Chicago and Omaha. What emerged in the 1980s in states like Iowa were corporate farms and meatpacking plants where unions were scarce and wages far less than they had been in urban unionized plants.[13] Farms across Iowa went bankrupt at the same time that the "Big Three"—meat-packers Iowa Beef Packers, ConAgra, and Cargill—set up shop in rural Iowa, discouraged unions, and depressed wages in jobs that were becoming ever more dangerous. Moreover, the corporatization of meatpacking led to an increasing rift between the producers, those who raised the animals, and the processors, those who killed them and packaged the meat.

In a sharp departure from 1960s–1980s meatpacking culture, today mostly nonwhite midwestern workers, primarily refugees from Central America and Central and East Africa, tend, kill, and package the animals that feed the world. And these individuals and their families, given the politics of race in U.S. history more broadly, are among the most vulnerable inhabitants of the state and the entire Corn Belt region. The Catholic Church in Iowa, among other religious institutions, has taken notice of these workers and their plight.

Increasingly, priests from around the state have become vocal leaders in what I am calling a "politics of inclusivity." Priests in the Hawkeye State, like Fathers Rudy Juarez, Greg Steckel, Bernie Weir, and Joseph Sia, want to make their state and their parishes more inclusive spaces—they want to transform the minds and hearts of Iowans. Father Rudy has led pro-immigration rallies; Father Greg works closely with the West Liberty school superintendent and city leaders, and Father Joseph has educated himself on ICE raid awareness and preparation. Their personal theologies that hinge on a preferential op-tion for the poor are part of a long-storied, if contested, history of liberation theology within a Roman Catholic theological culture. All four of these east-ern Iowa priests put themselves out in the public sphere and see themselves as advocates for their Latino and migrant Catholic parishioners. Moreover, these priests are reaching out of their theological comfort zones and are meeting with pastors from various Protestant denominations—including Baptist, Methodist, and Presbyterian—to work toward solutions. There is a popular slogan in Iowa today, seen on car stickers everywhere: ANF, short for "America Needs Farmers," created and popularized by the famous Hawk-eye football coach Hayden Fry. If the priests I have been working with had their way—and they might, given their stalwart constitutions—they would create a new sticker that reads "America Needs Latinos," or "America Needs Refugees."

Priests like Fathers Joseph, Bernie, Rudy, and Greg are among the many hands working to make the Midwest a place for all and have become vocal leaders in the politics of inclusivity. They advocate for Latinos' and refugees' rights in this fraught labor and racial context and acknowledge that they must be priests for "all people," yet balancing the needs and desires of their brown and white parishioners is a real challenge. Nevertheless, Fathers Rudy and Bernie remain public-facing in their activism on behalf of Latino parishioners; Father Greg continues his behind-the-scenes allyship and activism, most recently in his new role as hospital chaplain; and Father Joseph has expanded his allyship role on a diocesan level, where the bishop and staff are committed to migrants and underrepresented women and men.

Rural midwestern parishes fall under the United States Conference of Catholic Bishops' rubric of "special parishes." They are doubly "special" in that they are rural and are home to a mixed ethnic congregation. Tricia Mein Bruce and Brett Hoover, sociologists of Catholicism, respectively refer to parishes like the ones featured in this book as "special" and "shared," and in many ways this terminology is helpful as we work to understand the dynamics of mixed ethnic, linguistic, and rural parishes like the ones in eastern Iowa.[14] But given the demands placed on priests and the reality that there are all kinds of problems that priests like Fathers Rudy, Greg, Bernie, and Joseph deal with, it seems like *practical* might best describe these Iowa and broader midwestern parishes.

The most effective religious leaders, business owners, and plant operators, like those at Columbus Junction's Tyson Foods, at Tama's Iowa Premium Beef, and in rural parishes that dot the Midwest, are those that address diversity and do practical things to make all employees or parishioners feel welcome. The predominantly white American men and women who are in positions of power and authority, whether at church or in the workplace, not only must introduce practical measures to make their spaces welcoming and inclusive but also must go a step further and accompany their primarily refugee workers and parishioners on their journey. They must "walk the walk," as the middle-aged Father Bernie put it, and meet their more vulnerable community members where they live and work. They must accompany their employees and members of their religious congregations if they want to fully understand their struggles and needs. Father Bernie is all too aware of the growing divide between what he calls the "producing class" and the "processing class." The former tends to be made up of white farmers and corporate heads who raise the animals for slaughter, while it is mostly Black and brown women and men who kill and process the meat. Producers tend to be mostly white, middle- to upper-middle-class, and removed from the killing of animals. It is poor whites and refugees who process the animals and who are lower- to lower-middle-class at best economically. Father Bernie is deeply concerned with the stratification of wealth that he has seen expand during his long tenure as a rural Iowa priest.

When we turn our gaze to Corn Belt states like Iowa, we can gain a deeper appreciation of how Catholics—priests and laypersons alike—are taking concrete measures to address poverty, racism, workplace discrimination, and abuse in their parishes and communities. The rise of rural Catholic ministries and activist priests in states like Iowa should not surprise us, as it is in keeping with U.S. Catholics' historic predilections to aid migrants and their communities. Neither is the Latino presence new to Iowa or to the larger midwestern Corn Belt, dating back to the 1880s with migrant farmworkers. Sizable, long-standing Latino communities have contributed greatly to the economic and cultural well-being in the Midwest since the turn of the twentieth century. Latino migration, along with non-European migration, accelerated in the years following the Immigration Act of 1965, paving the way for a more diverse ethnic, linguistic, and cultural United States. Yet when we fast-forward to the first quarter of the twenty-first century, we find new implementations of restrictions and quotas placed on migrants to the United States, with clear preference being given to white European migrants.

In many ways, what we are finding in the United States today directly follows the race-based policies of migration set in motion by the 1924 Johnson-Reed Act, which gave preference to European and Canadian migrants. For nonwhite and Muslim refugees today, it is much more difficult to become a citizen, let alone reside in the United States, without conditions of extreme precarity in their home countries. The combined, interlocking forces of U.S. empire, instability in Central American countries, and U.S. policies that are anti-Latino leave many Latino individuals and families in perpetual limbo, not fully citizens but liminal inhabitants of a place they are not allowed legally to call home. Those who have applied for asylum and refugee status in the hopes of eventual citizenship endure endless waiting and the nagging insecurity of not knowing if or when they will be deported back to the very places they fled. For Latino families in the United States today, theirs has become a culture of anxiety and fear, as many have under the same roof citizens, asylum seekers, and undocumented women and men (those who have not sought asylum and refugee status out of fear of being deported). And Latino families and communities are divided, as neighbors have been known to call the police and other government authorities to "tell on" undocumented persons living next door or down the street from them. U.S. immigration policies have torn families apart and continue to do so. I have talked with many Latino individuals who have a family member at home who is afraid to ever go outside for fear of being deported.

The people I spent time with for this book and the priests who work with them as allies and advocates do not want these asylum seekers/refugees/migrants to be sent back to the lands of their birth because of the interlocking realities of violence and economic instability. Going home can mean rape, torture, or death for women and men deported back to violent countries.[15] For the thousands of women fleeing domestic or gang violence and migrating to the United States to seek asylum and refugee status, the violence inflicted on and toward them was declared ineligible for asylum by Attorney General Jeff Sessions in June 2018.[16] Precarity is part of life in the United States for Latino citizens, asylum-seeking refugees, undocumented persons, and DREAMers alike (those Latinos brought over as children by parents or guardians who have not been declared citizens). Legal status may soften the pain of racism and fear of being personally deported, but that legal status does not necessarily extend to family members or neighbors.[17]

While precarity is part of the everyday existence of Latinos in Iowa and the larger United States, growth also characterizes the Latino population. Latinos constitute the largest U.S. ethnic minority group. Religious organizations such as the Catholic Church, historically the favored church for Latinos going back to Spanish colonization, stand to benefit because of the population growth, as do evangelical nondenominational churches, Pentecostals, Mormons, Muslims, and Methodist-affiliated groups.[18] Between 2000 and 2018, the increase in the number of self-reporting Latinos in the state of Iowa was at 135.8 percent. As of September 2019, the most recent data at the time of the publication of this book, Iowa's Latino population was slightly above 6 percent of the statewide total population.[19] When we consider the geographic range of the broader Midwest and the Corn Belt, Latinos are clearly on their way to becoming the future of those states (and the country as a whole). Moreover, mainline denominations and religious institutions like the Catholic Church that have seen membership decline across the board in the past decade are vying for Latino membership.[20] And there is no doubt that Latino political and social clout will continue to expand. The League of United Latin

American Citizens sponsored its first-ever get-out-the-vote drive in the state, and its efforts paid large dividends. Latinos came out in record numbers and were visual and vocal opponents of Donald Trump (especially his "Build the wall" and "Mexicans are rapists" rhetoric) in Iowa's February 2016 caucuses.

Father Joseph

For Father Joseph Sia, the Postville, Iowa, ICE raid of 2008 was an epiphany and a wake-up call to action. Initiated by the U.S. Department of Homeland Security, the raid on the Orthodox-Jewish-owned-and-operated Agriprocessors meatpacking plant, at the time the nation's largest producer of kosher meat, was the largest single raid in U.S. history. A total of nearly 400 undocumented workers, primarily Guatemalan and Mexican, were arrested, detained, and eventually deported. Details that have surfaced about the working conditions of the kosher meat plant are chilling and confirm the perception that meatpacking is one of the most dangerous occupation in the United States. Men and women worked fifteen-hour shifts with few breaks, using inadequate and dangerous equipment that included dull knives. Moreover, allegations of mental and physical abuse and intimidation are on record, and employers took advantage of workers' undocumented status, knowing full well that they would not speak out because they would risk being deported. As a result of the horrors of the Postville raid and the aftermath, many Iowa churches—Protestant, Catholic, and nondenominational alike—became much more aware of and involved in pro-immigrant, pro-workers' rights. While some Catholic priests and laypersons, like those of St. Bridget's in Postville, were already aware of and concerned with the needs of undocumented Latinos before the raid, others throughout the state, including Jewish groups, were horrified and spurred to action and humanitarian outreach post-Postville.[21]

Father Joseph Sia was among the eastern Iowa Catholics and priests to be deeply shaken and moved by the Postville raid. Father Joseph, a Filipino who was pre-med at the University of the Philippines in Manila, admitted during our interview that he had not been sympathetic to undocumented, "illegal" workers before the Postville raid. Father Joseph came to Iowa City in 2002 to pursue his doctorate in genetics, but after arriving in the Midwest, he struggled. "I was living alone in Coralville and felt really isolated. My whole family was in the Philippines, and I was lonely. I knew I wanted to serve people, so I spent a lot of time in the hospital prayer room praying that I would find my vocation." Sia said he had always been attracted to the priesthood as he grew up in the Catholic school system and in the church in Manila. After spending much time seeking discernment, he had an epiphany while praying in his apartment on Pentecost Sunday in 2003: "My vocation came to me.... While I had fears, I had an assurance I hadn't had before. The very next day I contacted the vocation director and that next night I was in Davenport at a vocations dinner."

Sia attended Mundelein Seminary in Chicago and was ordained by Bishop Martin Amos in 2008 in the Diocese of Davenport. He has learned about the deep connections between Mexican and Filipino Catholicism and feels at home ministering to Latinos because of their home-based faith, their reverence for the Virgin, and their emphasis on family. He thinks that the rise in ordinations among Filipino and Vietnamese priests in Davenport bodes well for Hispanic ministry, as these priests are more acculturated and sensitive to the needs of minority groups and recent migrants. Father Joseph mentioned the sensitivity training he received as a seminarian that gave him the deeper empathy he said he "really needed" to be effective as a priest to women and men who were undocumented: "It was a voluntary immersion experience, and twelve of us signed up and went. We went in a van overnight from Chicago to Dallas and then crossed the border from El Paso to Ciudad Juárez. We crossed as a group and we crossed on foot. The most intense part was crossing on foot coming back into the United States, because we were able to feel what it felt like as a migrant crossing over. Of course, there are differences because we had papers and didn't 'really' have to fear getting caught, but we were still scared. I remember clearly."

Father Joseph was a newly installed parish priest in Columbus Junction's St. Joseph the Worker parish at the time of the Postville raid, presiding over two services at his own parish as well as delivering the Spanish-language Mass at St. Joseph parish in West Liberty, Iowa, twenty-four miles away. When the ICE raid on Postville's Agriprocessors plant was announced, some 145 miles from Columbus Junction, Father Joseph was still getting adjusted to the state of Iowa and his hectic schedule of three Masses every Sunday. As the Postville raid and post-raid events were unfolding and being reported, Father Joseph was deeply entrenched in Latino ministry. Yet as he reflected back on that time, he acknowledged that he was not really sympathetic and that he did not really understand the plight of undocumented workers.

I am an immigrant myself and I came from the Philippines. I have had to deal with a lot of paperwork, and I suppose that this was why I was unsympathetic to the undocumented. I thought, "Well, they should get their papers, just like I did." My eyes were opened after I took a tour of the Tyson plant here in town with other members of the ministerial association. It was in 2008, literally right after Postville. I saw how incredibly difficult the work is, how dangerous, and how horrible it is. I saw how incredibly hard the workers work—very, very few people can do this kind of work, and most Americans cannot fathom this kind of work.

Father Joseph remembered with horror what he called the "awful, awful smell" at the "horrible plant," the rudimentary looking knives that were used by workers, and the immense skill that a worker must possess in order to avoid being injured on the job. He talked about how a solid majority of the approximately 2,000 residents of Columbus Junction are Latinos of mostly Mexican descent (slightly over 60 percent in 2015). In addition, in the past several years, the town has welcomed a growing number of Burmese who have come to process pork at the plant, which pays good wages.[22] Father Joseph said that Tyson prefers to hire Burmese workers because they have their papers, unlike the majority of undocumented women and men who hail from south-central Mexico. He noted how, in a fascinating turn of events, the Postville raid has spurred the formation of interfaith alliances in towns and cities across Iowa. Churches and faith communities that used to ignore each other, he said, are now coming together in a common cause to aid workers and to promote workers' rights.

The interfaith alliances among Protestant Christians, Catholic Christians, and Orthodox Jews that began in Postville after the raid have inspired other small Iowa towns and rural areas to band together to come to the aid of refugees. Father Joseph was among those clergypersons in his small Iowa town who was motivated to "do something" after the 2008 raid. He saw how "literally overnight" ICE agents tore through the fabric of Postville and its multilingual communities. It was more than a packing plant that was shuttered: "Close to 400 people who were here to make a better living for their families were sent back to the places they had left for a better life. Families were destroyed." Father Joseph knew that "this just couldn't happen in Columbus Junction; I knew I needed to step up and help out to do what I could to help prevent deportations. This was my community. My people." Like Postville, Columbus Junction's economy is dependent on the meatpacking industry. The slaughter and packaging of animals is what keeps both towns going.

Columbus Junction's faith communities are part of a loose network of interfaith coalitions dedicated to putting aside theological differences for the common goal of aiding at-risk Latinos and other vulnerable workers. As he looked reflectively down at his adoring pet dog, Red, Father Joseph said that

Rural Iowa CAFO, 2020. Photo by Kristy Nabhan-Warren.

"Postville really brought ministers together." Members of the Columbus Junction coalition—pastors from Baptist, Methodist, Pentecostal, and Lutheran churches—meet regularly, and one of the issues they discuss is their preparedness in the event of a raid at the local Tyson plant. "While we can't stop or prevent a raid at this point, at least we can be prepared to offer humanitarian aid to families and make sure that the children are not traumatized in the way they were in Postville."

In addition to his deep commitment to the majority-Latino and steadily growing Burmese parish populations that mirror the town's demographics, Father Joseph is always mindful of his white non-Latino parishioners and constituents. Yet ministering to an ever-shrinking number of whites, a handful of Burmese parishioners, and an expanding parish of Latinos is anything but easy. He likens his service to a "schizophrenic ministry" because he is constantly trying to appease his non-Spanish-speaking as well as his Spanish-speaking parishioners. St. Joseph's at Columbus Junction offers two Masses, the first in English to approximately 50 white parishioners and the second in Spanish to a full service of approximately 200 Latino parishioners. While attendance is sparse at the first Mass due to declining birth rates, deaths, and aging white Catholics, the second service is bursting at the seams. Father Joseph has been working on ways to combine the Masses and to get some cross-over with the parishioners. He has experimented with a bilingual Mass with mixed results. Smiling at the thought of it, he said that "no one is truly happy, it seems," when he offers the bilingual Mass. "It's not 'Spanish' or 'English' enough and leaves everyone feeling unsatisfied." He remains committed to it, however, as he sees it unifying the parish. "The upside of the bilingual Mass is that is does bring people together. There are so many kids, and many of them do not speak Spanish, at least not fluently. I have been asked by so many parents to offer the Mass as a bilingual Mass so that their kids and now grandkids can understand and follow along, and so I do." Father Joseph is always careful, he said, not to offend "the Anglos"; a priest who served at the parish before him had made his preference for the Spanish-speaking Latinos clear and offended many of the non-Spanish-speaking Anglos. When Father Joseph talked about his time in Columbus Junction, he emphasized that the parish is a shared one. "I wouldn't say it is an integrated parish . . . no, that would not be the case. It is a shared parish, and as such it is a schizophrenic parish, because so much needs to happen at once and for so many people." He likened his role among Latino and Burmese parishioners as more of a respected authority figure, while his role among his Anglo, non-Spanish-speaking parishioners is more of "a friend."

Father Joseph is not sure if a truly "integrated" parish is possible, and for now he focuses his efforts on making sure St. Joseph's in Columbus Junction is a "shared" parish that is welcoming to his various constituents, old, middle-aged, young, Latino, Burmese, and Anglo. He relies on Deacon José Duran to help him in his ongoing efforts to reach out to all of his people. "My role as a spiritual advisor is to bridge the divisions that exist between Anglos and Hispanics. I have to go slow and not appear to be too much of advocate, you know, or else I will offend the Anglo community. It is a delicate issue, and I work very hard at maintaining balance in the parish."

Father Joseph spent some time talking about how more of the Latino youth from Columbus Junction are attending universities like the University of Iowa and Iowa State University and how the community's pride is tinged with sadness because "there is not much here for them to return to outside the Tyson plant, so they have to leave home after they graduate." For small towns like Columbus Junction, the "brain drain" that used to apply only to white non-Latinos now also applies to Latino youth, who, while they might want to return home to their families, do not want to work at the plants like Tyson. And for their part, their parents, as much as they want their college-educated children to return home, do not want them to work in the same grueling, dangerous jobs that they have occupied. They want more for their children. For his part, Father Joseph—spiritual advisor and mentor to Columbus Junction

Anglo, Latino, and Burmese Catholics—draws on his own position as an immigrant to the United States as a way to make connections with the migrants who come to the small town to work.

Working toward Inclusive Parishes

Father Joseph and other eastern Iowa priests are engaging in a politics of inclusivity, social justice, and ecumenical, interfaith dialogue and are challenging their parishioners as well as members of their larger communities not only to tolerate Latinos and other migrant groups but to welcome them. They are on the front lines of cultural, linguistic, and religious encounters and oftentimes take on the role of mediators and negotiators. Father Joseph, like other activist pro-Latino priests in Iowa, wants Iowa and its parishes to be places where a politics of inclusivity, social justice, and workplace reform is not just preached but practiced.

Recently, Father Joseph gave a Lenten season homily and challenged the parishioners at his different services to help create an inclusive parish.

> I would like to invite each Mass to attend the other Mass so that we can have an encounter with one another right here in church. We are all Catholics, and we have the same beliefs; we look to Jesus to save us. Even if we speak different languages, we have different traditions, we eat different foods, we belong to the same church. I know the situation out there—and unfortunately it has been magnified by some politicians, especially during this campaign period. They can debate about it on national TV and talk about it in Washington, but here in C[olumbus] J[unction] is where the rubber hits the road. We all experience it every day, as we have in the past thirty or so years, especially those of you who have been living here a long time. The situation in not simple, and there is no easy solution, but it is not only a political situation, it is a situation in our church. This is why I am talking about it here. Jesus Christ tells us to love one another, and one way we can do that is to get to know each other right here in the church and break down that border between the Masses, and our church is a safe place to have that encounter.[23]

Father Joseph encourages parishioners at both Masses to take what he calls "small steps": attending the English Mass if the parishioner's first language is Spanish, and attending the Spanish Mass if the parishioner's first language is English. I have observed this in action, as I am no longer the only non-Latino at the Spanish-language Mass but one of a handful. Creating inclusive secular and religious communities is hard work, but all of the priests I spent time with and interviewed in the rural Corn Belt believe it is possible. Religious leaders would like to have integrated churches—churches that are multi-ethnic and where Latino and white native-born churchgoers feel comfortable worshipping together—but they tend to preside over de facto segregated congregations. As Mary Jo Bane, sociologist of Catholicism in the United States, has noted, most parishes in America are segregated, and ethnic groups exist as parallel communities in the same parish.[24] As I have observed at St. Joseph the Worker in Columbus Junction, ethnic and linguistic boundaries exist between the minority white and the predominant Latino parishioners.

Most Latinos prefer to worship in Spanish because it "feels like home," said Abby, a second-generation Latina who was raised, baptized, and confirmed at St. Joseph's and who still lives in her childhood home. While she is completely bilingual in English and Spanish, English "just feels strange because it is not my language." And she wants her infant son to grow up to be proud of his language and heritage. A single mom, Abby and her baby live with her parents while she saves up money for a home of her own. Her parents, exclusive Spanish-speakers, take care of her little boy while she works and speak Spanish to him. Abby wants to reinforce that her first language and the culture her parents brought with them to the United States is beautiful, and attending Spanish Mass is part of her plan to ensure that her son is fully at home in the increasingly Latino Midwest and United States. At the same time, she is fully aware of and has been the victim of racist slurs, such as the white middle-aged man at a Chinese buffet asking her in a hostile way if she was "Asian" or "Mexican" and "how long I had been in America." As much as Abby is raising her son to be fully Mexicano, as she put it, she also wants him to be "totally comfortable" in what she calls the "white world." She hopes that his ability to speak two languages and operate in two cultural worlds will help him succeed in life. It is what she prays to la Virgen for every time she attends Mass with her little boy.

Abby knows she is fortunate to have her parents helping out with their grandson so she can work as a certified nursing assistant at a rural nursing home. She put herself through community college and hopes to one day obtain her nursing degree from the University of Iowa. She has experienced some upward job mobility because CNAs, like all health workers, are in huge demand, especially in aging white states like Iowa, where in 2016, 16.4 percent of the population was over sixty-five, and the percentage will continue to increase.[25] Abby said she has mostly felt welcome and appreciated by the elderly white women she cares for in the facility where she is currently employed.

But a turning point for her occurred when she experienced racialized slights at work: "One of the white ladies mentioned 'the brown people,' and then everyone started putting in their two cents about how we need to patrol the borders, etcetera, etcetera." As we sat on a park bench on a brisk fall day, Abby paused and said with passion,

> This makes me *so angry*, you know. I didn't say anything because I needed to keep a cool head and to get my work done, you know, but it is ironic. Yes, that is what it is, ironic. It is brown people like me who are taking care of the white people in our country, the people who live in nursing homes and assisted living facilities. Their own families in many cases do not visit them, and even when they have dementia they know. They know they are being abandoned. I am in the medical field because I take care of people, and I think I am doing something very important. I am taking care of *your* mother and father, you know. . . . How dare these people . . . people like Trump say that my people are "rapists." This is racist, and it is insulting. Without "brown people" this country wouldn't have people like me to care for the elderly.

Abby's passionate response to how she has been made to feel marginalized and ashamed of her heritage speaks to the age of Trump and how citizenship has become synonymous with whiteness. Abby was born in the United States, and her parents, proud of both their Mexican and American status, are part of a long-standing Latino population in the broader Corn Belt and Midwest. But Abby and so many second- and third-generation Latinos I have spent time with and interviewed over the past several years said they feel the sting of racism each day. "It's like we aren't seen as fully being *people*, let alone American," Abby observed.

One reason for the backlash against Latinos, regardless of their country of birth, is that any language that is not English is intimidating to our recalcitrantly monolingual nation. For the white Iowa-born Catholics at parishes like St. Joseph's in Columbus Junction, attending the Spanish Mass feels "very foreign." Even if they want to be there, they are "nervous" and feel "awkward" and "dumb" because they do not understand Spanish. While a handful of the white Altar and Rosary Society ladies I spent time with enjoy attending Spanish-language Mass every so often, they "don't get as much out of" the Mass as they do the English service because they understand very little of the language. Like Abby, who feels strange worshipping in English, her second language, these ladies feel strange worshipping in Spanish. And unlike Abby, who is completely bilingual and bicultural and operates in both

worlds each day, these white ethnic Catholics—Corinne Hargrafen's generation and younger—are monolingual. While racism and ethnocentrism most
certainly come into play for some parishioners, for the majority of white ethnic Catholics today in the Midwest, worshipping in Spanish just doesn't "feel
right," because they do not speak or understand *español*. Whites and Latinos share church space and come together for certain celebrations, but for
the most part, they are two separate communities, two distinctive churches,
under one roof.

St. Joseph the Worker in Columbus Junction is typical of midwestern parishes that have begun to diversify with primarily Latino parishioners, mostly
of Mexican descent. White and Latino churchgoers worship separately and
exchange pleasantries—briefly—in between Masses. Outside of parish life
and church time, though, they mostly remain separate communities, focused
on their in-group needs. The reality is complicated. While there is some stated
hostility, describing relations at St. Joseph's and the majority of Catholic parishes in Iowa and the broader midwestern Corn Belt region as racist or ethnocentric is incomplete. It is more accurate to say that insecurity, feelings of
awkwardness, and microaggressions in varying degrees reflect the state of
things.

I experienced some of this tension and awkwardness firsthand during one
of the post–English Mass potlucks at St. Joseph's. I had been in the basement
chatting with the white ladies I had grown to be quite fond of—Corinne,
Agnes, Julie—when one of my Latina parishioner friends came downstairs. I
got up to greet her with a hug and promptly switched over to speaking Spanish with her. My white English-speaking friends watched me as I left the table
and registered confusion as well as a little bit of shock as the words rolled off of
my tongue. They actually stopped talking for a moment, and it was disquiet-
ing for me. I had been attending Mass at St. Joseph's for well over a year at that
point and had been feeling as though I was continually code-switching—it
was exhausting, moving back and forth from conversing in English and in
español. I felt very uneasy and strange, as though I needed to apologize to my
white friends for speaking in Spanish. After my friend and I hugged and she
went back upstairs for the Spanish Mass, I felt my face burn, and I awkwardly
explained to my white friends what I had been discussing a moment earlier. I
felt that I had betrayed them in a strange way by leaving the table and talking
in another language—one they did not understand.

When I returned to my ethnographic jottings and thought about it some
more, I realized that the parish basement space, as with the parish itself, was
marked as "white" by those white Catholics who had been going for years

and whose family members literally had helped build the church. As a white woman, I was given a pass to be in the basement, but my Latina friend was not. Holding onto space as white is a marker of privilege, even in today's parishes where whites are vastly outnumbered by Latinos. The white rural Catholic population is aging and dying, and young white Catholics are not replacing them. By contrast, Spanish-speaking Masses across the state are bursting at the seams. As I mulled over what I had felt and experienced, I realized that parishes are places where a profound politics of place occurs. It comes across in side-eyes, stares, taking up the table space for longer than one should. Some would call these actions microaggressions. Latinos are continually being told—in small ways and big ways—that they do not belong, that it is not their parish, no matter how many Spanish-speaking parishioners there might be.

As Sujey Vega, anthropologist of midwestern Latinos, has shown, Latinos have continued to struggle to belong.[26] Even long-term Latino U.S. citizens are made to feel, each and every day, that they really don't belong here in "America." Abby, for instance, said that she has been told to "go home where you belong" and that her citizenship is under scrutiny with accusing looks and not-so-friendly "Where are you from?" inquiries. Beyond the walls of the church, Latinos and other nonwhite migrants and refugees often work as laborers for farmers and plant managers who are struggling to remain in the small towns that have been reshaped by mechanization, farm consolidation, and the fluctuating value of farm commodities. Are inclusive religious and work spaces possible in the twenty-first-century United States? When the CEOs of processing plants have close working relationships with priests and parishioners alike, the answer is a tentative yes, but only with on-the-ground, sustained effort on the part of many hands and many people. As U.S. Census data has shown, all but six states have seen Latino population growth over 40 percent, with many experiencing changes upward of 80 percent between 2000 and 2010.[27] And this growth shows no signs of abating. Social services, schools, churches, and work sites are on the front lines of addressing the influx of Latinos to their communities. A close study of Corn Belt Catholic churches reflects a microcosm of broader U.S. trends of ethnic and religious separation and division. In order to read the pulse of contemporary white-Latino relations in America, we need to examine the most dynamic places where people meet: the church and the workplace.

Latinos are now the largest minority group in the rural Midwest, as they are in the rest of the United States, and they do the hard work that feeds the world.[28] It is the hands of Latino refugees that keep the crops alive and harvest them. They care for animals, and they, along with other refugees, kill them for our consumption. In short, they do the hard labor, the unsightly labor, that whites wish to avoid. Meatpacking plant workforces are predominantly Latino and East and Central African. Iowa towns that are situated in the midst of rural America like Columbus Junction, West Liberty, Storm Lake, Denison, Marshalltown, and Ottumwa are economically thriving because of the Latino and nonwhite workforce. Workers purchase their groceries, fill their cars up with gas, buy homes, rent apartments, and contribute to their local economies in concrete and visible ways. They run laundromats, small grocery stores, and bakeries. Their shops are hubs for community and help asylum seekers and refugees as well as long-term residents and citizens alike forge community. Drive anywhere in rural America, and it is all but guaranteed that if you come across a prosperous small town, you will find a thriving Latino, African, Burmese, Vietnamese, or other ethnic and refugee community.

We must also focus our attention on working-class men and women. Class has long been, and continues to be, overlooked among scholars in their analyses of religion and culture. Yet an understanding of class and the power dynamics and stratifications of wealth that continue to exist is essential if we are to grasp the contemporary realities of religion, work, and food production in America. In the heartland, it is these individuals who grow the food, process the meat, and do all kinds of work that keeps America running. Mexican-descent Latinos in particular, who make up approximately 80 percent of the Corn Belt's Latino population, are bringing their talents, aspirations, and faith to a region of the United States long dominated by Western European Catholic and Protestant farmers and entrepreneurs. Ethnically diverse but racially homogeneous states such as Iowa, where white non-Latinos make up 85 percent of the populace, have become dynamic borderlands, and ethnic Catholic parishes, farm fields, meatpacking plants, and Latino-owned small businesses have become important sites of intersectionality and engagement.

In order to understand the increasing Latino-ization of America at large and the impact that refugees are having on the U.S. and global food production, we must look closely at the Midwest, which is ground zero for national trends in migration, work, and religion. In many ways, the future of ethnic and religious life in the United States is seen firsthand in the Midwest Corn Belt region, and a fine-grained study of the complex ethnic and racial relationships in midwestern fields and processing plants will help us to better understand the chasm that exists between brown and white America, as well as the social and economic disparities between urban and rural areas.

Since the early 1960s, hog and cattle factories have moved from urban centers like Chicago to more remote, rural locations in the Midwest like Denison, Iowa, to consolidate operations.[29] While operational costs were most certainly lowered, as anthropologist Deborah Fink has shown in her compelling historical and ethnographic work, the men and women who kill, cut, and package the meat have suffered.[30]

The vast majority of meatpacking industries throughout the Midwest are nonunionized and are in right-to-work states, where undocumented workers and refugees are especially vulnerable in a profit-hungry industry. Workers can be cast aside when injured, forced to sign medical waivers, and easily replaced by the waiting list of men and women hoping to make a decent wage. And the system has historically pitted ethnic groups against one another. While wages are relatively high at the plants, and there are savings plans like 401Ks and paid vacation after sufficient time worked, there is a nagging sense of vulnerability by many of the employees.

Of Melons, Corn, and Men

Hiding in Walmart, his heart beat wildly. Matteo had been working all summer for a small produce company, a family-owned rural business that bused in, each summer, several hundred Mexicanos like himself to work in the fields. It was a decades-old arrangement, a bracero-like, helping-hands kind of arrangement between Mexico and the United States. What many Latino and human rights advocates consider to be an inadequacy of the system, the H-2A visa for agricultural workers allows for seasonal, temporary workers to work for U.S. agriculture up to forty-five days. Since the 1940s, this government-sanctioned temporary work arrangement has been profitable for U.S.-based employers but not so good for employees. Matteo thought of the long sweaty days in the fields and the stifling hot warehouse without *aire acondicionado* where he and the other men slept all summer in bunkbeds. He could never truly cool down, no matter how many cold showers and cold cups of *agua* he drank. And the intense heat was an effective but dangerous appetite suppressant. He had to try to eat at the designated time in the cafeteria, even when he felt like throwing up from the heat and humidity. In Iowa, the summer heat index meant that you had to add ten to fifteen *grados* to the temperature to get an accurate sense of how hot it felt. Matteo imagined this might be what hell felt like, but he hoped and prayed he would never know for sure. This was as close as he ever wanted to get.

Like other rural farmers across the United States, Iowa farmers pay Mexican male laborers money to harvest their crops. In return for the workers' labor, the company houses them, feeds them, and guarantees them medical care. The work is hard—brutal in the heat and humidity of the Iowa sun. The men are out in the fields for fourteen hours a day, doing a job that Tom Bell, co-owner of Bell's Melons and Detasseling of Conesville, one of the businesses who hire seasonal workers, said is a job few want or can do: "They are hard workers and this is a miserable job." The wage of $10.44 an hour back in 2008, when he was interviewed for the *Muscatine Journal*, "is a hell of a wage in Mexico. All they gotta do is work."[31]

But not everyone wants to return home from seasonal work. Men like Matteo have no job waiting for them in rural Mexico, and few family members remain. And desperation can lead to desperate acts, actions that are out of the ordinary for the individual. Matteo decided he wanted to stay in Iowa. He liked the greenness, the vast fields, and the chance to start over. He had never been much of a risk taker but decided that he had nothing to lose. He overheard some bunkmates talking several weeks ago about ways to stay in los Estados Unidos. So he hid in the bathroom during the last company-sponsored trip to the giant retail store, as he knew many had before him on this pre-return trip to Mexico. He didn't want to spend his hard-earned money on televisions, clothes, and other things he didn't need. What he needed was a good job and to stay in the States. He wanted to plant his roots in a new land, one where there were many brown-skinned Latinos like him and jobs to work. Matteo was young and full of hope and longing for a fresh start. As the lights dimmed and the store employee announced that the store would be closing in ten minutes, Matteo crouched in a bathroom stall, planning his next move. He prayed silently to Mary and Jesus that the bus driver would not realize he was absent. He decided to slip out the back door of the store in ten minutes, before the last bathroom cleaning of the day. His stomach churned from worry; the acid bubbled up to his throat. But he had made his decision.[32]

Matteo is one of 500–600 male Mexican workers who are bused in each summer from Central Mexico to harvest melons in the small southeastern Iowa town of Conesville for the Bells, as well as for other Iowa farmers who hire them through the Bells. The men live in cramped quarters, and each is assigned a bunkmate. The warehouse building where they sleep, bathe, and live during their harvesting job has tall ceilings and is *very* hot. It opened in 2008 and is where the migrant workers rest and sleep when they are not working the fields in Conesville, Mediapolis, Morning Sun, Washington, and Waterloo.[33] The facility is directly across the street from the Rodriguez home, the

Catholic Latino family that hosts the migrant farmworkers' Mass and meal each summer, mentioned earlier in the chapter. Giant fans circulate continuously to create an artificial air flow to offer a reprieve from the hot and humid July and August Iowa heat. The unair-conditioned warehouse was, according to Tom Bell, "very expensive" and "is premiere in the state of Iowa for migrant workers."[34] After my own tour of the facility I was left thinking that if this is a "premiere" facility, I would hate to see what a "typical" facility looks and feels like. The Bells have been bringing in Mexican workers since 1987, first from Texas and later from Mexico. The couple was sued by Legal Aid in 1991 and won the court case. According to Tom Bell, "I ended up winning the case," but the case "broke" him.[35]

The adjacent building where the *trabajadores* go to eat their meals, receive health care from the Iowa-based nonprofit Proteus, and to grab coffee or water for the fields or bunks is open pretty much 24/7.[36] It is cooler in this building and is open and spacious. A short walk up the street from the warehouse sleeping quarters and cafeteria is a small convenience store, Bell's Mini Super. Here the men can get a cold can or bottle of Coke or *un cerveza*, wine, a slice of pizza, and other snacks/*botanas*. They can purchase cigarettes and chewing tobacco, magazines *en español*, and *tarjetas de teléfono* to call loved ones back home. The men can also do their laundry at the conveniently attached *lavandería*. The convenience store, owned by Tom and his wife Terri Bell, is not just the only store in town but the only one for several miles. There are no other options, especially for men who do not have transportation other than the buses that take them to and from the fields. They are effectively trapped at the labor camp.

It is these men that Father Joseph and the Rodriguez family serve food to each summer. After Mass, the men and other guests join the line to fill up their paper plates. Giant aluminum bins of steaming food are carried out by Rodriguez family members and friends. The foods are those that are familiar to the men and include *frijoles pintos y negros*, tortillas, arroz, carne asada, pozole, pan dulce, Coca-Cola, *limonada*, and other delectables. The men return to the line several times to refill their plates and are given hearty helpings with a smile. After the sun has set, the plates and trash have been picked up, and conversations have ended, the men file back to the warehouse to shower and go to sleep for the next morning's shift. On their way back to their bunks, they pass a woman who has a couple of piles of clothing—some for sale and some for free. A small group of men sort through the clothing and take some of the free stuff, mostly T-shirts.

Like most places, this small rural town has its share of identities and is complex. It is a destination place for seasonal Mexican workers who are bused in to work, as much as it is a destination location for the annual "Redneck Revival" festival where beer, bare breasts, and motorcycles are in ample supply for those twenty-one and over. The public space of this festival is white and advertised as "country," and over the four-day-long festival country music, motorcycling, and rural America is celebrated. This particular rural America, though, is one that does not include Latinos, who labor in the full sun in the fields throughout the festivities, unbeknownst to the white revelers. In most rural and small-town Corn Belt places, white and Latino worlds intersect in public spaces of churches, grocery stores, workplaces, and schools. But Conesville's population is in the mid-400s, and there are no schools, churches, or large employers where white and brown individuals would have encounters. In rural hamlets like Conesville, Mexican seasonal workers are cocooned in their own daily and weekly routines while they are in Iowa: they work, shop at the company store, and are bused home at the end of the summer. Their respites are walking up to the convenience store, purchasing some snacks and cans of Coca-Cola, and marking the days until they can return to their families with fuller billfolds than when they left.

While there are seasonal migrant workers in rural places like Conesville, the majority of Latinos in Corn Belt states like Iowa live in the state and region permanently. They migrate for work and better opportunities for their families and rent apartments in which multiple members of extended families reside. Like the Hargrafens, who rented their home for many years, numbers of Latinos—undocumented and documented alike—today rent their apartments and houses. Yet the differences in experiences and opportunities that are available vastly outweigh the similarities. The Hargrafens were reasonably confident that they would one day be able to purchase a home. They were able to bank their whiteness when they negotiated a rent-to-own deal with a white female farm owner who liked the family. White families like the Hargrafens lived as a nuclear family, whereas most Latino families live in multigenerational units. Unlike the Hargrafens, many if not most agricultural workers in the Corn Belt today are undocumented and cannot legally purchase homes. And even if they are documented, it is much harder today to save to purchase a home. As far as documented Latino workers go, there are many hurdles to purchasing a home, given the lack of an economic safety net, which is connected to systems of oppression.

What distinguishes the Hargrafens and nineteenth- and twentieth-century white farmers from their Latino counterparts is that the newer wave of migrants and refugees who work in agriculture have fewer mechanisms in place and far fewer opportunities to rent and to own land and homes. And, as a casual drive through rural Iowa and the broader midwestern Corn Belt reveals, the conditions of the trailers, apartments, and houses are decidedly mixed. While some are kept up by landlords, others are in poor condition, as an apartment complex in Columbus Junction that Lois Mincks and I drove by revealed. Burmese refugees and Latinos live in this particular complex, somewhat hidden and off the beaten path in the small town. Exposed wires dangled from open windows, some of which were cracked. Paint peeled off the window frames and sides of the building. It was a place in sad shape.

Extended family members often pool their resources and live together under one roof. Some families keep small gardens to supplement their diets, and there is a small but growing Latino gardener community and an even smaller but also growing Latino farmer community.[37] Many farming Latino families must travel the seasonal migrant circuit, from Iowa to Michigan, from seasonal crop to seasonal crop. Families follow the melon, beet, to-mato, strawberry, and blueberry trail, never able to settle down. The moving takes its toll on the families as children are uprooted from their communi-ties, schools, and friends as a result of these necessary, economically oriented moves.[38] Seldom are migrant farming families able to save up enough money to purchase a trailer, let alone a single-family home. And even if they were able to, they would not legally be allowed to own property based on their immi-gration status. There are most certainly overlaps in push-and-pull factors—poverty, state violence, precarity—when we compare white migrations with Latino and other refugees' migrations to the United States historically. But what continues to separate more recent refugees from earlier refugees is that refugees since 1965 tend to be brown and Black and as such are beholden to a state-sponsored racialization that makes their integration into society and their acceptance as "Americans" much more tenuous and difficult than it is for their white counterparts.

CHAPTER 3

Snapshots of Rural Priests

"Anglo Blood and a Latino Heart"

THERE IS ONE RURAL Corn Belt priest who sees his life's calling as ministering to Latinos. "I have Anglo blood and a Latino heart," he told me. Father Bernie Weir, or "Padre Bernie" as he is known to many, has long devoted himself to the particular needs and plight of Latinos in the Midwest. From staging demonstrations to providing food and shelter to Latino parishioners in need, Padre Bernie has long made his mission clear: to walk with his Latino parishioners. From the time he was a small boy, Padre Bernie always wanted to be a priest. The son of Scotch-Irish parents, one of seven kids, Father Bernie was raised in the small south-central Iowa coal mining town of Albia.[1] African Americans were a sizable presence in the mining corridor, yet while they worked alongside white ethnics, their coexistence was filled with unease and unofficial, de facto segregation that dated back to antebellum America. As historians have pointed out, Iowa's history of race relations between the majority white population and minority African American population was rooted in racism. Nineteenth- and twentieth-century "Black Codes" created separate and unequal societies, so much so that midwestern historian Robert R. Dykstra asserts that "Iowa was the most racist free state in the antebellum Union."[2]

Father Bernie does not remember a significant African American presence in his hometown. Weir grew up, as he put it during our conversation, "excessively white." "I mean, we had a couple of African American families in town, and we all knew Mr. Grayson, who was the janitor at the bank, but we really had no idea about race and injustices that Black Americans had in our society." In the small mining town of Albia, white and African American communities remained separate, as they did in the majority of towns across Iowa. On the surface, to white Iowans like Father Bernie, folks "got along," as he said, but the reality was a de facto segregation that had grown out of a de jure racism institutionalized by the Black Codes. The race riots of the 1960s were "incomprehensible" to a teenage Bernie, as he struggled to make sense of the world around him. Just about everyone in his town, save for about a dozen individuals, were "white."

Father Bernie says that his mother and father were "typical" hardworking Iowans, blue-collar workers in a blue-collar factory town. His dad "did what he had to do" to provide for the family, and his many jobs ranged from working for Iowa Southern Utilities to running his own small appliance repair shop. His mom was at home with the children when they were young and ran a small tailoring business out of the family home. As the children grew, she also helped her husband fix small appliances for his shop. His parents' income was enough to provide food, clothing, and shelter, but there were never many extras or luxuries.

The Weir family, like many other midwestern families, was hit hard by the farm crisis of the 1980s. Bernie's dad made the difficult decision to close his shop and found work in nearby Ottumwa, Iowa. "During the crisis, people had a hard time feeding their families," Bernie pointed out. His own family's prosperity was linked to those farming families who purchased goods and services from them. "If the toaster broke, well, then it stayed broke, so small businesses like my parents' were no longer necessary, and farmers just couldn't afford it anymore."

While economic hardship certainly impacted the Weirs, a greater tragedy hit when his mom died at the age of fifty-eight. Six of the seven children were in their teens by then, but her loss was deeply felt. Heart issues run in Bernie's family, and, like his mom, Bernie also suffered a heart attack when he was fifty-eight. As he thought back on his childhood and genetic predispositions, Bernie chuckled, ran his fingers through his shoulder-length white hair, adjusted the collar on his Hawaiian shirt, and said, "Well, I guess I was genetically right on schedule with mine." He added that folks on his dad's side "live forever," so he hopes there is a cosmic as well as genetic balancing out of sorts, so he is able to stick around and continue to do his ministry.

As he reflects on the midwestern and Catholic values he was raised with, Bernie appreciates how his parents encouraged each child to "live and let each other live as we chose." "My mom, you know, she encouraged us to follow our own path and to not get in each other's way if we just so happened to disagree with someone's path." Take for instance the day Bernie called his parents to tell them that he was going to the seminary—the same day his brother called to tell them he was joining the military. While it was hard at times, the young men had been raised to not interfere with each other's chosen paths. A self-described pacifist and "a guy just not into guns and hunting," Father Bernie wrestled with his brother's announcement to wear his uniform to his ordination. "But you see, it would have been wildly inappropriate for me to have told him that he couldn't wear his uniform." His mother's value of acceptance and understanding had taken root, and he and his brother, while they disagree on much, remain close.

Bernie's chosen vocation has been a deeply fulfilling one for him, so much so that he cannot imagine another life for himself. He is also thankful that he had the opportunity to leave his small rural community and said, in all seriousness, "If I had stayed in Albia, I would probably have been a drunk factory worker. No joke." Father Bernie never felt that he quite "fit" in the town of his birth. But a bright spot in his childhood was the Sisters of Humility nuns who taught him at his Catholic grade school. The Sisters' emphasis on social justice and doing God's work in the world resonated with him in his youth as much as Catholic social teachings did while he was a seminarian. He was hooked on the social teachings coming out of Vatican II that the women religious conveyed in class, as well as on stories of the martyrs.

It was in parochial school that his attraction to Spanish Catholicism was nurtured, as many of the martyrs he was introduced to were Spanish. The progressive, pragmatic Catholicism of his rural youth was tempered and challenged at his first seminary in Minnesota, which "leaned much more to the right." After the seminary "booted about half of my seminary class" for students' liberal leanings, Bernie and most of his evicted classmates made their way to Chicago's Mundelein Seminary, the same institution Father Joseph Sia attended, which was known for its embrace of Vatican II reforms and the kind of social teachings that had long appealed to Bernie. During his time there, Bernie became committed to helping the poor and applied to go work in El Salvador, where Archbishop Oscar Romero, Ursuline sister Dorothy Kazel, Maryknoll sisters Maura Clarke and Ita Ford, and lay missioner Jean Donovan had recently been assassinated for their liberation theology and their preferential option for the poor. While his request was turned down by Bishop Gerald O'Keefe of the Davenport diocese, out of concern for Bernie's safety and mortality, Bernie's determination to serve grew.

After his 1986 ordination at his childhood parish of St. Mary's with "pretty much every Catholic from the area present," Father Bernie's first assignment as a priest was at St. John Vianney in Bettendorf, Iowa, where he served as a parochial vicar, a kind of apprenticeship that prepared him to one day be the head pastor of a parish. From St. John's he was moved to St. Paul's in Burlington, Iowa, another parochial vicar position. St. Paul's was a very different kind of parish from the "wealthy, suburban, and white" parish of St. John's. St. Paul's was in Muscatine County, a blue-collar, rural area that resembled his hometown economically but had a more ethnically and racially diverse population. While most of his parishioners at St. John's had been white ethnics, about a third of his parishioners at St. Paul's were Latino, and there were small numbers of African Americans as well.

After Father Bernie had served some time as a parochial vicar, Bishop O'Keefe asked him if he would be willing to serve as pastor of the small rural "town parish" of Columbus Junction, a parish about thirty minutes west of St. Paul's. Columbus Junction, like most towns, rural communities, and small Iowa cities, had been overwhelmingly white since the mid-1800s. Irish, German, Czech, Bohemian, and Scotch-Irish families had settled eastern Iowa and the rest of the state from the mid to late nineteenth century. At the time that Father Bernie was asked to serve as pastor of St. Joseph the Worker, the community of Columbus Junction, like some surrounding towns in eastern Iowa, was beginning to experience demographic changes, which included higher numbers of Latino migrations.

As noted earlier, since the early 1960s the establishment of Columbus Junction as a meatpacking town effectively made it a destination location for work. Rath Packing in the 1960s, 1970s, and early 1980s reopened as Iowa Beef Processors in the mid-'80s, which was finally bought by Tyson in 2001. Right-to-work states like Iowa had become prime locations for nonunionized, vertically integrated meatpacking plants, and it was precisely during the 1980s that migrations of Latino women and men escalated. The rural and small-town Midwest and Corn Belt became browner as families chose towns like Columbus Junction to work and raise their families in. Such towns appealed to Mexicans for some of the same reasons they had appealed to the nineteenth-century white ethnics: they were seen as safer than big cities and as places where children could have space to run, grow, and learn. And Mexican migrants, while they lacked the financial resources to purchase land to farm, valued the opportunity to have backyards, where they could grow food.

The St. Joseph parish in Columbus Junction was not considered a "plum job" by anyone in the Diocese of Davenport, according to Father Bernie. It was a rural outpost and experiencing major changes, as was the town. White ethnic prejudices and resentments against the Mexican newcomers were starting to simmer. Parishioners like Corinne Hargrafen were taken aback by the rapid demographic changes in their town and were not exactly happy about it. While Father Bernie did not yet speak Spanish, he was chosen to minister in Columbus Junction because of his desire to serve Latinos. Bernie asked to be enrolled in an intensive Spanish-language program in Mexico as soon as the diocese could afford to send him, and the bishop agreed. Father Bernie said he was told by Bishop O'Keefe to "go there" and "make it work."

When he reflects on his thirteen years of service at St. Joseph's, Father Bernie said, "I made it work, but it just about killed me and the parish." In his first year as pastor, Father Bernie had a fourteen-year-old bilingual Mexican American girl assist him during the Spanish Mass. She translated what he said for the Spanish-speaking parishioners, and it "worked OK for a year, but clearly we had to do more." After this first year, Father Bernie was sent to Ceramax, a Spanish-language school in Guadalajara run by the Sisters of Humility. He remembers the two-week period as one of the most difficult times of his life. "I wasn't prepared, mentally, emotionally, or psychologically, for the experience." Father Bernie's "terrible culture shock" and the extremely difficult experience of being a "minority white, English-speaking guy" in a Mexican, Spanish-speaking culture humbled him to his core. His lack of even rudimentary Spanish skills made him vulnerable, and the bus ride from his apartment to the school was traumatic for him. "I couldn't even ask for basic directions. I couldn't order food. I felt like a complete fool." During each day's two-hour-long siesta, Father did not have enough time to return to his apartment, so he would walk over to the plaza and sit, contemplating his fear and intense loneliness. He located the Catholic Church but discovered it was locked, which astounded him. "After I returned after that life-changing two weeks, I literally threw out all of the keys at St. Joseph's. I thought, 'Why have a church if it is not open to people who need it?' I made a bold statement and vowed that no one who needed to find solace would ever be turned away. I never wanted anyone who felt lost to be locked out, literally speaking."

Despite the difficulties of his first language-school experience, Father Bernie chalked it up as one of his most important life lessons. He became acutely aware of his white privilege, he told me, and how it had protected him "pretty much my entire life." While he does not deny the difficulty of his experience in Mexico, he knows it was "nothing" when compared with that of Mexican migrants to the United States. "While I had a tough time in Mexico, I was safe. I am white. I had money to buy food, and I could have flown home anytime. It was my pride that kept me there—I was embarrassed to drop out and to come home early." He added, "When I thought about it, I realized that I have a safety net as a white guy. I will never be without a place to live. My bishop won't let me die. I always have a safety net. Always."

Father Bernie contrasted his own white privilege in Mexico with the experience of Mexicans who undergo "disorientation and culture shock all of the time—each and every day. Think about it. Young Mexican men cross the border into Texas and know no one. They know very little English. They know that they have an uncle in Washington, Iowa," but not "how far away Iowa is and/or how they are going to get there. So when I think about how most migrants find their way to their families here, I am truly astounded."

After his experience in Mexico, Father Bernie took "every community college course in Spanish I could find—some more than once just to make sure I knew it." He drove all over the state to attend classes. He attended Spanish-language gatherings, films, cookouts, and picnics. "I was a party crasher and could get away with it because I am a priest. I went to so many baptismal parties, confirmation parties, and quinceañeras. It was the best way to learn the culture and the language and to also show that I was committed to serving Latinos in my community."

When Father Bernie returned to Mexico two years later to study Spanish intensively, he was ready. He took Spanish-language courses in Morelia, Michoacán, for six months and was fluent by the time he came home to Columbus Junction. Once back in the States, he looked for a roommate with whom he could speak Spanish and found one in an El Salvadoran man, a friend who was not a parishioner. Indeed, the arrangement raised some eyebrows, he said, but Father Bernie saw it as furthering and maintaining his Spanish-language skills, one that was part of his commitment to complete fluency in Spanish and bilingualism. At this time, the Latino presence in town was just starting to grow, and there were a couple of Mexican families who lived on his street. The English-language Mass drew an average of 300 parishioners each Sunday, whereas the Spanish-language Mass drew just about 40 individuals. By the time Father Bernie left the parish, though, the demographics and attendance had flipped.

The town was changing, and Father Bernie said that the whites were "not happy about it." The downtown was starting to reflect the new Columbus Junction. Mexican-owned businesses started to open, and many whites complained that the center of their community resembled Mexico. Some were afraid to venture downtown and opted to drive to a neighboring town to shop for groceries and other necessities. Father Bernie was not exempt from the stress over changing demographics. Because he was so committed to including Latinos and to the Spanish-language Mass, he was seen as favoring Mexicans over the longtime white parishioners. While attendance at the Spanish-language Mass kept rising, attendance at the English-speaking Mass was dwindling. Father Bernie had, as he put it, "pissed off" a lot of whites because of his advocacy of the Latino parishioners. In fact, he upset them so much that he eventually left the parish. His successor was none other than Father Joseph Sia, who for his part has said that Father Bernie's departure has been a "cautionary tale" in how far he can go in his own advocacy, hence the "schizophrenic" feeling he has had trying to balance the needs and happiness of his two distinct parishioner populations.

As we talked in his office, Father Bernie stretched his arms out for a moment, paused, and said he realizes that he was "probably a bit too hard-core and a little insensitive at times towards the whites," but he has "no regrets" with the way he reached out to the Spanish-speaking members of the community. He shared that he was "so stressed out" trying to minister to the two parish groups that he started to have intense anxiety attacks. He worried that the whites "hated" him and was increasingly "paranoid" that the Mexican drug cartel was planting drugs in his Jeep to frame him "for God knows what." He was trying "to serve everyone but felt that no one liked me." Father Bernie admitted that he was "absolutely paranoid" and was having delusions of being targeted "pretty much all the time." The extreme stress of being a rural priest administering to whites and Latinos led him to move to nearby Muscatine, where he was already leading Sunday Spanish Mass at Saints Mary and Mathias Catholic Church. Toward the end of his time serving St. Joseph parish, he commuted to Columbus Junction regularly to meet with parishioners and to lead the English- and Spanish-language Masses.

Father Bernie's anxiety led to his request for a police escort each time he would drive from Muscatine to Columbus Junction after dark. "I was fearful; I didn't trust anyone and thought everyone was out to get me." Father Bernie's psychological, physical, and emotional health were in peril, and he acknowledged that it was harmful to the parish and its people. "I almost destroyed the parish, and it almost destroyed me." His focus on allyship and accompanying Latinos was met with resistance and hostility, and he said he "dug in my heels" and worked even harder for Latinos. It proved to be a losing battle of wills. While Padre Bernie does not regret championing his Latino parishioners, he does acknowledge that he could have handled his white parishioners with more finesse. "Yeah, I could have done better," he conceded. But Padre Bernie landed on his feet, and soon after his departure from Columbus Junction, he was asked to be parish priest for St. James parish in Washington, Iowa, a thriving Latino parish about eighteen miles from St. Joseph's in Columbus Junction. He hopes this is his "last stop" and said he is thriving at St. James, which is Latino-majority.

Padre Rudy

Father Bernie is part of a small group of rural priests who are focused on Latino outreach and making their historically white but now mostly Latino parishes more inclusive. The eastern Iowa Diocese of Davenport, of which St. Joseph's in Columbus Junction and St. James's in Washington are a part, has been proactive in reaching out to Latino Catholics. The outreach was initiated by the former Davenport bishop Martin Amos, who was the diocese's eighth bishop and who was brought in to make changes in the wake of the sex abuse crisis in the diocese.[3] During his ten years of being the cleanup man for the diocese, Bishop Amos began some new initiatives, which included establishing what he named the diocese's Hispanic ministries. The Davenport diocese currently has active Hispanic ministries in ten of its eighty-four parishes. The Corn Belt towns and small to midsize cities of Clinton, Columbus Junction, Davenport, Iowa City, Mount Pleasant, Muscatine, Ottumwa, Washington, and West Liberty have all become hubs for the diocese's Hispanic outreach initiatives.

Father Rudy Juarez, parish priest of St. Patrick parish, Iowa City, is currently the vicar of the diocese's Hispanic ministries and oversees regular meetings of priests involved in Hispanic ministries. Since the late 1990s, Father Rudy and eastern Iowa priests who minister to Spanish-speaking Catholics have met monthly to discuss and share ideas about serving Hispanics in their parishes. These priests find themselves having to balance the needs of their multiple constituents, namely white non-Hispanics of mostly German descent and English- and Spanish-speaking people of Mexican descent. Father Rudy, named the *Iowa Press-Citizen*'s "Citizen of the Year" for the way he ministered to his congregation and how he responded in the wake of the devastating tornado that leveled his downtown Iowa City parish in 2006, has made it his mission to make St. Patrick and the Catholic Church a more inclusive place for Spanish- and English-speaking Catholics. During my fall 2012 visit to St. Patrick's new location on a fourteen-acre site on the city's east side, Father Rudy gave me a tour of the church and was especially excited to point out the mural that blended the church's history of commitment to serving Irish Catholics and more recently of reaching out to Latino Catholics, who are the most predominant ethnic group of Catholics in the diocese, as in many U.S.

dioceses. The mural features St. Patrick and St. Juan Diego, and the Virgin of Guadalupe also has a prominent place in the gilded mural. Yet his outreach to Spanish-speaking Catholics and his work to make Iowa City a sanctuary city has been controversial, and some white non-Latino parishioners are uncomfortable with what they view as his excessive attention to Spanish-speaking parishioners, seeing themselves as a higher priority because of their greater financial contributions to the parish. Father Joseph Sia has experienced the same demands from white parishioners, who despite their dwindling numbers have felt entitled to privileges and decision-making powers because of their greater financial means.

Moreover, Father Rudy's outspoken pro-life stance and his pro-life messages during homilies have resonated with Latino Catholics in his parish, who tend to be more theologically conservative than their white cohorts, but have angered some white parishioners, who have been known to walk out during the explicitly pro-life homilies. While Latino Catholics nationwide tend to trend more theologically conservative but socially progressive, white Catholics are the inverse and tend to be more theologically "liberal" yet socially conservative.[4]

Overall, Father Rudy is widely held in high regard in Iowa City, in particular for his commitment to social justice and his outreach to Spanish-speaking Catholics. During our encounters, Father Rudy emphasized that he wants St. Patrick parish to be a place for all Catholics and wants Spanish-speaking Catholics to feel especially welcome. Father Rudy has been at the forefront of Hispanic ministries in eastern Iowa, a focus that really took off in the late 1990s, at the same time that dioceses across the country were beginning to be rocked by the seismic waves of priest sex abuse scandals. The Diocese of Davenport, along with several other U.S. dioceses, found itself in a public relations nightmare in the late 1990s and into the next decade as victims of sex abuse by priests came forward to tell their stories. Juries and judges across the nation, from Boston to Davenport, sided with the victims, and dioceses like Davenport had to pay out large sums of money to victims.

Under the direction of the now-retired Bishop Amos, the Diocese of Davenport has, since 2006, made improving its tarnished image its primary focus and has had some real success. Its campaign to clean up its image and to show its commitment to serving the needs of its parishioners includes its outreach to Hispanics and multicultural ministries initiatives. During his tenure as bishop, Amos was clear that ministering to Hispanics and other minority groups was a top priority of the Diocese of Davenport. He made Hispanic ministries his focus in a recently held diocesan council meeting, where Father

Joseph Sia gave a featured presentation, and this focus has been augmented by the addition of layman Miguel Moreno as the diocese's director of multicultural ministries. The diocese's commitment to Hispanic ministries will soon be followed by outreach to Vietnamese and Burmese refugees, two ethnic and migrant groups whose growing numbers are adding to eastern Iowa parishes.

For their part, Father Rudy of St. Patrick, Father Joseph of St. Joseph's in West Liberty and Columbus Junction, and Father Greg Steckel of St. Joseph's in West Liberty have emphasized in interviews and casual conversations that the overall health of parish life and the future of the Catholic Church rest on the success of outreach to Hispanics. As the largest ethnic minority in the state, Latinos in some towns and cities are positioning themselves as the future of the state of Iowa as well as of the Catholic Church. While their numbers are still relatively small when compared with the white non-Latino majority of Iowa and larger midwestern Corn Belt, the rate of growth among Latinos has been, by all accounts, substantial. With growing numbers, their political and social clout will continue to expand. Bishop Amos's successor, Bishop Thomas Zinkula, has made outreach to Latinos and vulnerable people his mission since he was named bishop in 2017. Bishop Zinkula works closely with Iowa City's Catholic Worker House and has been a vocal supporter of its outreach and care of refugees from Central America's Northern Triangle.

Father Greg

Like Fathers Joseph, Bernie, and Rudy, Father Gregory Steckel of West Liberty's St. Joseph parish—the only Catholic Church in town—is constantly thinking of how to most effectively address the needs of his Hispanic parishioners. A self-described "typical white guy" priest from Moline, Illinois, Father Greg has a sense of humor and doesn't seem to take himself too seriously. He is deeply self-reflexive and knows that he has a lot to do to reach out to the growing Latino population—the majority population, which has more than doubled in West Liberty since 2000—in his parish. He hopes to attain fluency in Spanish and is currently being tutored each week. For now, his friend and fellow priest Father Joseph Sia drives from Columbus Junction to West Liberty each Sunday to preside over the Spanish Mass.[5]

For his part, Father Greg sings in the Spanish Mass choir, he proudly noted to me during our interview. Father Greg is among a growing number of midwestern parish priests to find himself serving a growing and vibrant Spanish-speaking community, and aside from learning Spanish, he participates in local Hispanic advocacy groups like the West Liberty Coalition. He meets regularly with Steven Hanson, fellow Catholic and former superintendent of West Liberty schools, and has partnered with University of Iowa professors Drs. Barbara Vaquero and Jason Ulloa to bring cervical cancer awareness and HPV vaccines to his parish, along with diabetes screenings and dieticians' advice for his parishioners. While he is humble on many accounts, Father Greg speaks about a reality for twenty-first-century Catholic priests: if white non-Latino priests want to effectively serve their Spanish-speaking constituents, they must address more than spiritual needs. They must be culturally sensitive and must be conversant in Spanish. Father Greg has taken it upon himself to learn Spanish and puts himself in situations to expand his comfort zone. He understands and believes that today's Corn Belt Catholic priest must be in many places at many times to effectively minister. His parish boundaries are much more fluid than the boundaries of late nineteenth-century and early twentieth-century priests who worked with immigrant enclaves in inner cities, primarily in the north. And he must, as does Father Joseph, minister to the Hispanics of his parish without offending his white non-Hispanic constituents—a major challenge, it seems, for priests in towns and cities once dominated by Irish and Germans. White non-Latino Catholics remind their priests, as one of my Latino interlocutors told me and as Fathers Bernie and Joseph have felt acutely, that "they have the money and can call the shots."

West Liberty is the state's first Latino-majority city in large part because of its West Liberty Foods turkey processing plant, which, like Columbus Junction's Tyson, is a major draw for Latinos. West Liberty is a destination location for many Latino and white families alike because of its prevalence of jobs, reasonable cost of living, award-winning public education system, and proximity to Iowa City, a half-hour drive away. It is small but not too small, is walkable, has a vibrant downtown, and is close to major amenities in the university town of Iowa City. Residents can own a home in West Liberty and can live very well on Iowa City wages. Moreover, as Steve Hanson noted during our interview, West Liberty schools can draw on qualified teachers from the University of Iowa to teach in the dual language program. Importantly, West Liberty is thriving due in part to its acceptance and even embrace of Latinos, who are valued as individuals and families whose contributions make West Liberty a better place.

As an indicator of the town's positive view of Latinos and of Spanish as a second language, West Liberty schools' dual language program has been so successful that there is currently a wait list of children, and none of the kids enrolled are opting out of the program. The language program has become a model for other school districts.[6] Fewer families are choosing the non-dual-language track. The new challenge for the school system is how to expand the dual language program to accommodate everyone on the list. Graduating students are bilingual and even trilingual and are steeped in multiculturalism.

When we met, Father Greg talked at length about an issue that most consumes him at the moment: rural Hispanic ministry. While West Liberty is a growing town with a constant stream of Spanish-speaking Catholics who fill the church each week, many other eastern Iowa parishes are struggling to maintain membership since white non-Hispanic numbers are shrinking, and maintaining the buildings is costly for the diocese. Because of the continuing shortage of priests and the logistical and demographic challenges facing midwestern rural parishes, a current trend among rural Catholic parishes is to create "clustered" parishes. Parishes that are clustered combine their resources and share priests and their labor. While there is always a priest available to administer Sunday Mass and the sacrament of the Eucharist, in a clustered parish situation, the priest may not live in the parish rectory where he celebrates Mass on a given Sunday, which was standard before consolidations and clustering. The number of services offered during the week also tends to be fewer. Rural midwestern priests have always been travelers, and in many ways today's rural priests hearken back to the early days of Catholic missionization in the Midwest.

Father Greg is concerned about offering effective rural ministry in the midst of clustering parishes and said, "We've gotten so stuck in our parish model that sometimes it is hard to see the forest through the trees. We need to focus on what is best for the parishioners, and we are working on that right now. Bishop Amos has asked for a proposal to keep rural ministry alive, and that is what is keeping me busy right now." Father Greg recognizes that midwestern Catholicism is one of midsize cities and small towns. Latinos are among those migrants and refugees who are moving into these smaller cities and towns, and Father Greg, like Father Joseph, understands that if the church wants to effectively minister, then it must focus on rural ministries. Father Greg wants to be an agent of change in his community and brings his Quad Cities, Illinois, ethos of grit and determination to his job.

Like Father Joseph, he is under many pressures to serve multiple constituents. He understands that Hispanics are the future of the Catholic Church in the United States, and he is responding favorably and proactively. As of now his parish is a shared one, and he would like to see more interactions among Anglo and Hispanic parishioners, but he is pleased with how things are going at St. Joseph's. Like Father Joseph, Father Greg isn't sure if his parish will ever be truly "integrated" and doesn't know whether this is the right focus or what is best for his white and Latino parishioners. What he is concerned with at the moment is improving his Spanish, making sure his Spanish-speaking families feel connected and welcomed by the church, and working through the challenges of Iowa rural parish ministry.

> I think the hardest part of being a priest, at least for me, is getting over myself. I now realize that I am just one person and that to be successful I must take a pastoral approach. I have to give people what they want, and I have to be sensitive to their cultural needs and values. Hispanics want church to be a community. For Hispanics, the content of the homily is not the focus; for them church is the feeling they get at Mass surrounded by family, music, and community. I love working in Hispanic ministry and consider myself very fortunate.

Fathers Bernie, Joseph, Greg, and Rudy are Corn Belt priests, men who have devoted their lives to service in a region with rapidly changing demographics. They are deeply committed to serving the needs of their Spanish-speaking parishioners and are acutely aware of the challenges that meet Hispanics in America. A focus on the Corn Belt region and rural religion draws attention to some major trends in the contemporary United States, including the situation and plight of Latinos and how religious institutions choose to respond; the outreach and aims of integrating Latinos, whether third-generation or recent migrants, to Iowa life and broader midwestern culture; and issues of economic and social justice and how the church and its representatives and laypeople will choose to respond or not respond.

According to sociologist of religion Brett Hoover, how we talk about Catholic parishes does "not draw attention to the art of ongoing negotiated arrangement created by the presence of multiple cultural groups in the same parish space."[7] Hoover's use of the term "shared parish" is a helpful way to understand the dynamics of contemporary American Catholic parishes and fits the situation in eastern Iowa quite well. While the West Liberty parish space is certainly shared by Mexican-descent and white non-Latino Catholics, the parish is in reality made up of two distinct communities. Anglos and Latinos share worship space but seem to maintain ethnic, familial, and communal boundaries to a certain degree.

Fathers Joseph and Greg are especially concerned with the overall wellness and health of their Hispanic parishioners and work closely with University of Iowa Health Sciences faculty and Trinity Muscatine nurses. They are indeed part of a multipronged approach to addressing Latinos' needs, and they recognize the complexities and challenges that Latinos face, whether they are third-generation or recent migrants and refugees. The priests are well aware of the discrimination Latinos have faced and of the health risks impacting them (such as high rates of cervical cancer, colorectal cancer, diabetes, and heart disease) and see their role as representatives of the church who can help men and women in their parishes on many levels: faith, family, health, economics/employment. They are part of a broader historical continuity of priests reaching out to ethnic minorities and migrants and see their jobs as multifaceted.

Fathers Joseph and Greg work with employers, health services, professors, and educators and are part of a broader transnational coalition that seeks to address the needs of Latino and other migrant and minority Catholics. These priests understand that in order to successfully address Latino needs, they must partner with local agencies. While they would like to aim for integration, these parish priests understand, given intercultural challenges and sensitivities, that creating a shared parish space might be the most realistic and culturally sensitive option.

But creating a shared space is a difficult task, as we have seen throughout this chapter, especially in these fraught times full of verbal vitriol as well as aggressive actions toward Spanish-speaking migrants and longtime Latino residents and citizens alike. Making America "great" during Trump's presidency made life a living hell for many Spanish-speaking women, men, and children. Hawkeye priests like Fathers Joseph, Rudy, Bernie, and Greg have been on the front lines pushing back against the anti-immigrant America. They have worked overtime to minister to the needs of migrants and refugees, trying their best to make inclusive parishes for multiple ethnic groups and individuals. It is far from easy, and Father Joseph's description of his job as "schizophrenic" captures the stress that comes with negotiating the various demands and stresses. Part of his job is considering the work that his parishioners do each day and making himself present for the women and men who find their way to his parish.

The most effective priests and religious leaders must have meaningful encounters not only in parish and church spaces but also in places inhabited by the most vulnerable populations. Those who minister to Latinos as well as other vulnerable populations must visit homes and workplaces. Because working long hours and in a variety of shifts is a reality for Latinos and other Corn Belt migrants and refugees, religious leaders must be understanding toward those who cannot and do not make it to Sunday service because of work demands. For the women and men on the line at the packing plants, their religious faith can help ease the trauma of working in such a demanding, bloody place. Making space at work for prayer is an important part of the day for many refugees today, as well as for the white non-Latinos who serve as CEOs, CFOs, and managers. And the bloody work of the meatpacking plants can itself become a source of the sacred, not just the profane. Just as the priests in this chapter have worked hard to create meaningful encounters among their parishioners, so too do those who run the meatpacking plants. The CEOs and CFOs of the hog and beef processing plants see themselves doing the hard but necessary work of being cultural brokers and sacralizers of work and the workplace.

CHAPTER 4

The Work of God and Hogs

Work is a necessity, part of the meaning of life on this earth,
a path to growth, human development and personal fulfilment.
—Pope Francis, *Laudato Si'*, No. 128

DING! DING! DING! The alarm blares at five o'clock. It is still dark outside, but he likes this time of morning. It is a quiet, peaceful refuge before the rush of sounds, lights, and people. Alain stretches, rubs his eyes, and turns the annoying device off before rinsing his face and brushing his teeth. He goes downstairs to boil water for coffee and eats some *fufu* from last night's supper. The sweet bread reminds him of home in the Congo. While he waits for the coffee to steep, he gathers the lunch that his wife has prepared for him and fills a large bottle of water for his shift. He writes a note to his family, in French and English, telling them he loves them and will see them tonight *pour dîner*.

For the past three years, Alain has worked first shift at the pork processing plant in his adopted town in Iowa. He has recently been promoted to the job of shift manager. He oversees about fifty workers, forty men and ten women, all but two of them Congolese like himself. The other two are African American. He is thankful that he no longer works second shift, as he hardly saw Julie, Paul, William, and Sarah. That was a bad time. Now, he can share supper with his loves each evening and hear about the children's day at school. Alain is proud of his new position as he now makes more money. He thinks of the new shoes he was able to buy Sarah and how she squealed with delight to receive the purple Elsa and Anna shoes. Alain smiles; he doesn't think she has removed them except to take her bath at night and climb into bed.

At 5:45, an aging blue Toyota minivan, with seven coworkers, pulls up as it does six days a week. The men greet each other, and together they drive the forty-five minutes to work. They chat about their families, the news, and what they packed for lunch. As they exit the van at the plant, they are careful not to breathe in too deeply. They have trained their mouths and noses to guard against the intense stench of flesh and excrement. Hogs.

After he clocks in at 6:45, Alain puts on a hairnet, a white frock, and an orange hard hat. The bright color he wears on his head indicates his higher-level position. For over two years he wore a white one, indicating his new-hire status, and he is proud of the upgrade in color. After dressing, Alain walks through the shoe sanitizer station and slides the company-provided disposable covers over his feet. He slips on his sterile white gloves and enters the plant floor.

As he walks out, the smell of warm blood and flesh greets him. He still hasn't gotten used to it. He probably never will, he thinks to himself. The mixture of odors is a stew of heated and sterilized flesh, hair that is steamed off the hogs' bodies, and raw meat that moves through the line in the temperature-controlled environment. Thankfully, he thinks, his gag reflex is suppressed, and he no longer has to choke down his own vomit. He thinks back to how difficult it was the first six months and how he didn't know if he would make it. The smell, oh the smell. *Une odeur très horrible.* But the money and benefits are good, and the company sponsors regular meat sales where he can purchase a month's worth of family meals at a steep discount. Plus, he knows his coworkers and likes them. Alain greets each by name and ensures that each team member, as they are called here, knows his or her job and what to do. A section of women is in charge of sawing off the hogs' feet, another section is in charge of cutting off the hogs' ears, and a third station of men is in charge of sawing open hogs' bellies and pulling out the intestines and other organs. Body parts everywhere. Gruesome work, hard work.

Alain makes sure his team members work quickly and efficiently and that they know when to clock out for their lunch break. He is pleased that the company has expanded the lunchroom and has improved the cafeteria menu. The place has a food court feel to it, and he likes that. It makes him think of when he takes his wife and kids to the mall, and they always have a good time there. Target is his wife's favorite store, and his children like to get ice cream or popcorn. He smiles at the thought. While he is grateful he has a job that enables him to provide for his family, he begins to wonder how long he will

Downtown Columbus Junction. Photo by Kristy Nabhan-Warren.

work at the plant. The work is long and physically demanding. He is tired a lot, even though he drinks lots of coffee. And his clothes seem to always have a peculiar smell to them, and he does not like that—his wife has tried all of the detergents and fabric fresheners he knows. He has heard about company-sponsored ESL classes and the community college classes that are paid for by the company. Taking these classes could be a way to make himself ready for a job outside of the plant. But he isn't sure. He makes a mental note to investigate this possibility for himself and his coworkers as he walks out on the floor with a smile to greet his team.

Alain is one of thousands of men and women who work in U.S. meat processing plants today. Whereas Eastern Europeans dominated the industry's slaughter and processing floors of the nineteenth century, today the average worker is of Latin American or African descent. Where once big cities like Chicago were the epicenter of America's meatpacking, today small Corn Belt and southeastern towns claim that title. Small towns in Iowa, Indiana, Ohio, and Nebraska are the new "meatvilles." Indeed, the states with the highest concentration of jobs and locations in meatpacking and processing are, in order, Iowa, Minnesota, South Dakota, Kansas, and North Carolina.

The Midwest Corn Belt is today's version of Ellis Island for asylum seekers and refugees. Word of work travels quickly along migrants and refugees: where there is meat, there is work. And where there is meat, there is a Latino, Chin Burmese, and East African population that is globalizing the Midwest, long a bastion to white Protestant and Catholic women and men. Today's Heartland U.S.A. is an increasingly diverse global village, and the economically and culturally thriving towns are those that have accepted the new ethnic and racial realities. The future is in shades of brown and black. The towns and houses of worship, schools, and community centers that embrace the new social, cultural, and ethnic-racial intersectionalities will prosper. Those that do not will continue to dwindle and die.

What accounts for the shift from urban midwestern cities like Chicago and Cincinnati to rural America? For one, it is cheaper to build and operate in the rural Midwest. And the logistics of supply and demand are in the companies' favor: workers, land, and water are plentiful. And the states that attract and keep today's slaughterhouses are right-to-work states, unfriendly to unions. Local corn farmers, cattle ranchers, and hog confined animal feeding operations (CAFOs for short) are happy because their products are purchased. These companies embrace and capitalize on the "buy local" American mantra. Buying local from Big Ag and CAFOs means something new, however, and Corn Belt Big Ag has its own twenty-first-century version of "local." The animals who are killed and processed come from surrounding farms in what is typically a less-than-fifty-mile radius. As far as the workers go, they are plentiful. And the global and national demand for pork is on the rise. Think bacon. Think jobs with pay rates averaging higher than the national minimum wage. But there is an environmental cost of the slaughter industry. For several years now, local, state, and national groups have been calling attention to the uptick in water, soil, and air contamination and pollution as a direct result of CAFOs and pork plants. And Iowa's record of environmental stewardship in this area leaves much to be desired.

Corn Belt economies must deal with the environmental costs of the pork industry—and the costs are high. Currently, there are tons of pig fecal matter in Iowa. Open-air pits of hog shit literally greet those who drive into towns like Ottumwa. There is ammonia and hydrogen sulfide in the air. Soil is contaminated by high levels of heavy metals found in hog fecal waste. Residents who live near the plants and CAFOs smell the horrific odors on a daily basis. The air quality of rural Iowa has been seriously compromised by CAFOs, and rural Iowans themselves are "paying the price for industrial livestock operations that externalize the cost of pollution while their profits often go to out-of-state corporations."[1] Danielle Wirth, a professor of environmental science and policy at Iowa State University, lives along the Des Moines River in Boone County. Wirth is critical of Iowa's Department of Natural Resources, saying the agency has failed to protect the health of Iowans and the quality of the state's air, water, and land: "Clearly, Iowa's regulatory standards do not protect her citizens. Given the evident examples of geology, regulatory insufficiency, human greed, it is inconceivable that clean water for humans, native wildlife and native plants can be kept safe when CAFOs are constructed in this system."[2] CAFO-induced damage to Iowa's environment and the health of its inhabitants is real, and with the addition of several pork plants in Iowa in the past couple of years, the issues will only worsen for the environment and the people who work there, not to mention the residents of towns where the plants are being built. Some consider it a deadly combination: waste-producing and polluting hog CAFOs and pork processing plants are ruining Iowa's land, water, and air.

From the pork plants' perspective, they are upcycling waste and using it as beneficial manure in farm fields across the Corn Belt. There is a continuous loop within Big Agriculture that keeps cycling in states like Iowa. The cycle begins with the growing of corn, which feeds the hogs and steer, whose fecal matter is treated and then sprayed on the fields of corn and soybeans. And the corn that is not used to feed the animals is used to make ethanol to fuel the tractors and automobiles in states like Iowa and beyond. But the problem is that there is an excessive amount of manure and bacteria that pollutes waterways. The open-air pits of pig manure on site at CAFOs and slaughterhouses alike fill the surrounding airways with stench and pollutants and can carry odors miles away, if wind patterns are just so. And when the manure leaks and spills out of the CAFOs and the factories' open-air pits, then the damage gets in the groundwater. A recent Environmental Working Group report listed that of the almost 55,000 private wells in Iowa, 40 percent are contaminated with coliform bacteria.[3]

Companies like Iowa Select, the state's largest pork producer, claim that they are providing organic fertilizer for growers, bringing jobs to rural Iowa, and even "adding value" to grain operations. When asked about the environmental damage and pollution, these companies tend to deflect responsibility and blame onto "contracted facilities." Yet Iowa Sierra Club member Jess Masour sees it differently: "It's clear that these air releases are toxic and dangerous to neighbors, animals, and farmers, which makes Iowa Select bad neighbors."[4] The overabundance of fecal waste in the state of Iowa is harming airways, the quality of the soil, and waterways. Christopher Jones, a University of Iowa research engineer, has calculated that, while Iowa's population is 3.2 million people, when the waste from the nearly 110 million hogs, chickens, turkeys, and cattle is factored in, the fecal matter waste is the equivalent of 168 million people. Recently, the state of Iowa has been named, pun intended, as "Number one in number two."[5]

There is no doubting that the meatpacking industry is environmentally destructive and that change needs to happen now. Tama's Iowa Premium Beef has implemented more environmentally friendly measures such as a patented UV light treatment to treat the packing plant wastewater and remove solid wastes and bacteria before sending it to the Iowa River. Moreover, in many ways today's meatpacking industry hosts one of the most diverse workforces in America and has revived formerly stagnant or dying communities. The pork processing plants provides opportunities and jobs for thousands of Corn Belt workers, the vast majority of whom are immigrants and refugees. Compared with many workplaces across the country, one could say that the meatpacking industry—also known as the "protein industry"—is more inclusive than just about any other industry and workplace. A tough reality for many to swallow is that packing plants employ among the most—if not the most— diverse workforce in the United States today, even more than universities and colleges. Today's protein industry features a workforce ethnically, racially, and religiously diverse. But the plants most certainly pollute—a lot. Air, soil, and waterways are being compromised.

How can companies like Tyson, Iowa Select, Prestage Foods, and Seaboard Triumph be held accountable for the waste that comes out of their plants? How can small towns and their inhabitants be protected? For if they are not, we will return to the late nineteenth century and the journalist Upton Sinclair's historicized, nonfictionalized world of the Back of the Yards and meatpacking where there were no regulations. And without regulations, the quality of life for everyone—human and nonhuman species alike—is degraded. The pork plants that dot the Corn Belt and cluster in rural areas in Iowa are part of a 1960s nationwide shift: where once hogs and other animals were transported from rural to urban metropolises like Chicago and Cincinnati to be slaughtered and processed, now they stay in the Midwest in a vertically integrated process of raising, slaughtering, and packaging. As historian William Cronon writes of this shift, "There were strong economic incentives to slaughter and pack pigs near the place where farmers raised them. Pork packing was thus one of the earliest and most important frontier industries, springing up wherever people established new agricultural settlements."[6]

Rural Iowa today is what Chicago was in the nineteenth century, a hub for a meatpacking industry run by immigrants and refugees.

On a warm spring day in Columbus Junction, Esmerelda and I sat and chatted, *en español*, over coffee after the 11:30 Mass down in the parish basement. As she thought about the questions that I was asking about her life as a Mexican-descent Latina in rural eastern Iowa, Esmerelda smiled slightly and said, "My husband and I just want our children to grow up with the American dream that they can be who they want to be. We don't ask for much. We work hard, pray to our God, and love America. We want the same thing that *los* Anglos want for their children, and I pray to la Virgen and Jesús to watch over all of our families."

Esmerelda and her husband Juan are among the approximately 180,000 Latinos who live in the state of Iowa, a figure that is growing. Latino women and men choose to reside in rural areas and towns like Columbus Junction, where there are ample jobs in meatpacking plants and in agricultural work. Like Esmerelda and Juan, many Latinos work in the local pork processing plant, where the relatively high wages and 401K benefits are appealing, especially for young, growing families. Esmerelda and Juan work hard, give to their church, and are raising their four children as bicultural and bilingual global citizens.

Today, it is in small towns like Columbus Junction that we find the future of the United States. A future that is culturally and religiously diverse. A global, multilingual village. Men and women from different countries— Burma/Myanmar, Mexico, Guatemala, Vietnam, and the Congo—speaking various languages and working side by side in plants, factories, and fields to support their families. Working jobs that very few can imagine or will ever experience. If we want to understand what it is like to be an immigrant and refugee in today's United States, we need look no further than U.S.-based meat processing plants like the one where Alain works. For those of us who struggle with empathy for immigrants' plights, a tour of one of these many plants that dot the midwestern landscape can help in our understanding of what immigrants will do to survive and thrive and of their intense commitment to provide financial support for their extended family, in America and also in their country of origin.

What we also find on a meta-level at meatpacking plants like Tyson is the vertical integration of animals, migrants/refugees, and religion. The hogs at the Columbus Junction plant; the workers; and the CEOs, CFOs, and human resources heads work in tandem toward the goal of corporate American religion. This is the new religion in America today, and the Corn Belt is where it is being nurtured and raised.

Tyson Fresh Meats, Columbus Junction. Photo by Kristy Nabhan-Warren.

A Tour

It was all so very businesslike that one watched it fascinated. It was porkmaking by machinery, porkmaking by applied mathematics.—Upton Sinclair, *The Jungle*

The packer's triumph was to further the commodification of meat, to alienate still more its ties to the lives and ecosystems that had ultimately created it.
—William Cronon, *Nature's Metropolis*

The smell. It hit me like a bludgeon when I opened the car door. A violent smell. Warm, moist, and pungent. The smell of shit and animal flesh. Death.[7] My bodily instinct was to retch. I bent downwards and grabbed my knees. I told myself that I could not, absolutely *could not* faint or throw up on this tour of Tyson. I wore nondescript clothing, black pants and a long-sleeved blue cotton shirt from Walmart. My hair was pulled back snugly in a ponytail; old running shoes were on my feet. I wore what was recommended to wear for the day: comfortable, affordable, and practical clothing and shoes. I was ready for work. My legs trembled a bit as I walked with some fear and trepidation toward the check-in station, where I met my friend Father Joseph Sia and the plant chaplain, Joe Blay. Yes, you read that right—the plant chaplain. Tyson is a leader in a growing corporate movement to have men and women of God on the payrolls. The company is an important participant in the broader Faith at Work movement in the United States that can be traced back to the early twentieth century.[8] Tyson promotes faith in the workplace and, in a sense, packages and promotes a new brand of faith for its employees, who in turn draw upon this workplace faith to get them through their shift. A faith in hard work, grit, and determination that relies on a Protestant work ethic pervades the contemporary Tyson meatpacking plant and corporate culture. In rural meatpacking plants, animals are raised, killed, and sold in a pattern of vertical integration, much as religion, specifically evangelical Protestant Christianity, pervades the vertical integration process of animals from birth to slaughter. The "previously independent facets" of animals, humans, and religion are now in one sprawling place—the packing plants that contain animals, people, and workplace, corporate faith. An evangelistic fervor is present in companies like Tyson, where the food, faith, and the workplace are vertically integrated to form the American dream of values-laced success.

Once we were inside Tyson's check-in building, we signed waiver forms and presented our driver's licenses; then Father Joseph and I were given official visitor badges to clip on the white coats that we would be given in the administrative wing of the plant before the tour. As we walked to the main plant, we passed large signs of welcome in English, Spanish, French, Hakha Chin (a Burmese language), and Vietnamese.

The smells I experienced in the parking lot enveloped us on a concentrated level as we entered the main plant. Here it was even more palpable, concentrated. Trapped and stuffy air. A combination of flesh, hair, excrement. It was as the American realist Upton Sinclair wrote of the smell at the Chicago Stockyards: "It was an elemental odor, raw and crude; it was rich, almost rancid, sensual, and strong."[9] The smells bonded with our bodies, and we carried them with us throughout the day. The recently renovated administrative wing was a brief respite from the smell. After we passed through these doors, we were greeted by Dave Duncan, the human relations manager of the plant, who was to be our tour guide that morning. Waves of Febreze wafted over us, thanks to enterprising secretaries, hard at work combating the porcine stench.

Dave warmly shook our hands as we entered his office. He gestured toward the white lab coats, hard hats, hairnets, and gloves that were neatly laid out and ready for us. We even had special orange earplugs, as the floor of the plant gets very loud. Safety first—it is Tyson's mantra. We dressed according to Dave's instructions, covering or netting all hair on our heads (men with beards and mustaches must cover those as well), buttoning the coats all the way up to our necks, and inserting our earplugs in the way we were shown.

Dave prepped us with information, letting us know we would be walking through the cold rooms first before heading to the warm rooms. He told us there would be blood and body parts. When Dave turned to me and asked me point-blank if I was "squeamish" around this kind of stuff, without hesitation I said, "No, I am OK with it." I nodded, dug my nails into my palms, and ventured forth. Dave knew that Father Joseph could "handle it," and I was determined to handle it, too.[10]

As I wrote up my reflections on the day later in my notebook, I thought about the women and men I have interviewed who work at Tyson and have shared their stories. I thought about their sore limbs, their bodies that they massage each night after their shift, and the hot baths they take to relieve the pain and eliminate the smells their bodies have absorbed. But, at the moment of the tour, I sucked in my breath, exhaled through my mouth, and followed Dave out to the plant floor.

Walking out to a meatpacking plant floor for the first time is like stepping into an alternative reality. But this was real. Bloody real. It was loud, cold, and crimson red. There was a lot going on, and it was loud. There is an intense order to the plant, and each worker has a repetitive yet also highly skilled task. We walked by women and men with various knives and blades cutting through the now-chilled pork meat, slicing and cutting parts that would be sold at wholesale and retail markets. Their white coats were splattered with blood. The plant was cold and constantly surveilled by USDA inspectors. Fat, meat droppings, and the occasional eyeball washed down drains next to our feet. We walked and stood amid thousands of pounds of cold flesh. As I raised my eyes to look above me, a light spray of water, mixed with hog waste, managed to enter my mouth. I knew that I should not spit it out, so I swallowed it. I can still taste, smell, and see the meat as I write this.

At this particular pork processing plant, 10,000 hogs at 200 pounds apiece are killed—or, as the company prefers to say, "harvested"—and processed each day. Rows upon rows of sows with raised teats on their underbellies— they recently nursed and unbeknownst to them weaned their piglets—moved past us, slow enough so that we could take in their girth and their lifeless bodies. As we followed Dave's path through the cold cutting floor, the hogs' feet and hooves grazed my arms and shoulders and bumped gently into my white-coated side. They were heavy, rubbery, so heavy that I stumbled a bit at the first body brushing against me. Turning from the hogs on our right, I learned that the prime rib meat that we see in the stores is cut by a highly trained worker whose primary job is to slice blades in a very precise way. The Sudanese employee cutting the prime rib cuts used graceful and precise movements, slicing though huge slabs of meat that moved by him on a conveyer line. According to Dave, this was one of the hardest jobs on the line, one that required exact timing, a degree of swiftness, and graceful bodily movements. He also told us that African and Latino workers are the best because they have the "best work ethic." The worker we witnessed in action was like a dancer—but one who dodges blades and knives with precision and elegance.

Sharp silver knives proliferated along the line. Each worker wore a holster-like device on her or his hip that contained various knives used in the course of a workday. Dave informed us that a knife sharpener comes by at various points during the day to replace the team members' dulled knives for sharp ones. Sharp knives are a must-have for these team members.

It was very cold in the plant; we could see our breath. The damp air is kept at a constant temperature of thirty-five degrees Fahrenheit. If you have ever worked in a restaurant and have been inside the cold storage room where meats, cheeses, vegetables, and fruits are kept, that's what it felt like—almost like a freezer, but not quite. Dave informed us that meat rots from the inside out and that if it is too warm in this area, the meat will spoil. The team members all wore mesh gloves, but they were wet with blood and flesh, and they froze easily. From time to time another team member came around to replace the gloves with dry ones, and the cycle continued throughout the day. Wet and cold hands are slow and prone to accidents. Dry hands work better and faster and are injured less frequently.

The plant was orderly, and each person had a distinct role. Even the hard hats were organized by color, indicating what level and what job the worker represented. New team members had white hats, and when they graduated to new levels and jobs by experience and seniority, their hard hat colors changed. The plant floor was a sea of moving bodies and heads covered in white, yellow, red, purple, and blue. Always one to focus on productivity and streamlined work, Henry Ford would be proud of this crew.[11]

As we made our way through the cold floor, gingerly stepping over flesh that had fallen on the floor, we passed a neat line of women, all Latina and Congolese, who each had a little cart in front of her with the meat cuts she was generating. Their white smocks were splattered with blood. Each had a specified cutting task, and each performed her job with grace. We next climbed some stairs to admire a man whose sole job was using an ergonomic saw to cut through the hogs' torsos. His body moved in rhythm with the giant saw, up and down with the large electric blade. It was a feat that was physical and graceful. Dave informed us that this man was the best slicer on the floor and that his movements were impeccably timed. In the past few years, Dave said, the job had become safer and more efficient due to the ergonomic saw and platform. There would be fewer shoulder and back injuries, he said, thanks to engineering improvements. These contemporary marvels of efficiency and safety owe much to Henry Ford's chief engineer and father of the influential mid-twentieth-century scientific principles of management, Frederick Winslow Taylor.[12]

The plant's floor was a marvel of mechanization and specialization. The work was repetitive but also highly skilled; the workers had to perfect their bodily movements and be one with the hog. All around us, there was sawing, cutting, peeling, and disemboweling, the kinetics of light and sound. The entire process had to move quickly so that bacteria did not have a chance to invade the meat. Workers timed their movements with other team members' movements. Hogs were sawed in half and disemboweled by male workers. We were told that men tend to do the hardest jobs because of their "natural strength," whereas women did the more finely detailed work because of their predisposition toward this kind of work. The next set of employees harvested the organs and inspected them quickly and carefully, marking the good ones with a special USDA-approved purple ink and then placing them in a metal dish. The organs deemed unsatisfactory were called "compromised." Compromised organs include perforated intestines, fecal-matter-splattered organs, and unusually colored livers and were marked for nonhuman consumption. These rejects would be making their way into the food we feed our dogs. White-smocked, hair-netted USDA inspectors with official-looking clipboards and pens were all around to ensure food safety.

The hogs were thoroughly washed and hung from strong wires that carried them on their continued journey to be human food. We passed a cluster of women whose jobs were to slice, cut, pluck, and saw. Latinas dominated this area of detailed handiwork, and Dave told us that they had the focus, work ethic, and skill set for this type of job. We watched as one Latina carefully and quickly plucked the hogs' toenails from the hooves. The woman next to her then sliced the hooves off in one clean swoop. Another sliced the hogs' ears from their heads, and a fourth peeled off the hogs' eyelashes. A fifth woman plucked out the hogs' eyes. According to Dave, no body parts go to waste. The contemporary meatpacking plant is the ultimate recycler. Like the hogs' organs that were rejected for human consumption, the hogs' ears that lay in a growing pile on the plant floor would be roasted for dog treats sold at local and national feed stores. When I asked about the need for eyelash removal, Dave said that no hair can get into what will soon become meat that is packaged for human consumption.

We then walked over to a giant open oven-like device through which the hogs' bodies passed. High-powered lasers burned off any remaining hair on the bodies, giving them the clean, pinkish-white piggy look we adore. We learned that hogs are very hairy. *Very* hairy. Sometimes it takes a few runs through the laser oven to burn off the abundant hair. The air was heavy with a fried hair smell, and crisps of hair lay in piles on the floor in front of us. The smell of burned hair is not something you easily forget.

We then watched men and women slit open the dead hogs' necks and cut open the jowls. My takeaway from this observation was that every body part is used. This message was drilled into Father Joseph and me repeatedly. Rejected organs, ears, and eyes were joined by toenails, teeth, and snouts. American dogs are fed the ground-up and processed body parts that are mixed into those brightly colored bags of food we buy. Dave was quite proud of the fact that his plant uses all the hogs' body parts—even the rectum. We walked by a group of women—Latinas, Chin Burmese, and Congolese—who were cleaning and pounding out the rectum for shipment to Japan, where it will be grilled as a delicacy.

The pork processed at this small-town Iowa plant will feed people not only in the United States but also in China, Brazil, and Japan. There is a growing global marketplace for pork, and Iowa ranks as the top hog-producing state in the United States. As noted above, 10,000 hogs are processed at this plant each day—and this is a "smaller scale operation," according to Dave. There is one in Iowa and one in Indiana that process twice as many "head" of hog in a day, 20,000 to be exact, he told us.

Winning the Lottery

The journey to this plant, and many others, begins in far-flung global locales. In many instances, violence in migrants' and refugees' home countries lead them to the various packing plants that dot the U.S. Corn Belt.

All Maurice and Benita wanted was to raise their three sons in a safe environment. The South African couple had lived for the majority of their lives in the South African capital of Johannesburg and were mostly happy there. Maurice was a taxi driver and supported his family on the wages that he supplemented with "odd jobs." The family had a strong social network and attended one of the many evangelical-leaning Christian churches in the bustling city.

Yet their sense of happiness and security began to unravel the day their oldest son, David, had a frightening experience. The teenager had a craving for *droëwors* that day, the deliciously salty and cured sausage that the store up the street sold. Benita gave him some money, and he skipped along the familiar route, kicking small gray stones as he went, thinking about what had happened at school that day. But when he arrived at the store, a terrible sight greeted him. As he approached the entrance, a couple of masked men ran up and kicked open the door of the store. They shot the register clerk point-blank. David was close enough to see the man lying on the floor, a bullet wound in his head and bleeding on the ground. In panic mode, David fled the store faster than he had ever run in his life, said his mom. Benita remembers him crying and "shaking all over," unable to articulate what had happened. She was beside herself with worry. "I just rocked him in my arms like when he was a baby. It was so terrible and he was just . . . terrified."

David's brush with violence convinced Benita and Maurice that they had to leave Johannesburg. The couple stayed up all night talking about what to do. Even before the incident at the convenience store, they had been worrying about their future in South Africa. Crime rates had been steadily rising in Johannesburg, and they had been concerned that their boys would be recruited by one of the local gangs. By three in the morning it was decided: Maurice would go down to the U.S. branch of the Bureau of Consular Affairs that day and apply for the U.S. Government Electronic Diversity Visa Lottery, known as the "Diversity Lottery," an annual program that admits 55,000 men, women, and children into the United States from around the world.[13] It took a year, but the family was one of the fortunate ones—almost a year to the day of David's frightening experience, they were among the "winners" of that year's lottery.

It takes a lot of money to migrate to the United States. Maurice worked three and four jobs to save up money—doing small construction jobs, driving cabs, preparing food in restaurants—for his visa and a one-way flight to the United States. He and Benita decided that he would fly to Portland, Oregon, where he had an uncle with whom he could stay for free and save up money for Benita's and their three boys' visas and one-way airfare. Maurice was in Portland for six months and worked close to fifty hours a week as a cashier, repairman, and packer for a family-owned business. He loved living in Portland but wasn't making enough money, he knew, to support a family of five there, and he was aware of the high rents there. When Maurice finally had the funds to purchase tickets for his wife and boys, they flew to Sterling, Virginia, a half hour outside of the nation's capital.

Benita and the boys had to be there for three months while Maurice worked to obtain more funds to fly them out to be with him. Benita remembered her time in Virginia fondly. "I liked Virginia, really I did. It was warm, the people were friendly, and my boys liked it there." She also had fond memories of touring Washington, D.C., which she described as "beautiful." She had especially fond memories of seeing the cherry blossoms in the spring and walking around the National Mall with her boys and getting them ice cream. In fact, she liked it so much in Virginia that Maurice contemplated joining his family there, finding work, and putting down their family's roots. But he didn't yet have a job in Virginia, and his uncle had secured a job for him and a place to stay in North Liberty, Iowa. Maurice's experience with migration and movement is a common one among refugees and asylum seekers who join up with extended family and communities. Family ties help secure work, housing, and an extended network of care, while wives, children, husbands, parents, and grandparents wait to be reunited with their loved ones.

Maurice found himself in the fast-growing community of North Liberty, a suburb of Iowa City, doing light construction. He had worked construction for a few weeks when a coworker told him that a pork processing plant, Tyson Fresh Foods, was hiring. Maurice and his coworker decided to apply together to work at the plant, which was about a forty-five-minute drive from North Liberty. The pay at Tyson was good, work was steady, and workers received benefits and medical insurance. Maurice's construction coworker drove them down to the plant a few days later, where they applied for jobs. When the human resources representative looked at Maurice's application, she was surprised and pleased to see that Maurice spoke five languages: French, English, Swahili, Tshiluba, and Lingala. She wanted to hire him as a translator for the ethnically diverse plant where over twenty languages and dialects are spoken, a mini–United Nations in the heartland, surrounded by fields of corn and soybeans. The plant had just one translator and needed to hire more as more immigrants and refugees were coming in from Africa.

But Maurice would need to pass his driver's license examination with the Department of Motor Vehicles first, as the job of a translator included a company car for shuttling workers to doctor's visits and physical therapy appointments. He studied the manual and prepared to take the test in the evenings after working ten-hour shifts on the harvest floor as a "head dropper." For five days a week, sometimes six, Maurice would don his work uniform, which included safety gloves, and would slice the head off a hog until it was hanging by an approximately five-inch flap of skin. It was important to not cut the head off all the way as the USDA inspector, who stood beside him, would inspect the hog's head for disease and make sure it passed inspection. The work was difficult, cold, and hand-numbing. His fingers would grow stiff and swollen after the day's work, and standing all day made him fatigued. During our interview, Benita shook her head as she recalled how Maurice looked after a shift as head dropper. She held up her right hand and rubbed her fingers gently as she described her husband's hands after a work shift: "His fingers were so swollen, you know, like sausages. I would massage them and clean them for him each night." She worried that her husband was working too much and too hard, but Maurice did not want his wife to do the kind of hard, intensive labor that he did at Tyson. He supported her goal to become a nurse, and she took classes at a local community college at night. He loved her smooth, beautiful hands with their long, tapered fingers and wanted them to stay that way.

Maurice and Benita were happy to raise their sons in this small Iowa city that they felt was much safer than Johannesburg and had a slower pace of life than in Virginia. North Liberty seemed just right: it had good schools and a wonderful church about a mile from their apartment. Iowa City, where they now live, is also affordable and just a forty-minute-drive to Maurice's work at the Columbus Junction Tyson plant. The commute was made much easier as Maurice joined a carpool five to six days a week with a lively group of African coworkers from the Democratic Republic of the Congo. The only "bad" part of their new home, said Benita with a chuckle, is the cold. Her first winter in Iowa was "terrible, just like, I could not believe how cold it was." And it wasn't just the temperatures that made life difficult that first winter season; it was the cold wind that made Benita "just cry some days."

While he was happy with the wages he was making as a head dropper, Maurice was eager to secure a better paying and less physically demanding job at Tyson. He was motivated to secure the position as translator. While he passed the written part of the driving test on the first try, it took three tries to pass the driving portion. "I have been driving since I was thirteen, but it took a lot of focus for me to learn the driving rules here in the United States. We drive on the opposite side of the car in Johannesburg, and it is just so different driving here." He passed the test on a Friday, and on Monday he was officially a translator. "I went from the harvest floor to a supervisory kind of position in, like, two months and was so happy." Maurice likes his job because he meets a lot of different people and has "learned so much" about other cultures. At the pork processing plant, orientation of new workers occurs every two weeks, and for Maurice, it is an enjoyable part of his job to help train the workers and be of service as a translator.

They are a long, long way from Johannesburg, South Africa. The Iowa winter months with the bracing winds and the lack of sun have been tough to get used to, and Benita is not sure she will ever become accustomed to the cold, dry air. The small Iowa town where they have settled has many amenities, but "so many people look the same here, you know?" said Benita, with a chuckle. We laughed a bit more when I responded, "Yeah, a lot of white ladies like me, right?!" We giggled together, and she nodded affirmatively. But on a more serious note, Benita worried that her sons would not be accepted; she worried about racism and how it would affect her boys. The transition from Johannesburg to Virginia to Iowa was hard on her and the boys in the beginning. The older two, teenagers, missed their friends in Johannesburg and had started to get used to life in Virginia. The younger son was in primary grade school when they arrived in Iowa, and it was easier for him to adjust, Benita said. And the months when the family didn't have a car were especially hard as the bus routes are reliable only within a limited geographic area. What would normally be the simple task of purchasing groceries was challenging. The nearby gas station convenience store became all too familiar to the family and was where they purchased much of their food in the beginning. They tried to eat healthy in between trips to the grocery store, but it was hard to do. There are only so many Lunchables, crackers, Slim Jims, and packaged nuts that one can consume.

Yet despite their struggles adjusting to the Midwest, Benita and her Maurice consider themselves "very lucky." While they had enjoyed living in South Africa, it kept getting more dangerous, especially for dark-skinned young men like their sons. Rising crime rates and violence were the push factors that prompted them to apply for the Diversity Lottery and eventually migrate. We talked about school shootings and the availability of guns in the United States. Yet the couple acknowledged that while gun violence is real and on the rise in this country, they feel "much safer" in the United States, and in the Midwest in particular, where "life is just slower paced and people are just friendly and smile a lot."

Finding a church has been an important step toward making Iowa City their new home. Since November 2015, Maurice, Benita, and their now four sons—the youngest was born in Iowa City—have been attending Iowa City's All Nations Baptist Church, which has come to serve as their spiritual home. They like that there is a diverse group of people there, including, they said, "Koreans, Africans, Americans, and French." Maurice's skills and vocation as a translator is put to good use. For him, translating at church is not a job but is "for God and on God's time." The boys are involved with the youth group, and Benita is part of a women's group. Being a part of a church culture that celebrates global cultures was a must for the couple when they were trying out houses of worship. The vast majority of All Nations Baptist members, around

90 percent, were part of the Diversity Lottery, like Maurice and Benita's family. The deep desire to be in the United States is a bond that unites All Nations congregants.

Like many churches in the United States today, All Nations serves as a house of worship, community center, day care and preschool, and place to celebrate many languages and cultures. Maurice and Benita said they are "very happy" there and are confident that All Nations will assist them in raising their sons to be upstanding men. For Maurice, spending time at church with his wife and sons is a necessary respite from his stressful work at Tyson. The worship experience itself and being part of a community of believers helps to offset the physical, mental, and emotional stresses from his work week. Maurice said were it not for his family and church, he would not have survived at Tyson. Maurice and Benita's Christian faith is at the core of their family's identity, and they credit God and their church family for their ability to adapt and thrive in the United States.

For the South African family of six, getting around Iowa City was made much easier after Maurice passed his driver's test and secured a company car with Tyson. When he is not at work, he is able to take his wife and boys to the store, to school activities, and on Sundays to church. Benita will take the bus in town when needed, but she prefers to wait for Maurice. In this small university town, taking care of everyday tasks is made much easier when you own a car or truck. Unlike cities and towns on the coasts, which boast light-rails and accessible transportation, midwestern towns and cities are spread out and make auto ownership a necessity. For most immigrants, refugees, and migrants, obtaining reliable transportation is the number one priority after securing housing.

The absence of inter-town and city public transportation makes finding and keeping a job difficult for migrants and refugees in rural states like Iowa, as the vast majority of new immigrants lack the funds to purchase a car or truck upon arrival to the United States. While city buses are reliable and useful for women and men who work in these tightly bounded geographic areas, they are not an option for folks who work in the small towns and rural locations where the meatpacking plants, for example, are located. Maurice lamented the lack of light-rail trains and buses for travel outside of the larger Iowa cities. He misses the "excellent" public transportation systems in Oregon, his first U.S. state, saying that "transportation is a big, big issue for immigrants." He observed, "There are many accidents among immigrants because they are driving without their licenses or with just their permits. They do not understand the rules of the roads here, and sometimes even if they do know the rules, they disregard them because they need to drive to work and to live, and their job is far from their home."

Maurice and Benita said that there is a critical need for the Department of Motor Vehicles to have all of the information and exams available in multiple languages. For his part, Maurice plans on volunteering at the local DMV to help Africans understand what they need to do to obtain their driver's licenses. He wants the DMV to do a better job reaching out to immigrant and migrant groups and said he will assist the agency in its efforts because it is an important public service to immigrants and refugees. For her part, Benita serves as a translator for Johnson County, Iowa, and helps refugees and immigrants apply for food stamps, jobs, and "anything they need." She is especially empathetic toward immigrants without refugee status, because she understands what it is like to not have a U.S. sponsor and to have to "figure everything out" without the help of an individual or group.

Meatpacking Chaplaincy

When I asked him about his life's journey and how he ended up working at a meatpacking plant in small-town Iowa, Joe Blay contemplated the question as he ate his muffin and sipped his steaming coffee.

> You know, I never used to think about where my meat came from. When I went to the store, I would just buy it and not think about who prepared it. It was just meat. Now, when I go to the grocery store, I think of the men and women at work and what they do each day. I think of the kill floor. I think of the blood, the intestines, and the fact that this is a very, very hard job to do. I think of all of my team members at work and how hard they work for their families. All of them, I mean *all of them*, work overtime to provide for their wives, their husbands and children. Some for their grandchildren. It takes a lot, and I think . . . actually, I *know* . . . that most people cannot do this kind of work.

Joe has been the chaplain at the Tyson plant in this small Iowa town for the past four years. He identifies as Ghanaian by birth, a U.S. citizen, an ordained African Methodist Episcopal Church (AME) minister, and a former army chaplain. He and his family have moved over thirteen times during the course of his career, given the demands of the ministry and military. He was proud to share some good news with me: he and his wife Lora recently purchased a townhome in Iowa City, which is a forty-minute drive from his job in Columbus Junction. Their daughter and son attend public schools that have a diverse student body. They hope to retire here, and Lora hopes to not have to move "ever again," Joe chuckled.

Joe came to the States in the late 1980s to attend seminary in North Carolina. While he was in school he applied for and received U.S. citizenship. He was ordained with AME Zion a few years later and immediately began his ministry at the age of thirty-one. He was called to pastor a church in Tennessee, which quickly became three churches, and was there for almost seven years. While he enjoyed the many aspects of tending to his church community, Joe was feeling burned out and a bit stressed financially. "You see, I had to pastor three churches to pay the bills and have a little extra for my family." It was a pastor friend who told him about army chaplaincy as a career option. Joe looked into it and was impressed. The benefits were good, and the pay was more than he was making as a pastor.

> I entered the army for two reasons, really: for financial security and also to be challenged. I needed a change. I was administering many funerals when I was a pastor and did not have the opportunity to work with many young people. When I wanted to try new things as a pastor, I was discounted by the older parishioners who wanted to keep doing things the "same old way." I was becoming demoralized. I didn't feel useful. I needed to try new things. Plus, my denomination did not pay well. I had no health insurance and was on the state's insurance. I really got to know what it is like to be poor. I was making $175 a week and I had the parsonage to live in, but the pay was not enough for me and my family. So that is why I had to pastor several churches . . . to pay the bills, but it was still not enough. Somehow, we managed to live on $1,200 a month for quite some time. But it just couldn't go on forever.

The financial security the army offered was appealing to Joe. With his wife's blessing, Joe took the plunge and began basic army training when he was thirty-nine years old. He survived the training and accepted the offer to be an army chaplain.

He and his wife and their young children moved a lot in the course of his army career. While it was just him and Lora in the early days and they could pack up their things and move from Tennessee to Colorado Springs, later moves necessitated Joe living apart from his wife and two children for periods of time, which was stressful. The military mandated moves that included Bosnia (just Joe); South Carolina (family); Italy (Joe); a return to South Carolina (Joe); Fort Campbell, Kentucky (Joe); Iraq (Joe); a return to Kentucky (family); and Fort Lee, Virginia (family). While at Fort Lee, Joe was promoted to major, and later he was named brigade chaplain. As brigade chaplain, Joe oversaw 4,500 soldiers. During this time, he decided to pursue his master's degree in counseling at Columbus State University, Georgia, with a focus on family therapy. He graduated with his MA in 2010 and then did a mandatory "utilization tour" in Wiesbaden, Germany. The move was too much for his wife and kids, however, and they moved to Atlanta to live with his wife's sister. Lora, also Ghanaian by birth, liked the fact that there were many Black Americans in the city and felt more at home there than she had in other places they had lived. The kids liked it there, too, and felt like they fit in with Atlanta's Black youth culture. Final army stints for Joe included Frankfurt, Germany, where he gained experience in family life counseling with army families, and Huntsville, Alabama, where he was senior recruiting brigade chaplain.

While things were good, Joe was starting to feel a bit restless. He and Lora wanted to move to a place where they could retire and where the kids could graduate from high school. They were done with moving and living apart. It just so happened that the director of army chaplaincy was Joe's immediate supervisor, and he helped to arrange Joe's interview with several meatpacking plants that were hiring chaplains. Joe had never contemplated working in a factory—let alone one where animals were slaughtered—but he was open, as always, to a new experience. He interviewed at two meatpacking plants and was immediately intrigued with Tyson. "It reminded me of the army, with all of the focus on order and discipline. The plant, like the army, is a tightly run ship. I am the type of person who always wants a challenge, and this seemed like the next challenge. I get to work in a diverse environment, and I get to counsel and advocate for my team members." For Joe, returning to ministry was appealing, and this time around he would be able to make a decent living for his family, which he had been unable to do before even when he was serving multiple churches. The Tyson pay was good, he had a company car, and he worked reasonable hours—Joe couldn't believe his good fortune.

Tyson is part of a growing number of corporations that employ full-time chaplains. As the journalist Emma Green has discovered, workplace chaplaincy programs are on the rise in the United States as well as globally. Tyson Foods is unusual, however, in that it is a publicly traded company that runs its own in-house chaplaincy programs.[14] The company is at the forefront and is part of a larger Faith at Work movement in the United States that can be traced back to the postwar 1950s and the rise of corporate America, evangelical Christianity, and a new era of consumerism. In 1950s and 1960s America, a rising middle class was able and encouraged to purchase meat for growing families. Chicken soon became, thanks to Don Tyson in the 1950s and another chicken magnate, S. Truett Cathy, who launched Chick-fil-A back in 1964, America's most popular white meat. Tyson helped popularize a Christian business trifecta of family, work, and faith in his fresh meats conglomerate. For his part, Cathy applied the evangelical work trinity to his company, employees, and the popular chicken sandwiches, waffle fries, coleslaw, and ice cream cones they served by the millions each year.[15]

Tyson Foods also boasts, according to religious studies scholar David W. Miller, "the largest known private-sector corporate-chaplaincy program" in the United States and globally, with more than 115 chaplains based in different factories around the country. Company-wide, this works out to roughly one chaplain on staff for every 1,000 Tyson employees. According to Mike Tarvin, former military chaplain who directed chaplaincy services for Tyson, "When I first started here, John Tyson said something to me. He wanted people to be able to bring their whole selves to work. We provide our team members at Tyson Foods an opportunity to bring that whole self, including that spiritual side, and not [feel] like that they have to check that at the door."[16] The current director of Tyson Foods chaplaincy, Karen Diefendorf, is a Yale-trained, former army chaplain of over thirty-three years.[17] Diefendorf is in charge of leading and directing "more than 90 chaplains who provide pastoral care, counseling and support to team members at many of the company's plant and office locations."[18]

Tyson Foods, Inc., headquartered in Springdale, Arkansas, was founded in 1935 by John W. Tyson, whose family members continue to be actively involved in running the business. Don Tyson, John W.'s son, and John H. Tyson, the founder's grandson, have helped steer the now global company into a dominant producer of meats. John H. currently serves as chairman of the company's board of directors. Tyson Foods owns leading brands such as Tyson, Jimmy Dean, Hillshire Farm, Sara Lee, Ball Park, Wright, Aidells, and State Fair. It is a global leader in chicken, beef, and pork as well as prepared foods, including bacon, breakfast sausage, turkey, lunchmeat, hot dogs, pizza crusts and toppings, tortillas, and desserts. The company supplies retail and food-service customers throughout the United States and approximately 115 countries. The chaplaincy program has been around since 2000 and was founded to "provide compassionate pastoral care to team members and their families, regardless of their religious affiliation or beliefs."[19]

Tyson currently employs approximately 114,000 "team members" at more than 400 facilities and offices in the United States and around the world. Tyson

Foods uses not-so-subtle evangelical Christian terminology such as "values," "integrity," "faith-friendly," and "family" liberally in its public relations marketing. Its marketing division brands the company as caring and faithful and emphasizes that it looks out for the best interests of its workers. Through its "Core Values," "Code of Conduct," and "Team Member Bill of Rights," Tyson Foods strives to operate with "integrity and trust." Tyson's business approach is a blend of corporate paternalism, evangelical fervor, and capitalism. Workers are part of a "team" and, even more so, a "family." While Tyson advertises its corporate commitment to its workers, ultimately it is bound to "creating value" for its shareholders first, customers second, and team members third.[20]

As Americans have shifted from mainstream denominational affiliations —think Baptist, Lutheran, Methodist—in recent years, enterprising corporations have taken advantage of the "spiritual-but-not-religious"-identifying landscape in the United States and have rebranded their workplaces as religious sites. Dave Duncan and Joe Blay are active participants in a movement toward sanctifying workplaces for all employees and see this as their ultimate vocation. Together, Dave and Joe are working hard to make a profoundly profane place—a place where animals are killed in large numbers each day—into a sacred place.

The sounds, smells, and sights of death are not ignored but are rebranded as unfortunate necessities to meet consumers' dietary needs and employees' right to work. The horror of the job is downplayed with a focus on animals' existence to meet humans' needs and rights. Within corporate hog culture and the larger protein industry, animals exist to serve people, and the people who work at plants like Tyson are primarily refugees whose existence is legitimated as serving others' needs. How do workers at places like Tyson interpret the talk of "family" and "values"? Do they feel like they are a part of a family, and does the values-talk appeal to them?

In my fieldwork at Tyson and Iowa Premium Beef, I found that many workers appreciate the corporate focus on "family" and "values" and are grateful for the opportunity to work long hours to bring home a paycheck that provides material goods and housing for their families in the United States, as well as for those in their home countries. Remittances are sent home by every refugee I talked with at the packing plants, at coffee shops, and in homes. They are proud of the work that they do, but all of the refugees emphasized the difficulty and brutality of their jobs and did not romanticize it. Most survive by compartmentalizing their faith, families, and jobs. The women and men at packing plants like Tyson work long hours, are filthy when they return home, are sore, and always carry the slaughterhouse's pungent smell with them. None of the workers I talked with want their children working at the plant, absolutely none.

While the CEOs, CFOs, and human resources management at the meat-packing plants want to downplay the blood and violence and even sacralize it, the killing and cutting floors are not experienced as a religious space by the workers I spent time with. Religion *is* invoked by workers to deal with the onslaught of violence and the role they play in it—rosaries and scapulars are worn under smocks; prayers for protection are said—but the workplace itself is not experienced as "sacred" by the workers with whom I spoke. While I saw some women and men making signs of the cross and some of the Catholic Latino men wore scapulars under their T-shirts, religion is something the workers *carried in with them* that helped them cope with the horrors of their work. Religion works to make the blood, violence, and squeals of the hogs bearable. It works to get them through another hard day at the plant.

The workers I encountered considered the death of the animals a heavy thing—and they did not take their role in the killing process lightly. The violence is not sacred to them, and the women and men with whom I spoke undergo a cyclical loop of atonement. Their work at Tyson and Iowa Premium Beef is something that they must do to provide for their families, but it is not something that they love. The workers on the line talked about the physical pain they are in, the nightmares they have as a result of the violent work, and the smell of death that is always on their bodies. For as much as Tyson (and Iowa Premium Beef) sugarcoat and cloak what happens on the floor with feel-good language and employee freebies, such as baby blankets, squishy animal toys, water bottles, and lunch bags, the reality is that this is a terrible job. But this terrible job pays better than any other job a refugee or other vulnerable worker can get, because it is a gruesome job that white Americans, even the poorest, refuse to do.

The work of religion is no doubt being done in the packing plants. The paternalistic evangelical ethos of family, faith, and values permeates the entire operations of Tyson (and Iowa Premium Beef) and is all-pervasive on a meta-level. On the line, workers turn to their faith to get through the day, but the packing plant is not so much like a church or house of worship as it is a house of horror that they pray they can leave at the end of the day safely and return to their families. No, religion is present in their homes with their wives, husbands, and children and at the houses of worship that they look forward to attending. For as much as they borrow the language of faith and work to replace traditional "church," companies like Tyson have not succeeded. Tyson's "family values" cannot make the cognitive leap into the slaughter of animals. Family values do not include the cries of the swine and cattle before they are killed or the cutting and packaging of raw meat, and the refugees know this. While creating a faith-filled workplace that mimics church and organized religion may work for Chick-fil-A, where cooked animals are served on buns with pickles and mayo, it ultimately does not work at corporations like Tyson that deal with living animals.

Maurice has learned to compartmentalize his work for his family and faith. He told me he "cannot wait" to attend church with Benita and their four sons. His involvement at All Nations Baptist Church is a spark of hope and faith and keeps him going. If anything, the horrors of the plant lead to a more intensive and more introspective prayer life on the part of workers like Maurice. The line workers with whom I spoke all talked about the role of church and mosque as a refuge. The Sudanese Muslim women who crafted a prayer space in the women's locker room at Iowa Premium Beef (discussed in the next chapter) were fulfilling their obligations to pray five times a day to Allah and were doing their best to transcend a greasy, smelly, dirty place. They hung their prayer rugs on top of a metal curtain rod to keep them dry. But workplace prayer does not replace mosque prayer. It in part helps to transform— at least for the time of prayer itself—a gruesome place into a beautiful one. But it is naive and romantic of us if we imagine Tyson's corporate religion as appealing to and replacing religion of the home, church, and community. Making the sign of the cross, touching scapulars, and praying in the women's locker room on prayer rugs amplifies but does not replace religion in other more sanctified places.

For their part, Dave and Joe both reiterated that Tyson is a faith-friendly company that understands that individuals do not leave their values at home. They hope to provide a place where their "team members" feel comfortable and where they can express their faith. As self-described men of faith—both are practicing Methodists—the company's mission to honor workers' beliefs is a cornerstone of their vocational pursuits. Both men strive for a total integration of faith at work and are part of a broader Faith at Work movement in American religious history. As sociologist of American Christianity David W. Miller has written, integration is a view that faith and work are not meant to be isolated from each other: "Businesspeople want the ability to bring their whole selves to work—mind, body, and soul—and are no longer satisfied with sacrificing their core identities or being mere cogs in the machine, nor do they want a disconnected spirituality."[21]

For Joe, working at Tyson Foods is a way for him to put his pastoral and counseling skills to work each and every day. Joe spends his days at Tyson walking around the plant, ensuring that he makes personal connections with the team members. He meets one-on-one with employees who come to him for counseling and for help with everyday challenges, such as obtaining their driver's licenses, filing their taxes, making it to their doctor's appointments on time, and the like. Joe's job is multifaceted, and he likes it that way. "I never get bored with my job. Never. I am blessed to be here and to be working with all of these hard-working people." Joe also has a sense of humor. He sends weekly emails to the employees, and his messages are peppered with good-natured jokes. A Christian message is sometimes implicit, sometimes explicit, and he is not shy about sharing his own faith in God and in Jesus Christ. He does not, however, see himself as a "typical evangelist." "I mean, I don't want to be like those guys you see on television. No way." Joe prefers to approach his coworkers as a friendly guy who cares and is here to help.

Joe stands next to workers on the line, and if they wish, he prays with and for them. Joe prides himself on being accessible and approachable. He is pastoral in the sense that he is always smiling, is friendly, and has a warm, enthusiastic personality. I enjoyed spending time with him and came away from our conversations with an understanding that Joe is a man who is committed to a theology of accompaniment: a theology that emphasizes solidarity with those who suffer and who are on the margins. Joe sees himself as a pastor who helps the women and men who work at Tyson deal with the stresses and violence in the workplace as well as the stresses from their everyday lives.

Joe's office in the Tyson plant is always open to women and men who want to seek spiritual counseling, and he is always ready to pray with workers and for their families. He draws upon his army chaplain experiences aiding soldiers who had to prepare to go into dangerous situations. He has counseled soldiers who have been injured and who have seen violence and death. Army chaplains, hospice chaplains, and hospital chaplains alike deal with death and dying each day. It makes sense that someone with these qualifications and experiences would be able to handle the stress and challenges of working in a meatpacking plant. For Joe, his roles as an army chaplain and as a Tyson chaplain complement each other. In fact, the majority of Tyson chaplains are former army chaplains. They have seen blood, violence, and frightening things. They themselves may suffer from PTSD. They have empathy for those who serve and who risk their lives. And they also understand how women and men whose jobs are on the meatpacking line can experience stress from the daily grind of working with dead animal carcasses. Men like Joe are predisposed to know how to counsel men and women who work in industries of death.

Joe understands what Father Bernie Weir means when he makes the distinction between "producer" jobs and "processing" jobs. In the current farm-to-factory-to-table triad, the midwestern farmers in places like Weir's town of Washington, Iowa, raise hogs and other animals. Their focus is on tending to the animals they raise. They grow attached to the animals, and their children bond with them. They care for the animals—and then load them up to go to places like Columbus Junction, Tama, Ottumwa, and Marshalltown, processing towns that kill the animals from places like Washington. The farmers who raise the hogs in Washington do not witness the slaughter of the 10,000 hogs that are processed daily at the Louisa County plant. The hog farmers with whom I have spoken said that they "compartmentalize" what they do and "try not to think about" where the hogs go in the large trucks, but if they do, they think about how they will be feeding people and how their animals provide for their families' livelihood. Those who work in the "processing" business, as it is referred to in the protein industry, see and experience the animals in their last stage of life and postmortem. Psychologically, according to Joe and to Father Bernie, being part of the cycle of the killing and processing of flesh can be difficult and damaging to an individual's psyche. It is a "very different animal" from being a producer, and it takes a toll on workers.

Joe works hard to mitigate the stress of his job and says that he hopes that his onsite visits and social visits help make Tyson an inclusive place where people want to work. He is proud of the diverse workforce at Tyson and the many languages spoken there. When we ate a late lunch in the Tyson cafeteria, he waved his hand to demonstrate the national and ethnic diversity and beamed with pride. He said he is proud to work for a company that values people from all over the world. In addition to his physical presence at the plant, his exuberant smile and positivity, and his open-office policy, Joe communicates with his Tyson "family" via regular email correspondence. He is well aware of how "difficult and trying" the jobs are at the plant and says he wants to instill some humor in the day. His emails to Tyson employees are sent in English, French, Spanish, and the Burmese dialect Hakha Chin. His messages tend to pair Scripture with a cartoon or humorous photo and real-life narrative. A July 2017 email illustrates the blend of evangelical Christian piety, corporate paternalistic care, and humor he said he is aiming for:

". . . Know ye that the LORD, He is God; it is He that hath made us, and not we ourselves; we are His people, and the sheep of His pasture." Psalm 100:3 "Thought for the Day: The greatest act of faith is when man decides he is not God." So David is finally engaged, and is excited to show off his new bride. "Ma," he said to his mother, "I'm going to bring home three girls and I want you to guess which one is my fiancée." Sure enough twenty minutes later, David walks in the door with three girls following behind him. "It's that one," said his mother, without blinking an eye. "Holy cow," exclaimed David, "how in the world did you know it was her?" "I just don't like her," she replied.

Joe will sign off with a "ha ha" and "Have a great day."

Joe turns to Scripture to encourage hard work and determination. At times a subtle shaming ("Don't be lazy") accompanies the pep talks ("Have a great day!"). As a salaried Tyson employee who is part of the management team, Joe's work does not involve line work. He does not have to kill, cut, or package animals. He said that he tries to give his team members "pep talks" each week in person and online to let them know that the work they are doing is "very important" and that it matters. But as a Tyson employee, he said, he also "has to" send out warnings to them to not be "lazy," as there are daily and weekly production goals. Joe's job requires a tricky balancing act of pastoral care and corporate paternalism. He is friendly, approachable, and pastoral—but is indeed corporate because he is part of the Tyson management team.

Joe's annual Christmas message is sent to remind the workers that they are part of a bigger plan that God has in store for them. He uses explicitly Christo-centric "Jesus" language:

> Christmas is a depressing time for most people. An article written by a director of the California Department of Mental Hygiene warns: "The Christmas season is marked by greater emotional stress and more acts of violence than any other time of the year." Christmas is an excuse to get drunk, have a party, get something, give a little, leave work, get out of school, spend money, overeat, and all kinds of other excesses. But, for those of us who believe in the Lord Jesus Christ, Christmas is an excuse for us to exalt Jesus Christ in the face of a world that is at least tuned in to His name.

Joe ends his holiday message with the following: "Don't let us get ahead of ourselves. First things first. Yes, you will get to decorate your Christmas trees and do all the good stuff. But you have to work first in order to have the money to do that. So let us focus, focus, focus on what we are doing . . . safety first!!! Bye now!"

Joe loves to use emojis in his messages. After his chirpy "Bye now!" or "Have a blessed day now!," sprinkled with smiling emojis, Joe always attaches a quote from C. S. Lewis, such as this one: "To love at all is to be vulnerable. Love anything and your heart will be wrung and possibly broken. If you want to make sure of keeping it intact you must give it to no one, not even an animal. Wrap it carefully round with hobbies and little luxuries; avoid all entanglements. Lock it up safe in the casket or coffin of your selfishness. But in that casket, safe, dark, motionless, airless, it will change. It will not be broken; it will become unbreakable, impenetrable, irredeemable. To love is to be vulnerable."[22]

All of the workers I talked with at Tyson said that they try to not to get too attached to the animals. Joe's message is a cautionary tale against attachment to the hogs: workers are not to love them, or else their hearts "will be wrung and possibly broken." I thought about this message as I left the plant that afternoon, my heart broken. I couldn't undo the sight of huge, hanging hogs and all of the blood, or forget that nearly all of the line workers are refugees from around the world, some of the most vulnerable inhabitants of the United States. The anthropology I was doing was, to invoke the anthropologist Ruth Behar, "breaking my heart."[23]

When I asked Joe about why he chose this particular C. S. Lewis quote, he thought about it for a moment and replied that he knows that the employees—the team workers—at Tyson "have had very difficult lives. Very difficult. They are vulnerable people, and they have suffered so much." He sees his job as providing some daily and weekly comic relief as well as spiritual guidance, a guidance that recognizes the daily challenges and the complicated life histories of the Black and brown women and men at his plant. Above all else, he said, he desires to be a beacon of hope and love for the workers at Tyson. He hopes that his fellow employees can feel the kind of grace that he said he has felt in his lifetime.

Joe knows what grace feels like. He knows he is lucky to be alive. In 2007, while in the army and traveling with fellow soldiers in a caravan, an IED hit the truck ahead of his. Three soldiers died and two were wounded in this attack. "It was just surreal. We had just gathered as a group to pray before getting into our trucks to drive to the hospital. It was in Baghdad, about five miles from our base. We had left at night because it was usually safer to travel at night, so we were falsely reassured." Joe suffers memory loss and stress and was diagnosed with PTSD. He thinks that he feels at home at the plant because it reminds him in many ways of a war zone. Joe acknowledges that it takes a certain kind of person to be able to work in the plant. Blood, loud noises, knives, saws, and intense heat and cold surround you every day. There is death. Lots of it. Joe sees a connection between the horrors and stresses of the military and the bloody, difficult work of meatpacking, where taking the lives of living creatures is the job, day in and day out. "The work here is not for just anybody, just like the work in the armed forces is not for everybody. It is very hard to be in the army, and it is very hard to work in this plant. You have to have a special kind of stamina, and you have to be tough. The seminary prepared me to be a pastor and a chaplain, and the army prepared me for my work here at Tyson."

As Joe talked, he brought up the euphemism of "harvesting" hogs and the reality that they are killed. Yes, the pay and benefits are good at the plant, but the reality is that the work is bloody, smelly, and incredibly difficult. Chaplains like Joe are on the front lines attending to the workers' stresses. His job is a combination of counselor, cultural broker, mental health worker, translator, and pastor. He is also a grief counselor, a man who attends to the everyday stresses and challenges of the men and women who work in this rural Iowa plant.

Joe tries his best to make a profane place of slaughter a little more manageable, and he seeks to find divine purpose for himself and his team members, which he hopes will offset the violence. The fact is that 10,000 animals a day are killed and processed here. The emails and abundant emojis aside, Joe understands how difficult it is to work at a packing plant and does all that he can to normalize the job and to emphasize that it is important, meaningful work. He "gets" the ethical weight of killing, and he sees his role at Tyson as helping the 1,200 or so women and men who kill and process the hogs "find meaning" in their work and cope with the reality that they are part of an industry of killing. For it is here, in this remote, rural location, that predominantly Latino and African refugees harvest and prepare meat that will feed millions of people.

Dave and Joe aim to provide what anthropologists like Victor Turner have called *communitas*, a kind of community that has sacred meanings, or what sociologist of religion Emile Durkheim has called *collective effervescence*. In the bloody, fleshy, noisy world of the meatpacking plant, women and men from around the globe, speaking a dozen or so languages and dialects, come together out of necessity to provide for their families. The challenge is to find meaning and grace in a line of work that many would consider horrific. Cotton tunics and pants that are bleached and starched white when they begin their shift are red-splattered and wet with cold sweat by the end of the shift. Joe's job is to reinforce that their work has meaning and that they themselves, as brown and Black individuals, have meaning. Joe's frequent emails to the team members ask them to think about their jobs as part of their higher

Maurice Batubenga, Tyson
employee and plant *fútbol* team
player, 2017. Photo by Joe Blay.

purpose. Yes, they are part of a large industrial complex, one that survives on
slaughtering and processing animals, but Joe is an integral component in the
company's aim to sacralize the killing and to make it meaningful and worth-
while. He wants employees to feel as though their work matters in a carnal
and spiritual sense.

Joe goes so far to ask his teammates to find a deeper spiritual meaning in
their work. He says that his emails are a form of ministry. He is a minister of
ritualization, sacralization, and meaning. Joe is invited to try his team members' cuisines at work, to attend baby and adult baptisms, to join baby showers
and family parties. He also serves as the coach for the Tyson soccer team,
made up exclusively of Latino and African players.

Joe is also outward-reaching and makes sure that he maintains connections with agencies, organizations, and individuals who can help his team
members. He met Father Joseph Sia when the pastor visited the plant a few
years ago to learn more about the work that many of his parishioners do, and
the two have maintained a friendship ever since. Joe appreciates pastors like
Father Joseph who take the time to understand the complex lives of the men

and women who attend their churches. Joe said that he works with clergy from different denominations and that these women and men tend to become better at their respective ministries as a result of touring the plant and having follow-up meetings with him, because they can now visualize what their parishioners do each day to make a living. "They see how difficult the work is, how bloody, and how demanding it is, and they are more educated and enlightened as a result. They also get why their church members may be absent because they are too tired to attend church after a long week of this kind of physical labor." Joe stays in regular contact with these ministers at the monthly ecumenical Ministerial Association gatherings that are held at the members' churches.

What "drives me crazy," Joe shared, are "those ministers who preach so-called prosperity theology." He set down his cup of coffee at the coffeehouse where we met for pastries as he added, with emphasis, "It is unbiblical. . . . These men tell the people who go to their church that they have to give money to receive blessings. They put a lot of pressure on them to tithe and make these people believe that if they do not give their pastor lots of money then they will not be blessed." Joe shared a story of a local pastor whose congregation pays him $4,000 a month. "I tell you it is crazy, because these are poor people. They work so hard to support the pastor's lifestyle, which includes a very nice car and house. This guy is like a Creflo Dollar kind of guy—a wolf in sheep's clothing, let me tell you!" This particular pastor does not, according to Joe, attend the monthly ministers' meetings and is "living large off the backs of his congregation." As he shared the story, Joe shook his head in disgust for added emphasis. He sees himself in stark opposition to the gospel that is proclaimed by ministers and televangelists like Dollar.

As an African man, Joe said that he understands dark-skinned immigrants' struggles. Yet he also understands his privilege in relation to the average immigrant worker. "I came to the United States to attend seminary and have not experienced the degree of racism and struggles in the same way as many immigrants have, because I have a certain level of education." Joe was careful to avoid the language of "blessings," saying instead that he has been "lucky." He is as critical of the language of blessings and being blessed as he is of the prosperity theology that he sees and hears being espoused by some local preachers and that takes advantage of impoverished dark-skinned men and women.

Just as frustrating and damaging are white Americans who denigrate dark-skinned immigrants. "It frustrates me so much when I hear people badmouth immigrants, saying that they are 'taking' American jobs. It hurts me, it truly does, when I hear people say immigrants are like 'parasites.' This is just not true. I know that very, very few people could do the work that I see immigrants do at Tyson. Very few people can do the work that immigrant hotel workers do, and we should be very glad that they are doing the hard work that we do not want to do and that we do not want our own children to do."

Joe continued: "If we didn't have immigrants, brown and Black immigrants, most of the packing plants would just not exist. In Joplin, it is women and men from Togo; in Waterloo and Ottumwa, it is Mexicans; here, it is Sudanese and Mexicans. Companies and communities owe their continued existence and success to black- and brown-skinned immigrants and refugees. Without immigrants and refugees, many small towns would die." As he said this, he paused and looked at me for confirmation. I nodded my head in agreement, as my research has shown that what Joe was saying here about refugees reinvigorating—and even saving—small towns and rural America is correct. Without refugees, many—if not most—small midwestern towns would die.

Joe is passionate about his job and about his role as ambassador for "just being kind and appreciating each other." "We can all learn something from how immigrants treat their family members. Go to any Walmart on payday, and you will find lines of immigrant workers in the MoneyGram area sending money home to their parents, their children, at home." Again, my own ethnographic research confirms what Joe said. I have spent many hours talking with women and men who send remittances home to their families. These women and men, Latino and African, send a substantial portion of their paychecks to families back home: to mothers and fathers, brothers and sisters, cousins and grandparents. Sometimes the money goes to children they had to leave behind with grandparents because they could not yet afford to bring them to the United States.

Working with Hogs

Esmerelda was a stay-at-home mom when her boys were young "because, you know, I could not send them to daycare. No way. I wanted to be with them all the time." Esmerelda's sentiments here echoed the white native-born Iowan women I know and have interviewed. She now works at Tyson since her boys are older and busy with after-school activities. She is proud of the money she brings home each month, money that helps pay for clothes, shoes, school activities, and the many costs involved with three teenage boys—especially food. Esmerelda laughed and said she thinks that "about half, maybe more!" of her paychecks go to purchasing food to feed her growing *hijos*. Her husband Juan has worked at Tyson "por muchos años, muchos." When he saw that an entry-level position had opened up, he encouraged Esmerelda to apply, as he knew she was wanting to help with the family's income, especially now that two of their boys were nearing college-age. They work different shifts so that one of them can be home with the boys to help them get off to school in the morning and the other can pick them up from school and shuttle them to activities.

All of Esmerelda's girlfriends who work outside of the home—and most of them do, she said—are employed at Tyson or at a farm that supplies Tyson with its hogs. Her *amiga* Josepha—a fellow St. Joseph parishioner in Columbus Junction—also works with hogs, but with live ones at a large farm in Washington Township. Her daily duties include bathing them, feeding them, and keeping them clean before they have their babies. Josepha knows where the sows will go once they have delivered their piglets—to Tyson—and it is hard for her to think about it, she said.[24] She tries to focus on making them comfortable and keeping them clean. She loves the little baby piglets that are born, too, all pink and soft. But her work is hard, as she is down on her knees a lot. Her back hurts every day. And it is "very dirty work"—"sucios," she said with a slight grimace.

But Josepha feels as though she is doing something important. As a mother, she is drawn to the sows and wants them to feel her love for them and their babies. She is proud of what she does as a caregiver, and whenever she "gets down" about her job, she said, she thinks about her own five children and about helping them with their dreams. While she does not denigrate the work that she does, she said that she does not want her own children to work with dirty sows like she does—"No way," she said. She wants them to have a chance at going to college, and she smiled as she looked over at her youngest, a fourth grader who "loves school and loves to read." Moreover, she really likes working with the sows and has grown attached to some of them. She said that she does not experience the kind of stress that her friends who work at Tyson do because she does not have to deal with the killing of animals. She is part of the "producer" culture, and she is grateful that instead of killing animals, she takes care of them—she mothers the mothers.

While neither Josepha nor her husband Luís have extended family members in Iowa, they like living in the Hawkeye State because it is safe, "tranquilla," for their children. Josepha and Luís feel that their kids have a very good life—better than they would have had in Mexico—and Josepha dreams that they will have a chance at being what they want to be in life.

As with Esmerelda, Juan, Josepha, and Luís, Tyson and the pork industry have been a big part of Fidencio's adult life. From his youth working in the corn and soybean fields of Sandusky, Ohio, and then in Texas, where his family moved for economic opportunity, he spent "a lot" of his youth and young adulthood picking crops alongside his parents and siblings. Fidencio made money during high school as a weekend dishwasher and short-order cook in an Italian American restaurant. "I was never late, always on time for work," Fidencio proudly shared during one of our conversations. By the time he graduated from high school, Fidencio could make "a mean chicken parmesan, let me tell you," he laughed but said with pride. While he thought about going to college, it seemed overwhelming. Like many U.S.-born Latinos of his generation, he didn't have anyone in his family to ask for guidance with college applications. And no one really reached out to help him at his school, either. So Fidencio did what he knew best and could do very well: he cooked at various restaurants. Somehow, he found time in between long shifts making *enchiladas verdes y rojas* and carne asada at the Mexican restaurant where he worked to meet the woman who would become his wife. Fidencio knew that Catalina, a pretty and vivacious young woman with skin the smooth color of caramel, was "the one." It wasn't just because she was pretty—which of course helped, he said—but because he wasn't nervous around her as he was with other women. Fidencio, normally a "very shy" guy who became tongue-tied around women, could "be myself" with her.

Catalina was Guatemalan and had been raised Catholic, and that was also deeply attractive to Fidencio, who came from a "pretty irreligious" family. Fidencio was drawn to Catholicism as much as he was drawn to the woman whom he asked to be his wife. They were married by a justice of the peace in Texas, and a year later, once they had saved up money for the trip and the pre- and postnuptial festivities, their marriage was made holy in the Catholic Church in Guatemala City. The couple began their married life in Texas and were happy. Their three children were born in the Lone Star State, and life was good, Fidencio said. He was proud to work so that his wife could stay home with their children. But money was tight, and Fidencio was growing tired of the hard work for little pay. "I didn't want to work as a cook anymore and needed a change." Moreover, Fidencio was "embarrassed." "I made so little money and my kids were growing up, and I didn't want them to be ashamed of their father and the little money that he made." Fidencio was ready for something different. About three years into their marriage, Fidencio's cousin who lived and worked in Iowa called about a pork processing plant that was hiring—Tyson—in the eastern part of the state. Fidencio applied and was flown out by the company for his interview. He was hired immediately and moved his young family to Iowa in the fall of 1999. It was a big adjustment living in rural Iowa. The family rented a small home in the town of Wapello, where there was a very small Latino community.

In many ways, pork is at the center of the family's existence. It is a central ingredient in the carnitas that Fidencio and his Knights of Columbus brothers sell each year to raise money for the parish. The annual sale goes so well that the wives of the Knights can barely keep up with the orders. Fidencio's livelihood is with the hog industry. He has been with the Columbus Junction Tyson plant for over eighteen years and has no plans to leave the company, he told me. He has appreciated the opportunities to work his way up at the plant and to make more money to support his family. He started with the company "pushing hogs" down the line right after they had been slaughtered. Fidencio said this was a particularly exhausting, monotonous job. As soon as he had put in enough time to be considered for another job at the plant, Fidencio applied for that position, which was shaving hogs. But he soon developed a rash on his hands from this particular task. He thought that perhaps it was from chemicals that were used or the extremely hot steam emanating from the water.

After eighteen years of hot, exhausting work, Fidencio has graduated into what he calls "light duty" at the plant, receiving hogs and tattooing them once they have been unloaded by the tractor trailers and before they are corralled into the waiting rooms. Fidencio estimated that there are about 120 hogs on each truck, and the tattooers must work quickly once the hogs exit the truck. What he likes about his job, he said, is that the time goes by quickly and his work is never boring. But again, working in the hog industry is hard and can be psychologically difficult. During his early years with the company, for instance, truckers could be cruel to the hogs, indifferent to their squeals and rough with them. But today, truckers are required to attend company-sponsored classes and be schooled in how to treat animals. Fidencio said that the truckers treat the animals "much, much better today."

As far as his future with the company goes, Fidencio thinks he will continue with the kind of job he currently has, tattooing and corralling the hogs. He was recently tapped to be a supervisor and "hated it," he said, because of the increased stress and responsibility. His brief stint as a shift supervisor was so stressful for him that he had a panic attack and began taking antianxiety pills. He still takes a pill each day to ward off the stress from working at the plant. "You know, there are no incentives to be a supervisor. I guess you make more money in wages, but you are taxed more. You work ten-hour shifts and have more taxes to pay. And you have way more stress because you are in charge of a lot of people. There is a lot of responsibility and pressure being a shift supervisor. I tried it and will never do it again."

What ultimately keeps Fidencio doing the work he does is that he takes great pride in being a provider. His family is everything to him, he said. His Catholic faith, he added, is instrumental to his life, and he wouldn't be where he is today without it. Fidencio is involved in his parish in leadership positions and is a spokesperson for the Latino parishioners. He and Father Joseph Sia are good friends, and he is a trusted advisor to Father Joseph. Fidencio's involvement with his parish's Knights of Columbus chapter—notably, *en español*— has been an important religious and ethnic fraternity for him. He made a promise to la Virgen de Guadalupe many years ago that if she protected his sister, he would get involved with the Knights organization. The Virgin, "of course," said Fidencio, kept her end of the bargain, and for his part, Fidencio has been involved with the Knights for over ten years now. He has been president of the fraternity for several years and considers the men his brothers. The fact that the parish's fraternity is exclusively in Spanish is significant, for the Spanish-speaking parishioners greatly outnumber the English-speaking parishioners. Fidencio is proud that his compadres have raised money for the poor, wheelchair-bound, and "mentally challenged" individuals. And it is la Virgen herself who is the patroness of the Knights. The Virgin is the guest of honor who is understood as presiding over Easter season celebrations hosted by the Knights as well as the year's biggest event: the parade, matachina dancing, and post-celebration feast every December 12 in honor of the Queen of Heaven and patroness of Mexico.

So central is Guadalupe to the lives of Mexican-descent Catholics like Fidencio and his wife Catalina that her image dominates the home. "We owe everything to her and we give thanks to her each day. There is not a day that goes by that I do not pass by our little house shrine to her and freshen it up with flowers, candles, or something like that," Catalina told me. The highlight of the twelve-month calendar for the couple and their children and grandchildren is the December 12 celebration. "Guadalupe has been there for us since the sixteenth century, you know, when she appeared to Juan Diego. She came for us, for brown-skinned people, and we know she will always be here for us." Caring for their home shrine, planning and leading the annual December 12 parade, and cooking copious amounts of food for the post-celebration feast is "what we do" for the Blessed Lady.

Catalina is a leader among the Spanish-speaking women of her parish and helps organize the Grupo de Oraciones, the women who preside over

The Virgin of Guadalupe celebration at St. Joseph the Worker parish, Columbus Junction, December 12, 2017. Photo by Lois Mincks.

singing to the Virgin in the church in the December evenings that lead up to the twelfth. December 2 is an important day, for instance, because it is "the day when Mary and Joseph were out looking for a place to stay." To honor and recreate the night of December 2, Spanish-speaking women and men gather and meet outside the parish church to sing. Called a *posada*, the singing and post-singing feast symbolize the couple's search for a birthplace for the baby Jesus. For Catalina, the *posadas* are deeply meaningful because she is an immigrant, and almost everyone she knows is an immigrant. "As immigrants, and as Spanish-speaking people, we have a long history of looking for a place to stay and having doors slammed in our faces—like Mary and Joseph in *las posadas*, you see."

Yet even though Latino parishioners are devoted to la Virgen, Catalina is frustrated by the lack of help she receives each year planning and organizing the event. She understands that people are busy, but she just can't do the work alone. Catalina's dream is to have a chapter of the Guadalupana Society at the parish, but because it will take time and effort to get it started and maintained, she is not sure if it will ever happen. Guadalupana Societies are organized parish groups that focus on honoring the Virgin of Guadalupe all year. Catalina thinks that establishing one at St. Joseph's would encourage a sustained participation by a greater number of Spanish-speaking parishioners. For her part, Catalina organizes and leads the annual December 12 celebration. She is a constant presence at the Spanish-language Mass and helps her husband and his Knights of Columbus brothers with their events. She is a skilled cook and can be seen ladling out frijoles, arroz, and carne at every fundraising event. Most recently she has become part of the parish's religious education program for children. Catalina admitted that she does have more time now that her own children are grown to volunteer at her parish. But she wishes for more Spanish-speaking women and men to "get involved" with the parish events. Yet she also acknowledged that the majority of Spanish-speaking parishioners are employed at Tyson and, as such, work long, exhausting hours. Many work at the Tyson plant during parish events, and even if they do not, they may just need to be home to rest. Catalina understands this, but she worries for the future of Guadalupan celebrations and for the longevity of other cultural and *católico* events that are central to her people's history and, as she put it, their future.

For most of the Latinos I spent time with in Columbus Junction, the pork industry has defined, and continues to define, their lives. Pork provides the steady if difficult jobs and also feeds their families in traditional Mexicano dishes like menudo, which fills many a stove pot on Sundays. And then there are carnitas, savory pork cuts that are featured at late spring and summer barbecues.[25] Pork also lingers on bodies long after the work shift is over. Pork is in the air that they breathe: pungent and putrid smells from the processing plants waft into workers' homes that are situated near the plants. In short, for many a midwestern Corn Belt family, the flesh, fat, and by-products of pork are inescapable. Pork is not just what's for dinner. It is what feeds the family, what pays the bills, and what puts the kids through college.

Sickness

One winter morning I was sharing my research with a group of women and men at an Iowa City Protestant church and afterward was approached by Dave, a retired pulmonologist at the University of Iowa, who shared some insights into the pork industry and its issues with tuberculosis among some of its immigrant and refugee employees. According to Dave, such workplace environments are conducive to certain bacteria spreading. Dave mentioned that it is a well-known secret among pulmonologists and other healthcare specialists in the state that the big meatpacking companies have done a bad job testing their workers before they are hired and do an equally bad job reporting cases of TB.

I followed Dave's advice and reached out to Dr. Douglas Hornick, pulmonologist, with the University of Iowa Hospital. According to Dr. Hornick, an expert on TB, the bacterial disease (*Mycobacterium tuberculosis*) is transmitted by coughing, talking, and sneezing. The bacteria usually reside in the chest cavity and specifically in sputum, and in an individual with an active case of TB, it can spread rapidly. When an infected individual coughs, sneezes, or talks, the bacteria become airborne and can attach to others and infect them. "When you get sick enough, you cough and you spread the disease," said Hornick. And the disease can remain latent in an infected person's body for years or even for a lifetime. But it can also manifest itself and can kill the person.

What does TB have to do with the meatpacking industry? Plenty. The protein and packing industries are dependent on refugee labor, and the women and men who work in meatpacking are from the very countries that have high rates of both active and latent TB. In the language of the World Health Organization, these are nations with a "high TB burden": Burma/Myanmar, Honduras, Mexico, Vietnam, the Central African Republic, and the Democratic Republic of the Congo.[26] Because of the close quarters of the line work, packing plant workers can transmit the disease to each other fairly easily.

Having latent TB means that the disease is present in an individual's system; those with the latent form of the disease have a 5 to 15 percent chance of it developing into active TB without treatment. Individuals with active TB exhibit symptoms of the disease and can spread it. Whether one has latent or active TB, the best way to discover the disease is by a blood test and chest X-ray. Yet meatpacking plants do not have a system in place to check new hires for TB, so if a new hire has latent or active TB, chances are the disease will not be detected. If a worker displays active symptoms of the disease, the employee is usually let go or leaves voluntarily, according to Dr. Hornick. In the worst-case scenario, TB can spread and sicken workers and can create a workplace nightmare.[27]

Treatment takes months, and for active TB cases, the infected individual must go through what is called a directly observed therapy. What this means is that a person with diagnosed active TB must be given the treatment drug each day at the local health department. In cases where the infected individual has to be at work all day after the two-week quarantine, a nurse will bring the drug to the workplace and watch the individual take it. Once an individual is diagnosed with latent or asymptomatic TB, that person is quarantined for two weeks and started on an antibiotics treatment that will last nine months. Latent TB is "tricky," according to Dr. Hornick, because the disease has a tendency to "hide itself" and thus requires a longer amount of time to treat. An individual with active TB is also quarantined for a period of time and is given a six-month treatment of a combination of four drugs.

But the nurse is not able to make sure that the infected individual is eating properly, getting rest, and drinking lots of fluids. The drug is very strong, and common side effects include dizziness and nausea, feelings of pins and needles, skin rash, and flu-like symptoms. And because the drugs are hard on the kidneys and liver, jaundice can result from the drug treatment.[28]

One piece of good news is that the animals slaughtered in the packing plants, whether hogs, cattle, chickens, or turkeys, cannot be infected with the bacteria. But the workers can, and according to Dr. Hornick, the industry is not driven by a commitment to the health of its workers. Given the time and care that companies like Tyson spend on building their brand, telling their story, and appearing committed to the welfare of their workers, it might seem surprising that they do not become more invested in TB screening and the treatment process when workers are diagnosed as sick. After all, Tyson specifically puts a lot of effort and resources into advertising itself as a family-focused and friendly business, a company that puts people over profits. Even a cursory glance at the company's websites and marketing materials confirms the company's purposeful branding as people centered. In my experiences with human resources at the Iowa plant, spokespeople were insistent that the Tyson brand means that "people come first." The industry must comply with OSHA standards for its employees and USDA standards for its products, and Tyson is incredibly cognizant of maintaining its brand.

Yet meatpacking plants in America do not routinely screen their new hires for TB and do not conduct other screenings to ensure that their workers are healthy. The tests are admittedly expensive, as Dr. Hornick pointed out. The high cost of the testing is why most countries do not test individuals but give out antibiotics that in the end produce drug-resistant strains of TB, because the patients are not monitored as they are in the United States. And these drug-resistant strains of the disease are carried to the countries where migrants and refugees travel. Is it not the responsibility of giant corporations that claim to be family-focused and friendly to provide the testing and treatment that would be required to keep its workers—"team members," members of the "Tyson family" and their families—healthy? While a focus on hygiene and following federal health standards for the live animals and resulting meat for consumption is strictly followed at Tyson and at other packing plants, there are very real challenges to workers' health that remain insufficiently addressed.

A White Rural Farm Woman and Hog Producing

Jenny and her two daughters get up each morning at the crack of dawn. The girls, aged eleven and nine at the time we met for coffee at her farmhouse, have lots of chores to do before the bus picks them up for school. They have to feed the cows and chickens and make sure that they have fresh water and bedding hay. They bottle-feed their calves and groom them. Finally, they gather eggs to make breakfast—this is their favorite part. But sometimes the hens get a little irritated with them, and they have had to learn to approach them "just so." The girls put in a good hour and a half before getting cleaned up for school. Emma, the oldest, is a "foodie" and enjoys making breakfast for the family, which her parents happily oblige. It gives Jenny a tremendous amount of joy to see her daughters at work as fourth-generation farmers in Iowa. She and her husband Justin want them to know the "value of hard work, grit, and determination" so that they can be successful in life. Both girls show two calves apiece each July at the county fair and are involved in the local chapter of 4-H. And Jenny makes sure she is actively involved with the girls' farm education by taking on leadership roles in groups such as her younger daughter Claire's chapter of Clover Kids. She sometimes feels "a bit too stretched, you know what I mean?" but keeps volunteering because maintaining her family's connection to farming and animal husbandry is of utmost importance to her.

Jenny has fond memories of growing up farming. She recalls helping her mom with the henhouse chickens and her dad with the sows in the farrowing house. She and her sister were their dad's assistants when it came time to castrate the piglets—not something she enjoyed, to be honest, but something she was proud of doing. It was hard work and work that she embraced because she loved her dad and always wanted to show him that she cared about the farm. She and her sister also helped their mom weed and feed her garden, which supplied tomatoes, green beans, onions, peas, and potatoes for the family in season; the vegetables were canned for the colder months. The gardening ended, however, after their mom went to work as the school secretary when the girls started school full-time. Jenny credits her mom with teaching her how to grow vegetables and herbs and how to properly can vegetables and summer fruits. Today, her own larder contains the fruits—no pun intended—of the days they spent canning in the warm summertime kitchen. Spreading some fresh strawberry jam on toast in the fall and winter makes the hot, sweaty work of canning "totally worth it," she told me with a smile.

Today, Jenny and Justin own the building and "contract the pigs out" to well-known businesswoman Heidi Vittetoe in Washington, Iowa.[29] For her part, Vittetoe, an "Iowa Master Pork Producer," runs her family company with husband Jerome. JW Vittetoe Pork, Ltd., is an award-winning farrow-to-finish sow operation that markets over 200,000 hogs each year. Jenny and Justin are among the many Iowa farmers who supply the Vittetoes with hogs that make their way to processing plants like Tyson. Theirs is a small confinement building, compared to many that dot the landscape, a smaller version of a CAFO. Jenny understands why there is "a fuss about the larger CAFOs" but said that hers is "a good way to raise pigs" because it is "safer for the pigs" than keeping them open range, which makes the piglets more susceptible to being trampled. Plus, the manure is pumped out from under the building to fertilize the cornfields. And the pork meat is exceptionally tasty, according to Jenny. Their freezer is stocked with meat from the hogs and cattle and supplies them with antibiotic-free, farm-raised meat all year long. Jenny said that she and Justin take "a lot of pride" in raising their animals "in the best way possible."

Farming is in her and Justin's blood. Justin attended Iowa State University and, like many young men who grew up farming, majored in the agronomic sciences. He was involved in a fraternal organization, Farm Operations, known to locals as "Farm Op." He and Jenny met during college and instantly connected because they were both from farming families and wanted to keep the lifestyle and traditions going. Both get irritated by the stereotypes of farmers and farming life. "Justin gets so frustrated by the cheesy ads on television, ads for the dating site FarmersOnly.com. Ugh! And a few years ago, there was a farmer on *The Bachelorette* who was so darn cheesy. He cared more about his appearance and looking hot than he did his work. Our farm men are NOT like that; I mean, they don't spend hours on their hair and they don't spray men's cologne all over themselves!"

Loyalty. It is a quality that Jenny said is special to farming families. "When you grow up not seeing your dad very much because he was working the land and caring for the animals 24/7, you grow to appreciate that kind of hard work, work that benefits a lot of people. And I knew that I wanted to marry a man like my dad. A man who is loyal, hardworking, and true to his farm roots." Part of the loyalty is loyalty to one's spouse and making marriage work. Jenny and Justin's family is typical of today's Iowa farm families—fewer children, smaller tracts of land, and a blend of owning and contracting out with larger businesses to stay solvent. Jenny and Justin own the building where the pigs live and the hundred acres on which they grow feed corn for Iowa cattle and hogs. The 1980s farm crisis and crash devastated many Iowa farmers, including Jenny's father, who, like many Corn Belt farmers, went bankrupt.[30] He managed to rebound from complete financial devastation, thankfully, and today he farms 2,000 acres of cattle and hogs in eastern Iowa with Jenny's brother. Jenny is thankful to her parents for showing her how to work hard and how to survive tough times, "because, let's face it, we all have them." Sometimes being apart from each other is hard, and Jenny misses her husband. "It's different as a wife of a farmer. Justin leaves each morning at 6:30 and doesn't come home until 8 at night. When he is harvesting or planting, I take him a hot meal. It is very important to me to take my husband a home-made hot meal once a day. It maintains that connection I have to him, and I give him the food that I made. It is a way that I show him that I love him."

And like many farm women, Jenny has a full-time job outside of her vocation as wife, mother, and farmer. She has been an art teacher for twenty years, currently in the county elementary school. Specializing in glass blowing, acrylics, and oil, Jenny said she absolutely "loves to give kids experiences with all kinds of mediums." She is a farm woman, an ambassador of art, a wife, and a mom and loves all of her identities. She also hosts painting parties at eastern Iowa businesses like Iowa City's Brush and Barrel for fun and to make some extra spending money. Jenny is part of a growing number of American farmers taking on extra jobs to maintain and keep their farms. Her family needs her teacher's salary to survive, and her extra income from teaching art classes helps out with things that her girls want and need. It costs a lot to run a farm operation today.[31]

Another important facet in Jenny's life is her Catholic faith. While Justin is not Catholic—he was raised Methodist—he fully supports her and the girls' involvement in the life of the church and attends when he is able to, but not often, she said, given his demanding job. "Justin reminds me so much of my dad in that he works so hard and all the time. He comes to church for the big events and supports our faith." Jenny and the girls attend St. Joseph parish in Columbus Junction. Her mixed-faith marriage is common for her generation, as Catholics and Methodists in particular intermarried from the early twentieth century to the present. Jenny's Catholic and Iowa roots run deep.

Her German Catholic great-grandparents on both sides worshipped at St. Mary's parish in Muscatine, Iowa, a rural community about thirty minutes from where she currently lives. Her parents live in nearby Riverside, where she and her two siblings were raised on a farm, and her parents still live and worship there today. They sometimes come to St. Joseph parish to see their daughter sing as cantor.

Like many Catholic women, not just in the Midwest but globally, Jenny has taken charge of her children's faith formation. The girls are altar girls and have experienced the three Roman Catholic sacraments of initiation: infant baptism, First Communion, and confirmation. They help their mom prepare food for the first Sunday potlucks, and they are proud of her as she leads the 8:00 A.M. Mass in English as cantor. Jenny loves to sing, as it enhances her faith and spirituality, and she sees her vocations as teacher and artist as extensions of her spiritual and nature-centered self. She is grateful to her rural Iowa school for "being so great at giving me big projects to do with my kids." Her elementary kids collaborated on ideas for a mural, and they did a "tremendous job" painting it. They also worked with artists from all over Iowa to create a tree sculpture in front of an elementary school. The kids made the leaves for the metal sculpture tree and helped fire the leaves in the kiln and attach them with the assistance of the metal sculptors.

For Jenny, making public places more beautiful and teaching kids how to value the land and world around them comes from her Catholic spirituality as much as it does her identities as artist, wife, and mom. And because she teaches in a diverse school with half of the student population Mexican-descent Latinos, Jenny said she has learned to really value other cultures. She realizes that her parish, like most American Catholic parishes that have a substantial number of Latinos, is segregated by language and culture. Even though she does not speak Spanish, she understands a little bit, and when her priest, Father Joseph Sia, challenged his parishioners to "try out" the Mass they did not usually attend, Jenny said she was excited to take up the challenge—though admittedly a bit nervous. She tries to go several times each year, and while she knows it is "not enough," she said she is really trying to show the Spanish-speaking parishioners that she values their culture and their presence. She acknowledged that most white Iowa Catholics "have a long way to go" in accepting diversity in their parish and in society. It frustrates her when she sees more Spanish-speaking parishioners trying out the English Mass and "not enough" whites trying out the Spanish Mass, but she will keep doing her part, trying to live and serve by example.

There are many white Iowans in the Corn Belt like Jenny, trying to raise their children and to uphold a faith, all the while being good citizens. Most of the white Iowans I have interviewed and have spent time with said they value the work that the minority women and men in their communities do and that they try to be good neighbors and live by the Golden Rule. And some, like Jenny, are working to welcome their newest neighbors. Attending a Catholic Mass in Spanish is for many a first step toward appreciation and acceptance.

CHAPTER 5

Cattle

STEERED BY FAITH

THE CAMP CONDITIONS were "horrible, horrific." It was hot, so hot that people were just "lying around" because they were so weak, worn down from thirst and hunger. Black flies were everywhere, as were mosquitoes, and not the kind we see in the Midwest but giant ones, undeterred by the heat. Babies and new mothers died on a routine basis as malnutrition and dehydration were life destroyers in the tent city. Close to 8,000 people at the time James and his family lived there were exhausted mentally, physically, and psychically by their refugee existence. Disease, despair, and disillusionment claimed lives each day in the encampment.

Mugombekere Mugereke, called James, and his family have lived a life very few Americans could imagine. In the Democratic Republic of the Congo (DRC), the country of his birth, James was a sixth-grade teacher. When he talked with me about his former life in the DRC, James smiled broadly and said he "loved" being a teacher. Then his smile faded a bit as he became wistful, for the memories, both good and bad, came flooding back. He had wanted to be a teacher since he was a small boy. He and his wife had what he called a "comfortable" existence until the ever-present political instability and ongoing war forced them to escape the DRC in 1998. The Congolese refugee camp in Tongogara, Zimbabwe, was the second place they sought protection.

At the Tongogara camp, his family's new home, James found meaning in his work and in his faith. Shortly before he fled the Congo, James and his wife became Jehovah's Witnesses, and James is unwavering in his belief that it was Jehovah who saved his and his family's life: "Jehovah was watching over me."[1] Armed with the protection of the Lord and a strong will to live,

James worked as though his life depended on it. And it did. James's job at the camp was to work toward improving hygiene and sanitation, which he said was a very difficult job since the water—dug up by boreholers—was quickly contaminated. "The water was yellow, but the people didn't care because they needed to drink. But the contaminated water of the camps led to deaths."

The family's home was put together with old bricks and plastic sheeting, which made it unbearably hot during the day. There was no ventilation, and the floor was dusty earth. Inhabitants of the city literally had just the clothes on their backs. And food was scarce. At the time he was there, monthly rations included 250 grams of sugar, 750 grams of oil for cooking, 500 grams of dried beans, and 10 kilograms of yellow cornmeal. "It was not enough, it never was enough," he said. During his family's stay at the camp, the system changed from commodity allotments to monetary allotments. Each individual received eleven dollars a month, so his family of four received a total of forty-four dollars. For the entire month. And the camp stores "charged way too much money for the food, so people always ran out of food before the end of the month. You always saw people sleeping . . . sleeping for most of the day . . . the last week of the month because the food always ran out." Stores in nearby towns charged less for the same commodities, but the problem was transportation.

The most heartbreaking thing for James was to see dying babies and children: "Their bellies were bloated from malnutrition, from kwashiorkor. Their mothers' milk dried up early because they had so little water. Life was very, very hard in the camp." James received a small stipend for his work as a camp hygiene worker, and he used his meager pay to supplement the monthly family cash allotment. The money always went for food and water, the basics, but to James and his family they were luxuries. Still, despite the supplemental food and water, his children were "always" hungry and thirsty. The camp school was a five-kilometer walk from the camp, and his children, like the others, went with no food or very little food in their stomachs. "My daughter, she say to me, 'Daddy, I do not want to go to school because I am so hot.' When she come home from school she just lie down and close her eyes." There was not enough water to pack with his children for school, and no food was served at the school. "The children would usually not eat at all until they come home from school in the afternoon." And none of the kids had shoes or backpacks. They walked barefoot for over six miles round-trip to school. James said he prayed every day to Jehovah to ease his family's and so many others' sufferings. It was his and his wife's "Christian faith," he said, and faith that others had in them that got James and his wife Naomi through the horrors of the camp and eventually to the United States as classified refugees. When the forces of Jehovah, Catholic Church Charities, and the U.S. government came together, James and his family were "blessed" and were granted refugee status in the United States.

How in the world did James and his family end up in the midsize eastern Iowa city of Cedar Rapids? When Catholic Church Charities, which sponsored his family's journey and helped with rent and food for the first several months, asked James if he had any family in the United States with whom they could live upon arrival, James told the agency that he had a cousin who lived in Iowa. This set the wheels in motion, and in the spring of 2016 they arrived in Cedar Rapids. Representatives of the church helped James obtain his temporary official refugee work permit, Form I-94. The church also assisted him with the filing of Form I-765, Application for Employment Authorization, so that James could receive his Employment Authorization Document. James said he is "very grateful" to the Catholics who helped sponsor his family and to help them get started in their new life in eastern Iowa.

While life in eastern Iowa wasn't difficult in the ways it had been at the refugee camp, it was "overwhelming" for James and his family at the beginning. For one, it was COLD. Used to the intense heat and aridity of the camp, the Iowa spring seemed like winter. The dampness and chilliness of the early mornings were hard for his wife, who walked the children to the bus stop. While the family members spoke English, everyday tasks such as going to the grocery store and laundromat were made difficult because the family did not own a car and were unsure of the bus stops and the bus schedule. Like Maurice and Benita from the previous chapter, who experienced adjustments upon coming to eastern Iowa from South Africa, James and his family were specially challenged by Iowa's weather and need for a car. Said James, "I remember walking from the apartment to Casey's [a convenience store] and buying lots of food and drinks for my family and then hurrying back to the apartment. I was so happy to be back in the apartment, because I was afraid. I didn't really know anything about what was around me, and I just wanted to be with my wife and children." His cousin had a car, but he worked all day, so James and his family felt stranded. He is grateful to the family's caseworker, Caleb, assigned by the state of Iowa, who took the family to the store and to the school where they could register the children for the school year.

James's cousin worked at Iowa Premium Beef (IPB), a slaughterhouse and distributor in Tama. He drove James to the company for an interview a few months after James arrived in Iowa and "guess what?! I was hired that same day." James experienced a mixture of surprise and relief and said he was "so happy" when the carpool driver picked him up for work a few days later. His first shift was in the area of condensation, where he had to clean up the animal waste—fat, meat, blood, and renderings—and make sure the waste made it into the proper bins.

His strong work ethic and linguistic abilities soon caught the attention of management team member Michelle Baumhover. "I heard this man switch languages several times and thought to myself, 'This is one talented individual who needs to be moved up.'" Today, James wears a blue hat, which indicates that he is a shift supervisor. He is also a translator, and a small white label attached to the right side of his helmet lists the four languages he translates: Swahili, English, French, and Lingala. James pointed out that he actually speaks eight languages in all: the four listed on his helmet and also Kirundi (Burundi dialect), Kinyarwanda (Rwanda dialect), Shona (dialect in Zimbabwe and Rhodesia), and Kifuleao (his "mother tongue"). Like Maurice at Tyson in Columbus Junction, James's linguistic gifts were instrumental to his upward mobility at the company.

James said that he and Naomi are "grateful" for the supportive and caring people in their new communities of Iowa. "My coworkers here at IPB have been so good to us, and they always ask how we are doing." In addition to his "work family," as he calls it, James and his wife and children join with fellow brothers and sisters in Jehovah and Christ at their house of worship several times a week. It is at the Jehovah's Witnesses Kingdom Hall in Cedar Rapids that James and his family come together to praise God and to offer their thanks and praise. While his job puts food on the table, clothes on the backs of his wife and children, and money in the bank for college tuition, James said he knows that "Jehovah is behind all the good things that have happened and that keep happening in my life." Being hired at IPB and getting a higher-paying and prestigious translator's job at the plant was "all Jehovah. All Jehovah," he said with the same broad smile that he shared when we first talked at the plant.

Managing Refugees

While Latinos still dominate the meatpacking industry, de jure refugees like James, from countries like the Congo, Liberia, Sudan, and Burma/Myanmar, are in many ways the future of the meatpacking industry in the midwestern Corn Belt. Since the infamous Postville, Iowa, Agriprocessors plant raid of 2008, the "protein industry" has been in a state of high alert regarding potential raids of factories. A consequence has been a sharp decrease in the hiring

Iowa Premium Beef plant, Tama, Iowa, 2020. Photo by Stephen Warren.

of Latino workers, who often come from the countries of Central America's Northern Triangle, which are not officially designated as refugee countries, and a greater scrutiny of workers' papers. It has become much harder for companies to hire undocumented workers, and as a direct result of Postville, fewer de facto Latino refugees are hired and more de jure refugees—those formally classified as "refugees," such as the Burmese, Congolese, and Sudanese workers at Iowa's meatpacking plants—are hired, because they have the legal status and required paperwork to work in the United States.[2] Now and in the future, it is primarily refugee women and men from African nations and Burma/Myanmar who kill, process, package, and ship the red meat that Americans and global citizens eat. They are the backbone and the future of the U.S. protein industry.

IPB is also a place where documented and native-born Latinos and, increasingly, African refugees have leadership positions. White Americans are a small minority of hourly employees at Tyson and IPB, although the majority of the upper management team is white. There are more African workers than African Americans and very few Native Americans, despite the close proximity of the Meskwaki Settlement. Whereas Iowa outside of the plant is rather white in terms of ethnic and racial categorizations, inside the plant the world is in shades of black and brown.

Iowa Premium Beef is considered by business insiders to be a high-end, smaller scale operation, with 830 men and women employed.[3] This particular plant based in Tama features family-farm-raised Black Angus meat from Iowa farms. At IPB, 1,100 head of cattle are killed and processed each day, making it a far smaller operation than Columbus Junction's Tyson plant, where a little over 10,000 hogs are killed and processed each day.

The plant's management team—CEO Jeffrey Johnson, human resources supervisor Steve Armstrong, and marketing director Michelle Baumhover—are proud to be a part of the protein industry. All three have backgrounds in farming and agriculture and were hand-picked by a group of investors at TBI Capital, LLC, in 2012 to lead the new plant in Tama. While rural Iowa was not their idea of an ideal place to live, they agree that what drew them to this small community were the possibilities to "provide premium meat, to be good stewards of the community, and to work with a diverse group of people," said Steve when we met for our interview.

The plant features 100 percent Black Angus beef, and the management team is proud of the high distinction of their product. Corn-fed, Iowa-raised cattle from family farms make their way to this plant, where they are killed, processed, and packaged for what Michelle called "higher-end" consumers. "This is not beef you will find in your mainstream or your discount groceries but in pricier venues where consumers can say, 'Wow, this is different.'" Steve, Jeff, and Michelle know their cattle and their cuts of meat. Michelle was raised on a "diversified family farm" in Plymouth, Indiana; Jeff, on a dairy farm in Green Bay, Wisconsin; and Steve, on a farm in Missouri.

All three worked their way up the corporate ladder from the fields and factory floors. Jeff started as a sweeper on the floor of a meatpacking plant in Wisconsin when he was fourteen years old, spent time loading meat onto the refrigerated trailer, and eventually became a minority owner in the company. And as is par for the course in the meat industry, the formerly family-owned business went through a couple of mergers, from Smithfield Foods to JBS, and with the change in ownership the company moved westward, from Wisconsin to Colorado. Then, on a day that Jeff considers especially auspicious, a group of investors who had formed the group TBI Capital called him up and told him that he was "their man" to build a plant in Tama and run it. When Jeff discovered that the new plant would be following the philosophy and in the footsteps of his business mentor, John Stewart, founder of the premium Angus beef Creekstone Farms, he was hooked and soon found himself in Iowa.[4]

For his part, Steve also started on the factory floor around the same age as Jeff and, like his colleague, worked his way up the production line. Neither of the men went to college, thriving in the factory setting and making more money each year to support their families. Michelle went to Purdue to study agricultural science and graduated with a bachelor's degree. We teased each other as rivals—I am an Indiana University grad from a small Indiana town north of Plymouth, and the rivalry between the Boilermakers and Hoosiers goes back many years.

Jeff, Steve, and Michelle are passionate about meat. They love talking about it and eating it, and they wear clothing with the Iowa Premium Beef logo, happy to promote the company they believe in. One could say that they are the Black Angus trinity and advocate for the holy grail of red meat. According to Michelle, 95 percent of the beef produced in the plant qualifies as choice cut, a high-end cut of meat that is marbled and tender. And here in the Hawkeye State, cattle can eat lots of Iowa corn, which in turn makes them appeal to consumers who, Michelle said, "know a good steak when they see one."

The origins of the Tama plant date back to 1971, three years after "boxed beef" was introduced to consumers by Iowa Beef Processors at the Denison plant. In the past, mostly big urban meatpacking centers like Chicago would ship carcasses to butcher shops across the country where they would be cut to customers' specifications. The Tama Meatpacking plant, as it was known at the time, was part of a midwestern-based revolution in beef processing and packing. Yet the business was difficult, and "cattlemen, who knew one part of the business, that of raising cattle, weren't always the best processors or businessmen," said Michelle. A trifecta of interrelated events—the global mad cow disease scare, lower consumer demand for beef, and poor management—led to the Tama plant's closing.[5]

The plant sat dormant for ten years after the closing; 540 men and women lost their jobs. After TBI Capital purchased the plant in 2012, it made extensive renovations and additions and reopened in the fall of 2014. The current plant is twice the size of the original operation. The Tama City Council voted to approve tax incentives for the new Iowa Premium Beef by agreeing to rebate up to $3.6 million over the first ten years of operation. At the time the rebate was approved, IPB planned on employing 550 in the first few years with a goal of 950 employees in the first three years. By January 2018, the plant employed 830 workers.

The best stories are the complicated ones. They are the ones that keep us up at night as we think about the various players and the multiple perspectives involved. The story of Iowa Premium Beef is, on the one hand, a story of commodification of flesh and death. It is one about the vertical integration of animals' and humans' bodies in the plant. But it is also a story of hope and opportunity for the 830 women and men who work at the plant, the vast majority of whom are recent immigrants and refugees. The men and women who want empathy, not sympathy. The women and men who want respect for the difficult and exhausting work that they do. In this true story, red meat from choice Black Angus steer makes its way from a living, breathing animal to attractively wrapped plastic and Styrofoam packages in high-end grocery stores across the Midwest and in select locations abroad. The bright red, marbled meat at the end of the line in no way resembles the living mammal from whence it came. Consumers do not have to think about how an animal has been slaughtered.

Critiques of the protein industry (primarily cattle, pork, and poultry) have pointed out the environmental degradation from overgrazed cattle, diminishing grasslands, polluted water, methane- and carbon-dioxide-filled air, and acres and pits of swine feces. The hog and cattle industries—sites for my fieldwork—are absolutely polluting the waterways and airways of Iowa and surrounding states. The overproduction of animal feces is staggering, is stewing in open-air pits, and is sprayed on farm fields in vast quantities, yet no one seems to know for sure what "safe" amounts are. There is indeed much evidence to support the critics' claims. Iowa's landscape is slowly being inundated with swine manure and filled with heavy metals and other toxins that are harmful to the air, soil, and water.

But cattle are another, if related, story. The environmental footprint of IPB is less than its Iowa kin Tyson. Cattle feces are not as toxic and are processed into manure for contracted Iowa farm fields. The cattle that make their way to IPB are not from CAFOs, which is significant, as CAFOs are contributing to immense environmental issues that spread throughout Iowa and the Midwest, and down to the Gulf of Mexico. But certainly, there is a lot of waste, and a lot of water is used. There is no getting around the fact that the contemporary meatpacking industry leaves a very large footprint on the natural environment.

Good Work

Meat processing and packaging plants such as Iowa Premium Beef provide jobs for men and women who have experienced poverty and violence—refugees like James, who was starving in a refugee camp with his family. Employees are trained in intensive detail work, such as boning, slicing, or cutting—or even slaughtering. Translators wearing green helmets are on hand as employees of the plant and are called upon many times throughout the day to help with a recent arrival. Many of these refugees consider the job a blessing. James brings home a salary that allows his family to thrive. He and his wife are able to give their children a chance in life that they did not have in the refugee camp in the Democratic Republic of the Congo.

For Nam, a Cambodian refugee in his early sixties, the meatpacking industry has provided good work for close to twenty years. Nam told me he has lived a "very sad life but a happy life too." His Chinese-descent father died in a plane crash when he was seven years old, and his mother and younger brothers were killed by soldiers with the Communist regime three years later. A "big boy for my age," Nam was taken by soldiers to a children's camp in the jungles of Cambodia; he escaped and found his way with some help to Vietnam, where he was placed in a refugee camp. He took classes and found out that he was skilled at the English language. Nam was adopted/sponsored when he was nearly fourteen by a wealthy white couple in Seattle, Washington, but said he was raised mostly by the maid, since his parents traveled a lot. When he was eighteen he went to Sacramento to live and to work. He met the woman he would marry, and they moved to Minneapolis, where Nam had found employment at a furniture factory. When the factory closed down, Nam had a lot of time during his unemployment to take fishing trips to Lake Ahquabi in central Iowa, where he chanced upon fellow Cambodians who were fishing there as well: "I was fishing by myself and overheard Cambodian being spoken and went right over to the group of men and introduced myself." In the course of the conversation, Nam found out that there was a thriving Cambodian refugee community in Des Moines. And just as important, his new friends and countrymen told him, there were jobs to be found at JBS, a pork processing plant in nearby Marshalltown, Iowa. Within six months of his auspicious fishing trip, Nam, his wife Min, and their two youngest children moved to Marshalltown, where Nam and Min had secured jobs at JBS. The three oldest children elected to stay in Minneapolis.

The work at the plant was good but hard. Nam has vivid memories of rubbing camphor ointment on his wife's hands each night when she returned home from work. "Her hands hurt so much, and I just rubbed that lotion into them to make them feel better." After a few months her hands "toughened up," but for his part Nam said he lasted only "one year" doing the kind of line work that Min was doing. He switched to loading pallets and moving boxes, which suited him much more, he said. His wife still works at JBS. But when he heard that Iowa Premium Beef was hiring and that it paid more than his other job, he applied and got the position.

For many workers, IPB provides a good living. While they may not go so far as to call their work and the plant a "blessing," as does James, men like Joe, from the U.S.-Mexico borderland, and José, from Cuba, say IPB is "a good place to work."

For Joe, the work shift goes by quickly because he is a forklift driver. He enjoys lifting the crates, filling orders, and picking orders for customers. "I like it, you know, because my day goes by fast and I can help provide for my two girls." Joe also appreciates the small-town feel of Tama and sees it as a good thing for his daughters, since class sizes at the school are small, the neighbors are "nice" and look out for them, and the cost of living is affordable.

Since moving to rural Iowa several years ago, Joe has seen his life change. He found work at IPB, went through the Rite of Christian Initiation of Adults (RCIA) with the local Catholic Church and was baptized a Catholic, and recently married his longtime girlfriend, the mother of his daughters. The structure of his workday, the "laid-back" pace of his Iowa community, and his status as a husband and father make Joe satisfied with his life. Working at the plant has also opened his eyes to cultural and religious diversity. He works with refugees "from all over the world," he told me, and has learned "to look at people as people and as like me more than they are *not* like me." For Joe, his job has taught him that similarities outweigh differences. He has become close friends with a couple of Congolese refugees and also with a member of the Meskwaki tribe of Iowa. "I recently went to a pow-wow he invited me and my wife to, and so we went with my wife's cousin. It was a really good time, and I enjoyed the food, the dancing, and the music there." For Joe, working at IPB has been an entrée into cultural and religious diversity, and his view of the world around him is more complex and nuanced. He sees difference not as "bad" but as "a pretty good thing, you know, because we are really all alike when it comes down to it." He credits his workplace environment for introducing him to cultural diversity.

For José, his journey from Cuba to Miami to Omaha to rural Iowa has been adventurous, to say the least. Never one to shy away from working hard, José has experienced mostly disappointment from previous employers, he told me during our interview. Some have paid too little, some have withheld wages, and others have paid well but the wages did not go far in the local economy with inflated housing, food, and services. The wage theft that José has experienced is an acute national problem. Vulnerable populations such as refugees, economic asylum seekers, and the poor are targeted by employers. In the state of Iowa, a 2015 Iowa Policy Project report authored by University of Iowa history professor Colin Gordon characterized wage theft in Iowa as "shockingly commonplace."[6] While neither Tyson nor IPB have been formally accused of wage theft, this practice was one of many egregious charges filed against the former Postville Agriprocessors kosher packing plant.[7]

In Miami, José said he was earning a good wage as a car salesman, but the cost of living was too steep to "get ahead" financially, and he was never able to purchase a home. When I asked him how he made his way from Miami to rural Iowa—"Why Iowa?"—he smiled and said he gets the question a lot. "It is tranquil here, quiet here. My wife and I both have good paying jobs here at the plant. We bought a house, can buy food we like, and we can send money home to our families in Cuba and Peru. God willing this facility never shuts down because I am here for life. For life." José went on to mention that the human resources employees have helped him out a lot and that his floor manager treats him well—rare, he said, in the meatpacking industry. "My manager, well, he is very flexible. He understands that people will sometime need a day off. In all the places I have worked in my life, and it has been a lot, let me tell you, I have never seen people like [CEO] Jeff [Johnson] and Steve [Armstrong] saying 'hi' to workers. I mean, they are the heads of the plant, and they talk to us with respect." He turned to Michelle Baumhover and said, "And we workers are always being given gifts, as tokens of the company's appreciation. At the other plants where I have worked"—he named Cargill and JBS—"I never received anything. Nothing extra, you know, to let you know you are valued and appreciated. Those little things can really go a long way to keep workers feeling important and valued."

José has been with the plant since its opening and reconfiguration as IPB, when he recalled there being just 320 cattle a day. "Look how far we have come." José now makes $17.50 an hour and has benefits. He works on the kill floor, a very hard job, but one that he said he does with respect for the animals. José said he feels safe at the plant, something I press him on. What does that mean, exactly, given the dangers of his job on the slaughter floor? Working in close proximity to knives, hooks, and thousand-pound-plus carcasses that move continually by on "the line" is not an environment most would think of as "safe." José clarified and said that of all of the places he has worked, he feels as though his bosses "give a damn" about his well-being and that it is in their best interest to have a factory that is clean, safe, and well-run. He believes that the training he received and the consistent communication between him and his fellow kill-floor workers during their shift make it a good, safe, and lucrative place to work. "We have each other's backs here, you know? And I make good money here, good enough so that I was able to buy a home for me and my wife." And as far as his relationship with his coworkers goes, José feels confident that his stuff in his locker will not be stolen and that his car parked outside for the long shift will not be vandalized, as it was at another plant where he worked. "I recommend this place to people for work all the time. I mean, it is a good place, a good job, and good people."

José's and James's stories of workplace pride and satisfaction put a wrinkle in prevailing narratives about contemporary meatpacking plants. All of the workers I interviewed expressed a sense of satisfaction in their work and the fact that they made incomes that provided for their families. They talked about how hard their job is, but they do not feel like they are victims. They know that their work is "dangerous," but they are proud of the work they do and how they do it well. In fact, all of the women and men I talked to in the course of research for this book stressed that they do not want anyone to "feel sorry" for them. Rather, they want respect for what they do. All of the workers I interviewed talked about how their hard work is rewarded with a good salary and benefits, such as a 401K, paid vacation time, and affordable health insurance. And many of the women and men at IPB and Tyson expressed their gratitude for upper management's care and concern for them and their families.

The management's paternalism was viewed mostly as beneficent and as something that sets IPB apart from other employers. Employees repeatedly mentioned how they felt "cared for," "listened to," and "taken seriously" by all levels of management at the plant. The company-sponsored picnics, soccer games, and gift-giving on major holidays was cited by the women and men I spoke with as indicators of a healthy and caring work environment. Indeed, the hourly wages at Tyson and IPB are far higher than at any other industry in the area. Carpooling also builds camaraderie, and the women and men who ride to and from work together become good friends. Many of them live in the same apartment complexes, such as the Sudanese workers at IPB. They are part of a tight network of Sudanese refugees in the Cedar Rapids–Coralville–Iowa City "Corridor" area. Their families are close, and their children attend school and play together. They attend the same mosque. And the sizable Congolese population of workers at Tyson also share rides to and from Columbus Junction. The African refugees have made their new homes in Iowa and across the midwestern region, and they have formed a network of support.

Right to Work

Worker satisfaction is certainly an important barometer of the overall success of an industry and surrounding geography, yet it is also important to take a look at some of the larger issues surrounding the microcosms of packinghouse workplaces. While those I interviewed registered satisfaction, it is still important to delve beneath what they said and look outward to broader macro-issues. For example, today, most plants are nonunionized and are located in "right-to-work" states—states like Iowa. Currently, twenty-two of the fifty U.S. states are designated as right-to-work, which means that workers have the right to work at unionized workplaces and the choice to either join or not join the union. Advocates for right-to-work laws argue that they are pro-worker and give workers "a choice over where their money goes." They contend that under right-to-work law, unions are "forced to earn worker's respect" and are "ultimately better" because they are held more accountable. Right-to-work advocates like the Heritage Foundation conclude that "the law should not force anyone in America to pay union dues as a condition of employment."[8]

Those against right-to-work laws argue that under them, wages and the economic well-being of all workers is lowered. Moreover, according to this perspective, the laws "make it easier for more of the economy's gains to flow straight to the country's wealthiest people."[9] The Center for American Progress asserts, "The name 'right to work' is a lie. The federal government already protects workers' freedom not to join a union. Workers can decide to opt out of membership at a unionized workplace and pay a reduced fee that covers the costs the union pays to negotiate for wages and benefits and represent an employee if they have a problem at work."[10]

The vast majority of U.S. meatpacking plants are located in Iowa, Nebraska, Kansas, Texas, and North Carolina, all right-to-work states where unionization has been hotly contested and seen as suspect by management. The industries that operate within these states' borders are under the aegis of the Taft-Hartley Act, which outlawed "union shops" and favored management's rights over workers' rights. During the late 1930s and up to the passage of Taft-Hartley, the major meatpacking industries of the time, which included Swift, Armour, Sulzberger, Cudahy, Morrell, and Morris, lobbied hard to reverse the earlier pro-workers' rights act, the Labor Management Relations Act of 1935.[11] Since the 1920s, unions such as the Amalgamated Meat Cutters and Butcher Workmen of North America saw their efforts challenged by the companies. Despite the 1935 act, which upheld workers' rights to collective bargaining, the big companies met efforts to unionize with intense resistance, resorting to hiring nonunionized workers from other states, outright firing, or refusing to meet any of the union's demands.

As anthropologist Steve Striffler details in his book *Chicken: The Dangerous*

Transformation of America's Favorite Food, the vertical integration of companies in the early twentieth century gave more power to companies like Tyson to focus their attention on anti-unionism and a right-to-work ideology. While Tyson was not the first, it was one of the earliest vertical integrators and has proved to be the most successful at bringing "previously independent facets of the emerging industry... under the control of a single entity."[12] The company became an industry model for how to combine multiple segments of an industry (raising chickens, producing feed, killing the birds, processing) under one company and, increasingly, under one roof. The company maximizes its profits, as most of the labor that goes into processing the meat is done in-house. Keeping labor issues in-house is also part of the vertically integrated corporate ethos of the chicken industry and, I would add, the broader protein industry that includes hogs and cattle. Companies like Tyson locate in right-to-work states that at best discourage unionization and at worst are overtly hostile to workplace unionization.

Corporate leaders like Don Tyson, whose Tyson Foods took over Holly Farms in the then-biggest corporate merger in 1989, offered a kind of populist appeal in his anti-union, pro-worker rhetoric that he shared with his employees: "Why should you and I, as individuals, have to have somebody work between us? It's like hiring a lawyer, and both of us paying him, when we could have thrown him out the window. In the last few years, of the companies that came with us, five plants that were union voted them out, where they belong." Don Tyson went on to describe himself and his newly expanded company as "pro-people."[13]

Similar pro-people rhetoric is used today at the rural Iowa Tyson pork processing plant and at Iowa Premium Beef. The CEOs and management team of both packing plants cite the higher-than-local-standards hourly wages, the company-sponsored benefits, and the care and concern that they have for their workers as evidence for a superior model to unionization. Indeed, the paternalism and ethos of stewardship for the workers, the animals, and the land is promoted in a mantra-like way. Positioning themselves as caring individuals who work for a caring company is a powerful and convincing story indeed for management and owners. Company mottos reflect the corporate ethos of stewardship, paternalistic care and concern, and commitment to people above all else.

The geographic realignment of the meatpacking industry from urban to rural mid-America, the rise of vertical as well as horizontal company integration, and the steady dismantling of unions did not happen simultaneously. They occurred as interrelated and interdependent components of the new corporate-driven packing plant that claimed to value people over profits—but the underlying reality of the rhetoric and branding was profits over people. The exodus of the meatpacking plants from Chicago to the rural Midwest began in earnest in 1954 and was the beginning of the demise of Chicago as the center of meatpacking. By the 1980s, the protein industry was thoroughly decentered, and plants were scattered in what were right-to-work states.

Iowa Beef Packers was a key player in the seismic shift from urban to rural meatpacking operations when it established its state-of-the-art plant in Denison in 1960. Key to the shift and to its success as a template for late twentieth- to twenty-first-century meatpacking was the location of the plant next to feedlots and cattle ranches that supplied live cattle. Iowa Beef Packers represented the new, modern meatpacking plant: it was rural, near the animals and their food; it was only one story, for efficient processing; and it facilitated a comprehensive processing of a live animal to boxed beef. The industry was streamlined in all ways possible. Moreover, the shift from urban to rural also ended the reliance on the railroad industry and switched the mode of transporting beef to refrigerated trucks. Iowa Beef Packers streamlined the entire process of meatpacking and combined all facets: slaughtering, fabricating, and distributing to retail and wholesale. It also marked the shift from retail-ready carcass beef to boxed beef.[14] As the labor historian Jimmy Skaggs writes, Iowa Beef Packers "installed the latest capital equipment in a sprawling, highly automated one-story facility made practical by cheap energy."[15] The Denison facility became a template for other Iowa Beef Packers plants, which included those in Dakota City, Nebraska; West Point, Nebraska; Luverne, Minnesota; Emporia, Kansas; and Holcomb, Kansas.[16]

The U.S. meatpacking industry's major shift from urban to rural, carcass to boxed beef, and unionized to nonunionized workforces also coincided with something else—the beginnings of the farm crisis in rural America. As the price of farmland plummeted and farming states like Iowa, Nebraska, and Kansas saw their economies begin to shift and falter, new employers and industries like the meatpacking plants were welcomed with mostly open arms. These comprehensive slaughterhouses and fabrication and distribution centers needed corn, animals, and workers. Corn-rich states like Iowa had crops and animals to sell but faced an issue with a lack of workers willing to perform the dirty, dangerous work. In the early years of the plants, white ethnics populated the line as well as management positions at the plants, but by the 1980s and 1990s, most of the plants had ramped up production due to increased demand in beef and needed more workers. The solution to the meatpacking industry's labor shortage has always rested in waves of recent immigrants:

whether it was Eastern Europeans in the late nineteenth- and early twentieth-century Chicago Back of the Yards; Mexican-descent, Chin Burmese, and Vietnamese women and men in the 1980s, 1990s, and first decade of the 2000s; or, most recently, East African refugees.

Most of the employees at Tyson and IPB I spoke with have worked at other meatpacking plants and are protein industry veterans. They are familiar with the layouts of the factories and tend to move to higher paying positions when they arise, even if that involves moving their families. They advocate for themselves and their families, who depend on their income. If they know of a better job at a rival plant, they apply for it. Their families come first. If they are dissatisfied with their job, they know that more than likely they can find similar work at even higher pay in the industry. Because there are several packing plants in Iowa and nearby states, workers here have options to leave and go elsewhere.

Brenda is a woman who sees herself as always moving for better opportunities for her family. When we spoke, she had been at IPB for almost three years and said that working at the plant is a family affair for her: she was hired the same week her sister, two brothers, and brother-in-law. Iowa is the fourth place Brenda has lived. Originally from central Mexico, she moved to Garden City, Kansas, at the age of twenty-two to work at the beef processing plant there, and then to Colorado after she was laid off for taking "too much time off when my youngest son was sick." She was disappointed that she was let go, because she said she worked hard and had proved herself a good and reliable worker. "It wasn't my fault that my son got sick, you know, and it wasn't fair that I was let go because I took too much time off to take care of him. I mean, I am a single mom; what could I do? I had to take care of my boy." For a while she cleaned hotels, but she made "little money for hard, backbreaking labor." Her mother helped out with her two boys while she cleaned. But Brenda felt bad about her job; it seemed to be "low, you know. I was not proud of my work and maybe even embarrassed if I really think about it."

After she had been cleaning hotels for about a year, Brenda caught wind of the ICE raid on a Greeley, Colorado, meatpacking plant. Fed up with cleaning hotel rooms, Brenda drove to Greeley to apply for a job at the plant, which was hiring workers with documentation. "This Mexicana with papers was hired on the spot" in 2007 at the beef processing plant. "I interviewed on a Friday, and the next day I sent for my mama and my boys." Her sister and brother-in-law were also hired at the plant, along with her brothers, who joined her when she moved to Iowa. Brenda worked at the Greeley plant for six years, working her way up to Quality Assurance. It was a good wage, but the cost of living in

Colorado was always going up, and Brenda physically could not work more hours. She did lots of outdoors activities with her boys and loved the outdoor lifestyle that her family experienced there, but money was always "really tight." She constantly worried about paying the bills, let alone getting ahead. Moreover, she was stressed out because her brothers were being targeted by local gangs as recruits.[17] In the early 2000s, Greeley and nearby towns were experiencing spikes in gang activity. Brenda, the oldest of eight, looks out for her siblings—she calls herself their "second mom"—and knew she needed to get her brothers out of their gang-infested town.

She heard about the Tama plant opening and decided to give it a chance. Word travels across state lines when there are openings at packing plants that pay well and that treat their employees better. There is intense competition among the plants for a concentrated pool of workers, and companies offer incentives like hiring bonus pay, help with rent, and other perks. After I talked with workers at Tyson and IPB, it became clear that there is a communication circuit that moves from plant to plant—from Kansas, Nebraska, Iowa, and Illinois all the way out to North Carolina. Workers talk a lot outside of work. A cousin of a cousin may have heard of an opening in another state, and the tip can prove to be instrumental to a family's success in the United States. I talked with dozens of workers who, like Brenda, were open to moving their families across state lines to new jobs that paid better and had better benefits. While workers can indeed see online job postings, more effective, it seems, are informal lines of communication that travel via cell phones and personal email correspondence.

After Brenda was hired, so were her brothers. At first, she left her sons with her mom in Colorado, not wanting them to leave their friends and school, but after living and working in Iowa for six months, "I couldn't stand being away from *mis hijos* anymore. I missed them so much and felt sick from loneliness." Today her boys, ages ten and seventeen, seem to like Tama and the "slower pace" of life than they had experienced in Colorado. For her part, Brenda really misses the outdoors and the views Colorado offered. She acknowledged that she traded a "beautiful, expensive place to live for a more affordable, sometimes boring place."

What worries Brenda today is the complacency she sees in the younger generation. Her boys' lack of drive concerns her, and she knows she is part of the problem because she has always wanted to give them everything and to not experience hardships. A single mom, Brenda knows she has "spoiled" her boys, but she told me she did this out of love and a desire to protect them from struggles. But she knows that this backfired in a way. "My son, you know, wants to be a YouTuber when he grows up. His role models are the rich YouTubers. I tell him that this is not realistic, but he doesn't listen to me. . . . My eleven-year-old works harder and has a paper route and babysits each week." She said the children of the Latino workers, mostly second- and third-generation—like her older son—do not want to work on the floor. If they want to work at the plant at all, "they want to start in human resources right away and not work their way up. They just do not have the work ethic." Brenda started on the floor in Kansas and moved up to a higher-grade position in Quality Assurance in Colorado and then to her current office position in human resources with IPB.

Interestingly, although Brenda is fluent in both Spanish and English, she said that "knowing just two languages doesn't mean squat here." While Spanish is important, French and African dialects are more important to know at meatpacking plants. The average refugee of the new workforce speaks several languages, but Spanish and English are not among them. James has been able to thrive because of his linguistic skills and acuity. He speaks English fluently and translates for human resources. James is definitely the new face of today's upper-middle management and the globally situated protein industry. His linguistic gifts, skills at handling difficult situations, and refugee past most certainly have prepared and situated him to work in this new American workplace.

Orientation

IPB holds two orientations each week for new hires, and each session runs two days. Every Tuesday and Wednesday, orientation is conducted in English and Spanish, and each Thursday and Friday, it is led by James in French and Swahili. I was allowed to sit in on orientation for my research. During that particular week, the English-Spanish session was smaller than usual, which typically runs closer to fifteen to twenty new employees, we were told. The winter months and icy roads might have been one reason for the smaller group, as we were in between snow storms in this area. US 31, the two-lane highway that connects part of the state to the route that leads to the eastern Iowa "Corridor," as it is known, can be a dangerous highway. Indeed, a Congolese employee died in a van accident several days before our orientation. She was going home after a nine-hour shift at the plant with four fellow Congolese workers when the van skidded into the median ditch while trying to pass another vehicle. Aziza Nikuzi, forty years old and the mother of five children, ages two to twenty-one, died from injuries sustained from the crash.

Her children were left orphans, as their father had died several years ago from an illness. The other four employees were uninjured. This tragic occurrence, almost exactly two years to the day after another crash that had killed four other Congolese workers driving home after work, served as an entrée into our session, which focused on worker safety. We were implored to be safe drivers and to "always wear your seat belts." A collection had been taken up by Congolese employees, and the collection box was placed on a table in the hot side's break room, which was right outside the cordoned-off orientation area. Pictures of Aziza were taped all over the box.

Eight of us convened for the two-day English- and Spanish-language mandatory orientation. The new hires in our group were Alicia, a young Latina mother who had been rehired after taking time off from work after the birth of her youngest child; Daryl, a middle-aged woman who had been rehired after taking FMLA-approved leave for a medical issue; Scott, another rehire and young married father of two daughters; Gunner, a recent high school graduate and veteran worker in the industry; Marceline, a young Congolese woman; Josephine, a Congolese mother of five, whose high-school-aged son Geoffry was accompanying her and Marceline as a translator; and Nam, the Cambodian refugee discussed earlier in this chapter.

The focus of our two days of training was personal safety and food safety, which are interrelated and essential here at the plant. Veronica, a bilingual Latina who works in IPB's human resources department, led our session and translated everything from English to Spanish for Alicia at a rapid and continuous pace. We covered a lot of ground in our eight hours of training each day, and by the end of the second day we were all out on the floor working in our new jobs. Marceline and Josephine were on the hot side, working with the freshly killed carcasses; Alicia was working on the cold side, trimming meat; Daryl was a quality control supervisor on the cold side; Scott was in the barn, caring for the cattle before they are moved to the slaughter room; Gunner was in maintenance, making sure all of the machines are running smoothly and completing necessary repairs; Nam was in distribution; and I, as an observer, rotated through all the parts of the plant. Once our new-hire paperwork was signed and turned in, we were given the employee handbook, which we could refer to during and after the training sessions.

The first day of training contained a lot of instructional videos and PowerPoint slides that conveyed important information that employees are expected to know. After each session of training was completed, we were tested on the information in a quiz show type of format. Teamwork was emphasized, and we were not allowed to progress to the next unit until the group's score was 100 percent. There were incentives to doing well; the winner of each unit was given a prize, which was an IPB product such as a lunch bag, a beverage koozie, or a T-shirt. Scott did very well and scored two koozies, a T-shirt, and lunch bag. We teased him, telling him that he would soon have a koozie set for weekends watching Hawkeye games.

Teresa served as moderator of the information and translator for Alicia, who spoke Spanish exclusively. The speed at which she translated and conveyed the information was admirable and showed her skill and experience at this work. The overarching focus of the first half of the first day's session, bodily safety, touched on being safe around fellow workers, not intruding on coworkers' physical space, and being respectful at all times to ensure safety. Interestingly, the danger of the work itself (cutting, slicing, packaging) was not discussed as much as the emotional and physical dangers of sexual harassment and the stress that can arise out of employee relations gone awry. The videos emphasized worker-on-worker verbal and physical violence and how to report such violence rather than workers getting injured on the job, though the jobs that the women and men perform there are potentially very dangerous. The videos broached the topic of danger primarily in terms of keeping clean and wearing appropriate footwear (steel-toed boots with good treads or company-issued rubber work boots). In our orientation, worker hygiene, respect for fellow workers, and commonsense safety (two knives maximum in your metal scabbard, wearing gloves) equaled a safe work environment.

The actual dangers on the floor itself—where all of the new hires would be working—were addressed later in the training. Raúl and Edith, both supervisors on the "hot side," also stressed the importance of safety during their visit later in the day and took all of us out on the floor after we "suited up" in our frocks, helmets, and safety gloves. But before we got the new-hire tour, Raúl shared stories of workers being careless and unintentionally injuring themselves with their knives. The focus of their presentation was how to use knives and hooks properly and how to sanitize them regularly with the 140-degree Fahrenheit water and a chlorine solution. Walking, not running, on the floor was emphasized, and using the handrails was a must. What was not discussed were the 1,200-pound whole carcasses that move, suspended by giant hooks, on the hot side and the dangers these massive bodies pose to human bodies; the danger of standing too close to the massive carcasses before and after they are sawed in half; and the danger posed by body parts that are being cut and processed all around you as you work in your small area on the line. There was, in other words, a disconnect between the videos shown, the "quiz shows" and testing, and the constant motion on the line.

The factory shown in the video, for example, featured a tidy, quiet, and seemingly solitary place where the clean and orderly workers have a lot of space that separates them from each other, giving them room in which to perform their particular task. Significantly, these fictionalized workers put boxes and products together in slow motion. They do not kill, cut, slice, and basically disassemble a large animal down to parts that will be packaged and shipped across the states and globally. In contrast, workers in real time at IPB and other meatpacking plants work quickly, efficiently, and in very close proximity to each other. They have very little space in which to work and a much smaller room for error.

Toward the end of our first orientation day, we transitioned as a group from the video tutorials and quizzing to actually touring the plant. We put on white frocks, hairnets, beard and mustache nets (for the three men in our group), earplugs, and safety helmets. Helmets at all meatpacking plants are color-coded and correspond to the particular job and rank of each employee. The colors that corresponded to our group were light blue (for cold and hot side workers) for the probationary ninety days before graduating into white helmets; yellow for maintenance; and orange for Quality Control. Other colors used by the plants are black, indicating the most highly skilled employees; dark blue, indicating supervisors; green, for translators; and brown, signifying the cleanup crew. Everyone was given a decal with his or her name to stick on the helmets. My helmet simply indicated "Visitor." I was the only one without a colored helmet—I wore white—and full name.

Daryl was a rehire, a tough, petite, middle-aged blonde who had to take some time off for surgery to repair tears in her arm, which resulted from the repetitive motion of cutting that was part of her former line job. Her insurance covered the surgery, and after physical therapy she came back to work at a different job: inspecting the meat in the position of quality controller. Now Daryl makes cuts only when other workers have missed cutting fat off the meat. Daryl exuded confidence during our orientation session and had a can-do attitude. When we talked during our lunch break, Daryl said that she can't eat during a shift. "I can't eat breakfast or lunch, I don't know... but after a shift, I shower and make a big meal for myself." Daryl loves to cook, and a hobby of hers is to make "big pots of soup and chili." She said, "I don't mean to brag or nothing, but I am a pretty darn good cook." She also loves to take long, rambling rides on her Harley, a vintage model that she cherishes and carefully maintains with her earnings.

Gunner was another rehire, an Iowa native raised by a single mom. He worked in his last years of high school as part of the maintenance crew for another packing plant in nearby Marshalltown as well as for a pork plant in rural Minnesota. He moved back home recently because he was homesick. Gunner's dream is to become an engineer, but he isn't sure he ever will because, he told me, "college just costs so much. When I looked at all of the costs it just sort of scared me, and I thought that I just can't do this right now." He would love to attend Iowa State or the University of Iowa one day, but for now he is gaining job skills and expertise as a lead maintenance worker. Part of his daily routine will be maintaining the trolley system, the boilers, and "pretty much everything that makes the plant run." An earnest young man, Gunner was not much older than my oldest son when we went through orientation at IPB. During our group tour of the plant, he kept asking me if I was "OK" as we stood next to steaming carcasses and cut body parts. My orientation cohort all knew I was there to work on a book, and Gunner joked during lunch one day, "Hey, maybe you can give me a shout out in the book—say something like, 'And here's a shout-out to my buddy Gunner.'" I have thought of Gunner many times and how he is an engineer without the formal training. I have thought about how much he could command in earnings compared to what he makes now and how low-income white families like his are also treated as fungible commodities, as are refugees.

Scott was a third rehire in our small group. Born and raised in Iowa, Scott joined the army shortly after graduating from high school. "It is a great place to be if you are single and young," he told me. Another draw is that the army pays for college, and once he is caught up on bills, Scott plans on enrolling in some online community college courses that he can take at night. He worked in the receiving area with live cattle for a few years before he and his wife decided to move to California to "try something new." They had lived in Iowa their entire lives and had always wanted to move to a warmer climate. So they packed up their things and moved to sunny California with their two daughters to try their hand at an organic farm. His wife worked with the produce and Scott with cattle, sheep, and goats. Working at a California farm was "very, *very* different" from working at IPB, he said. They loved living in California and had free housing at the farm, but the pull of their extended families drew them home. Plus, their girls missed their friends and their school. So, back to the Midwest it was. Scott had left IPB on good terms, and the company hired him back for the same job. "So that's why you kept racking up the wins!" I exclaimed. Scott shyly nodded and answered, "Yes ma'am, I pretty much knew all of the answers to the tests because I took the same test before." Scott was looking forward to resuming work at the plant for a lot of reasons, and one of the big ones for him and his family was the health insurance. Scott said it is "so much better" than the school district's health insurance program. His wife is a teacher, and Scott said "her insurance benefits are so bad that they are really not worth having." IPB will provide them with "excellent" benefits, and he even thinks that his retirement will be a good one thanks to a rigorous 401K program. Plus, he really likes working with the cattle: "I love animals and just can't see myself working on the slaughter side of things." Scott knows that he works for a packing plant and is well aware of where his live cattle are going, and he wrestled with that reality. But he thinks it is a good company, he "feels good" about what he does, and he knows the meat product is "quality, pure and simple."

Workers at packing plants are transient and move for better jobs on a regular basis. Like Brenda, who moved from Colorado to Iowa for a better opportunity for herself and her family members, Scott and his wife moved back to Iowa for the lower cost of living and higher pay than they had commanded in California. IPB offered him a "very good deal" to "come back home." For all of the workers I spent time with for this book, being close to their families was an important pull of the Corn Belt, as were higher pay, a lower cost of living, and the ability to own a house with a yard.

After our conversation about the pull of Iowa and the packing plant, we went with our respective supervisors to have our first real-time job experience. Scott went to the farm; Gunner went to maintenance on the cold side; Josephine and Marceline went to the hot side; Daryl went to Safety on the cold side; Nam went to the distribution center; and Alicia went to the cold side. I was told to join the cold side group, and we were led there by Edith and Raúl.

Benefits

Workers' benefits were explained in detail during orientation. We learned that for rehires, health insurance and 401K benefits "kick in" right away, and for new hires, insurance and 401Ks are activated after they have worked for ninety days. Rehires have already been through the three-month trial period, and new hires must go through it as well. Brenda, who was leading this part of orientation, explained employee benefits to us clearly and effectively. Hourly employees have the opportunity to work their way up the pay scale ladder from an entry-level "Grade 1" job at fifteen dollars per hour to a "Grade Six" level job, which pays twenty dollars an hour. She told us that we should think of the 401K as a savings account for our retirement and that it is "a good thing that this company provides. We want to take care of our workers." She talked

to us about vesting and how employees can become vested in, or part owners of, the company. At IPB, employees become vested after working for the
company for five years. "The longer you work here, the more money you make
and the better retirement that you have," Brenda told us.

As Brenda talked about the intricacies of health insurance, 401KS, and
other employee benefits, I could not help but notice the amazing smells of
international food wafting into our orientation area. It was break time for the
hot side workers, and as the employees microwaved their meals, the sweet
and savory smells of cumin, cilantro, rice, beans, and vegetables filled our
area. For a moment, I imagined that I was at a restaurant—it smelled that
good. Scott, who was sitting next to me, agreed. "Man, it smells so good!" he
exclaimed. The overall message we received that afternoon was that if you
work hard enough and want to increase your pay, it can happen at IPB. Economic uplift was possible through hard work and determination. As I looked
around the room, everyone was taking notes.

The Producers: Faith, Family, and Cattle

For the Kieswetter family of eastern Iowa, raising and selling cattle is a family
affair. It is as integral to their lives as is being Catholic. The family is very involved in their parish—St. Joseph the Worker in Columbus Junction—where
Bruce was president of the parish council for several years. Raising animals is
"in our blood," I was told by Bruce, Cara, and their youngest son, Will, who
was fourteen at the time of our interview. Bruce and Cara have been married
for twenty-five years; Cara, raised Methodist in southern Indiana, converted
to Catholicism when they wed in a small Indiana parish. Bruce, a romantic
at heart, proposed to Cara in a southern Indiana pasture. Cara recounted his
proposal: "It was a dewy morning and Bruce asked me to stay in the car—he
said he had a few things to get done. As he was, unbeknownst to me, lighting
candles in the pasture and making everything look pretty and romantic, I
watched as the cows milled around. It was just beautiful." Cara, who said yes
to Bruce's proposal "without hesitation," was raised Methodist in Indiana.
Bruce joked, "Man, I was pretty jealous of her when we met because she knew
the Bible in a way that I did not. I was raised on the Baltimore Catechism
where it was more like questions and answers about Catholic faith, but we
didn't learn the Bible when I was growing up." Cara smiled at this and said
what impressed her about Catholicism was the rituals and the beauty of them.
She also really liked the priest who married them and with whom they took
their required pre-marriage courses. "He was really accessible and down to

earth in a way that my pastor really hadn't been. And he came to our wedding reception that was on my parents' Indiana farm." For Bruce and Cara, the kind of couple who finish each other's sentences and hold hands when they are together, family, faith, and raising cattle are entwined. Cara was raised on a farm in rural south-central Indiana, and Bruce grew up cattle ranching and cattle fitting in southwestern Illinois.

For both of them, religion was at the center of their lives. Converting to Catholicism was a big deal for Cara, for she had been raised in a devout Methodist home where church picnics, Sunday school, and choir were integral facets of her life. She admired how Bruce was committed to his religion and wanted to raise their children as a couple and attend church weekly. And Cara loved Jesus and knew her husband did too. Her family, she said, accepted her conversion and saw in Bruce a fellow devotee of Jesus. When Cara visits her parents in Indiana, she attends the Methodist church of her youth, and it brings back a lot of happy memories for her. Raising her own sons in a faith has been extremely important to her, and of all of the things she has done in her life, raising good Christian men is the thing she is most proud of. They have raised their sons, Cale and Will, in the Catholic faith.

Bruce and Cara lament what they see as a decline in religion in America. "Religion seems to be in second, third, or no place for many of today's families," Cara said. The two value Latino culture and admire how "so many Spanish-speaking women and men work hard to provide for their families." Bruce and Cara lived in Argentina when they were newlyweds, as Bruce, only twenty-one, had "an opportunity of a lifetime" to live and work on a cattle ranch there. As a fitter, he washed, dried, and brushed the cattle's hides to prepare them to be shown in competitions. Neither Cara nor Bruce spoke Spanish, and Bruce had an interpreter during his time working on the ranch. He said it was one of the "most amazing, powerful experiences of my life so far." The Argentinians' love of food, wine, and family left an indelible mark on the couple, and Cale's godparents are members of the family that hosted them during their yearlong stay.

Bruce and Cara are critical of white ethnic Americans, whom Bruce refers to as "Anglets." But both speak favorably about Mexicans and other Latin American–derived women and men, noting that family is more important to Spanish-speaking cultures. "I really respect how family-oriented the Hispanics are. You really see it. It comes through in how they treat each other. Younger Hispanics really take care of their older family members and vice versa. We could really learn a thing or two from them, let me tell you," said Bruce. Cara shared how much she loves the Hispanics' devotions to the

Virgin Mary. "As a teacher, I often make home visits, and I see how devoted they are to Mary. Statues of her are in homes. Flowers are around her image. Candles are burning. The mother of Jesus is really celebrated in their culture, and I respect that so much." Taking in what Cara just said, Bruce paused a moment before speaking critically about his own culture: "Yes, there are a lot of 'woodworkers' in the Anglet culture. What I mean by this phrase is that so many Anglets—whites—come out of the woodwork and attend church just once or twice a year. You know, at Christmas and Easter." He took a breath and continued, "We Anglets have grown away from family. The internet, technology, and sports pull us away from each other." Cara chimed in and noted that "this younger generation communicate through texts and Snapchat. They can't write, and this really worries me." The couple has worked hard, they said, to instill in their boys a strong sense of family and faith. And they take the time to eat dinner as a family as often as they can. Cara tries to feed her family home-cooked meals as often as possible. She takes great pride in being a mother and wife and is very proud of her boys and the men they have become. Bruce loves to grill and has easy access to the freshest meat as a cattleman. "Life is good, and we are grateful for what we have," said Cara. Bruce nodded in agreement.

Being around cattle and on the farm has taught young Will "a lot about life. I understand life and death and how connected they are." Like his parents, Will sees life as "a miracle" and has helped many cows as they have birthed their calves. He spoke reflectively about his generation, which he called a "bipolar generation." "I mean, some days we are nice to each other, and the next day we are not. I think that the Internet has a lot to do with how we treat each other." Will said that while he doesn't go to church all the time, especially during calving season, he tries to go often and truly enjoys it because it is so "different than what I experience each day." At church there are no cell phones, no distractions that he has at school and with his friends. Church is like his work on the farm and with cattle, where Will is centered, focused. He loves to farm and work with cattle because he feels "really in touch with nature." He has learned "the facts of life" living and working on a farm, and he believes he has a "pretty good" work ethic. Will took me through his daily routine: he feeds the show heifers at dawn, cleans out their stalls, and helps his dad with anything he needs help with—all before breakfast, showering, and taking the bus to his rural consolidated school. Will has worked on the farm for as long as he can remember. When he was a bit younger, at age ten, he remembered getting up even earlier, at five o'clock, riding the tractors, putting feed in trailers, and feeding the cows. He would work with his older brother, who helped teach him a strong work ethic.

Will is grateful to be raised on a farm in rural America. He says he appreciates his mom and dad for "raising me like they are doing, I mean, I feel like I have good values and accept people for who they are. I want to honor my mother and father like it says in the Commandments. I see how animals, people, and nature are related and connected. And I see my faith as a way to keep me centered and grounded." And working with cattle also keeps him grounded, as it is physically demanding work. As a member of 4-H and the Future Farmers of America, and a junior member of the National Angus Association, Will has gained valuable skills in showmanship, public speaking, and sales. He is proud of the way he has been raised and is confident that he will parlay his talents into a career in farming and raising cattle when he is older. For now, he is focused on succeeding in high school, taking care of his cattle, and being confirmed at his parish. He hopes to continue his family's tradition of farming and raising cattle.

The Language of Stewardship: Faith at Work

Bruce, Cara, and Will see themselves as stewards of the land and animals they cultivate and raise. Their identities as farmers, ranchers, and Catholics are deeply connected. They see themselves as following the teachings of their faith in caring for the land and their animals. They raise animals that are consumed in global locales, and like Jenny and Justin, they are personally removed from the slaughterhouses where their animals will go. The producers I spent time with talked about their role in feeding people and their gratitude for their animals, for providing their families with a living, and for the ability to feed others. They use the language of "calling" and "vocation" and believe that their Catholic faith gives them spiritual strength to raise animals for the Corn Belt and global protein industry. Raising animals for consumption is in their blood—they are connected to earlier generations of kin and to the animals themselves.

At the Tyson and IPB packing plants, religion and faith are still present, albeit in less obvious, less denominationally specific ways. What I observed and heard at the Tyson and IPB plants from middle- and upper-management women and men is a pronounced sense of desire and duty to embrace servant leadership. Servant leadership is the idea that arose in post–World War II America that businesspeople must lead by example and must run their businesses as caring institutions. In this ideology, religion—usually Protestant Christianity—is interpreted as necessitating a social contract between the management and the average worker. Those in positions of power and authority—in the case of meatpacking, the CEOs, CFOs, heads of human resources, and middle-management women and men—must demonstrate care and concern for their fellow workers and employees. They must run their business in a way that demonstrates compassion. Postwar American visionaries and prophets of corporations in their new form of American communities were espoused by popular authors such as Howard Bowen in his 1953 *Social Responsibilities of the Businessman* and Peter Drucker, an influential managerial theorist.[18] And even more recently, as scholars of American religious history Amanda Porterfield, Darren E. Grem, and John Corrigan have argued, Robert Greenleaf's 1970 essay "Servant Leadership" repackaged as well as popularized for a new generation the belief in business as salvific for people when it is run according to the principles of "servant leadership" and continued the postwar championing of seeking "cults of beneficent corporate personality, inspiring the hourly employee and middle manager alike to emulate the service to God, country, company, and employee, that executive stewards and servant leaders ostensibly modeled."[19] And throughout the 1990s, Stephen Covey's bestselling *Seven Habits of Highly Effective People* solidified Christian-laced ideas that religion and religious people were good businesspeople, even the best kind. As Porterfield, Grem, and Corrigan note, "In business schools and in the books lining the shelves of Barnes & Noble, business 'values,' 'ethics,' and 'character' became watchwords, each supposedly based in selective readings of various religious texts."[20]

At Tyson and IPB, the theology and ideology of servant leadership, with its values-centered language and references to high standards of character for all levels of employees, was front and center. As IPB's CEO Jeffrey Johnson and human resources supervisor Steve Hanson talked about serving the workers and their "duty" to provide good work at good pay for the plant's employees, faith was and is most certainly at work. This is the new face of religion in America. Historian Bethany Moreton shows just how postwar retailers came to infuse their capitalistic messaging with Christian morality in her masterful book *To Serve God and Wal-Mart: The Making of Christian Free Enterprise.*[21] Walmart set the bar for companies wishing to serve up products with morality messaging, and IPB is one contemporary business that adopted Walmart's messaging in the Hawkeye State. IPB fashions itself as a moral company whose leaders serve their clients and employees alike, and the profit is reward for their good efforts.

As scholar of American religions Robert Wright has written, religion has always been, one could argue, akin to a "service industry," one that "sells salvation, spirituality, and so forth."[22] Service industries, as we know, change and morph over time, as do churches, and new leadership emerges that reaches out to the marketplace. Churches and businesses alike, according to historian of American religions Lawrence Moore, "sell God." They sell the idea of God, and the idea comes through in the heavy usage of language that references values, morals, family, and character. With church attendance on the decline, in part because Americans are working more hours than ever before, are attending their children's sports and other recreational activities that take place on Sundays, and are disillusioned with traditional trappings of church and religious places, religion is embraced as well as reworked in the places where people congregate. One of these places is work. Porterfield, Grem, and Corrigan put this succinctly in their assertion, "As the church's role as an arm of the state withered, religion's role as a form of free enterprise expanded, opening give-and-take between religion and commerce, stimulating innovative forms of outreach and marketing in both areas, and blurring boundaries between sacred and profane."[23]

Industry heads such as Iowa Premium Beef's Jeffrey Johnson and Steve Armstrong work in the same spirit that earlier leaders such as nineteenth-century American religious entrepreneurs and salespersons Charles Finney, Aimee Semple MacPherson, and Washington Gladden had. These Protestant Christian leaders all believed that there is a direct link between business success and faith, and today's packing plant leaders follow in their footsteps.

At Tyson, as we saw in the previous chapter, with its company-wide network of chaplaincy, *character* matters very much, and it is a *values-based* company that employs chaplains to maintain workers' morale and spirit and to attend to the whole person. Also on display at the packing plants is a religiously laced paternalism. Members of the management team all express genuine care and concern from the positionality of a parent, and they take seriously the task to oversee and care for the workers, team members, or line workers (as they are interchangeably referred to at the plants). All of the upper-management and middle-management employees at Tyson and IPB expressed their assumed roles of parents during our discussions. Moreover, they take on other roles as spiritual leaders, men and women who are at the plant as people to whom the workers on the line aspire to be like. Tyson's Dave Duncan repeated several times during our conversation that the company wants workers to be able to "celebrate their faith" at work and to feel comfortable expressing "their whole person." Chaplain Joe Blay picked up on Dave's comment and reflected on declining church membership and the aging church populations, adding that "we want our workplace to be a new kind of church, and you do not have to be Christian to be a part of it, because this is about celebrating values and morals in a safe and supportive environment."

While this kind of language isn't "religion" or "spirituality" in their more traditional forms, what they represent is an emerging new religion, religion of real life. Religion of the workplace. Religion of the home. What we have seen so far is that religion and faith are relevant for people today, whether they are crossing the border to be with their family, harvesting corn and melons, working on the kill floor, or serving as a plant chaplain. This is religion and faith in new forms for a post-church America. Religion in the Corn Belt is ground zero for the new religiosity of everyday life. With Mass and church attendance down nationwide, companies are providing religious-like services and benefits to their employees, who spend the majority of their waking hours at work. Yet this turn to a business-inspired religion is not exactly new. Business leaders as servant leaders is not a new idea; the current packing plants' management takes the concept to the next level. Higher-than-average wages for the rural communities in which they are located, 401Ks, and health insurance are all part of the new corporate meatpacking religion. Membership has its benefits, and work is rewarded with perks such as flashlights, cute little squishy pigs and cattle toys with the company logos, baby blankets, koozies, jackets, and T-shirts given out as incentives and tokens of thanks to the workers. Family-themed picnics, company-sponsored *fútbol* games, and monthly meat sales at steep employee discounts represent the business leaders' care and stewardship.

Recall Joe at Tyson, who sees his job as divinely inspired. In one of our email correspondences, he likened his job and mine as an author chronicling the lives and work of Latinos and Africans. He wrote, "To God be the glory who has enabled us to be part of His plan to show His love and tender care to those who are less privileged."[24] To Joe, who has overcome obstacles to make it to his current life in the Corn Belt with his family, he has been blessed and is duty-bound to share his good fortune with the less privileged. He also feels that he was "called" to a company to minister to workers' bodies and souls and to assist them at the job and in the outside world. Whether it is helping them work with government agencies, driving them to the doctor's office for checkups, or taking them to the grocery store, Joe is present. He is pastoral and a self-described "servant leader." During our time together, Joe mentioned that he has the "heart of a servant" and that he wants to lead by example. He takes his overlapping roles as husband, father, and employee all very seriously and sees himself as being in the fortunate position to take care of those less fortunate than himself.

For James, like for Joe at Tyson, God is present at work all the time. James feels that God called him to work at IPB and sees the management team as made up of godly women and men. James, a Jehovah's Witness who converted with his wife and children in the Democratic Republic of the Congo, lives his entire life focused on Jehovah. James brings his faith to work and feels "blessed" to have his job to provide for his wife and children. While he is not technically a chaplain, as IPB does not have a chaplain on site, he assumes the role of counselor, spiritual guide, and friend to IPB's employees. In fact, James was introduced to me as having a "heart of a servant" by Steve Armstrong, who shared IPB's philosophy with me: "We are very proud of what we do here at Iowa Premium. We produce a premium product and we treat our employees with respect. We have to have the heart of a servant if we want to have a successful business."

James is highly respected for his grit, determination, and positionality as a man of God at his workplace, and like Joe, he is seen as a special servant of God.

Halal and Good Business

While both Tyson and IPB embrace faith at work and freely use the language of values, character, and family to demonstrate that they are superior companies, there are some differences. IPB, a small, privately owned company, in contrast to the large, multinational Tyson, does not have a chaplain and has no plans to hire one. When I spent the afternoon talking with Jeffrey Johnson and Steve Hanson, they differentiated embracing and supporting faith with showing preferential treatment to one faith over another, which they see as a danger of a chaplaincy program. IPB is a religiously and culturally diverse workforce with a rising number of Muslim employees, who, like followers of Judaism, are forbidden by religious law to work with pork. At IPB, there is a small but growing number of Muslim employees, and human resources works to accommodate their religious needs "within reason," as one HR employee told me. The small number of Somalian Muslim female employees and larger number of Somalian Muslim male employees—close to fifty Muslim workers total—are able to leave their line, when their supervisor approves of it, to go pray, as part of their five-times-a-day obligation. I discreetly watched, in awe, as two Somalian Muslim women tidied up the small area they had created in the women's locker room on the "hot side" before one of them knelt on her prayer rug to pray. Now, I need to mention here that despite the janitors' herculean efforts to keep the plant clean, it always smells of flesh, and the floors are always a bit greasy from the animal fat and waste that cannot help but be brought into the locker room. As I toured the women's locker room I watched as a female janitor scrubbed the outside of the lockers with hot soap and water, trying to remove the film of fat that constantly collects. The locker room floor, like all of the floors on the hot side, had just been sprinkled with Quat, both to freshen the smell and to also cut down on the grease and make the floor less slippery.

The Muslim women at the plant, Somalian and Sudanese, made a sacred space for themselves in the women's locker room by sectioning off a small area in one corner of the entrance with a rounded curtain rod and long dark-blue drapes that can be closed to shield them as they pray to Allah. A dozen or so colorful woven prayer rugs were neatly stacked in the corner, and two women cleaned the floor before unrolling a rug. Both women proceeded to wash their faces, arms, and hands in the restroom sink before going back to the prayer corner. One of the women sat on a locker room bench while her coworker entered the prayer corner, pulled the drapes, and prayed. Trying not to stare and interrupt their sacred rituals and preparations, I jotted observations and thoughts in my notebook. When I spoke with Jenny Mora in human resources later that day, she affirmed that management wants to respect individuals' religious needs and that

> everyone at the plant has the right to practice their faith and be who they are here. We totally support their religious practices and their right to pray and to practice their faith here. We just don't want them abusing the privilege, but you know, so far no one has. When it is OK with their shift manager for them to take a break from the line and pray, we are good with that. We feel that as long as we respect everyone's desire to practice their faith, they do not abuse it. We have not had any problems so far.

As part of its respect for and accommodation of various religious faiths in the workplace, IPB is one of few beef processing facilities to offer certified halal beef. Following his Creekstone mentor and friend John Stewart, Jeffrey Johnson wanted to make sure that the beef he and his team would produce at IPB was halal. Creekstone Farms beef had long been considered top in the industry for its juiciness and tender flesh, and its halal certification most certainly broadened its appeal and sales.[25]

Halal certified beef, like any halal, or "permissible," meat, like chicken, must adhere to strict guidelines and standards set forth in the Qur'an and as monitored by international governing bodies such as the Halal Food Authority and the U.S.-based Halal Transactions of Omaha, which focuses specifically on the beef industry.[26] According to the Halal Food Authority, halal-certified meat must also come from a place that recognized and adhered to "humane treatment" of the animal. Animals must be fed and given water as they would normally be given; animals must not see each other be killed; the knife should be four times the size of the neck and razor sharp; and "as far as possible the slaughterer and the animal should face the Qibla or Mecca and the animal must not be suffering from any ailments or any lacerations."[27] Processing halal-certified beef makes good business sense from multiple angles and is yet one more way that IPB and the broader protein industry demonstrate the American propensity of "braiding . . . religion with business."[28] IPB carries on an American tradition and with gusto. It is a small, high-end producer of family-farm-raised beef that is certified halal. This designation is part of a combined marketing and interfaith awareness outreach to the growing numbers of Muslims in the United States, as well as globally. Producing halal-certified Black Angus beef makes good business sense as much as it represents corporate goodwill and is yet another way the company sells religion in today's marketplace.

In 2014, the news that the then soon-to-be-opening IPB plant in Tama was going to offer halal-certified beef was met with enthusiasm from the Halal Transactions of Omaha group, which defines itself as "committed to helping the food industry produce Halal products and helping consumers locate authentic Halal goods since 1992. We are approved and recognized by various authorities to certify meat/poultry and other consumable goods produced in North America and across the Muslim world."[29] The group was eager not only to announce the halal certification of IPB but to tout the plant's state-of-the art, environmentally conscious design.[30]

A major feature of the new design was a more humane way to kill the cattle. Killing at IPB is done via a handheld penetrating captive bolt gun.[31] According to Temple Grandin, the leading expert on animal euthanasia and humane killing practices, a captive bolt gun "kills the animal by concussive force and penetration of the bolt."[32] At IPB, double knocking on each animal is utilized, which ensures that the animal is indeed dead, that it does not suffer, and that it dies instantaneously. What follows immediately after the double knocking is a process known as exsanguination, in which a knife pierces the thoracic cavity of the cattle and severs the carotid artery and jugular vein. The cattle is then strung up by chains on an overhead moving trolley and bleeds out. As the animal moves along, its blood runs down to the floor, pushed down drains by workers wielding large squeegees.

Iowa Premium Beef is attempting to satisfy animal rights activists, veterinarians, and Muslims who believe that the captive bolt gun followed by exsanguination method of killing used at IPB is acceptable as halal. Iowa Premium Beef's slaughterhouse was designed in direct consultation with Temple Grandin, the famous animal rights scientist who has drawn on her autism to make more humane conditions for animals in farming and slaughter. Grandin's own sensitivities to light and noise helped her design what has become the gold standard of slaughter in the protein industry. According to Grandin, "It was easy for me to figure out how animals think and how animals would react because I think visually. Animals don't think in language. They think in pictures. It's very easy for me to imagine what would it be like to go through a system if you really were a cow, not a person in a cow costume but really were a cow, and autistic senses and emotions are more like the senses of an animal."[33]

Humanely killed animals also means better-tasting meat, as stressors elevate levels of stress hormones that include adrenaline, cortisol, and other steroids that cause the meat to taste bad.[34] It is literally a bad investment for companies to treat and kill their animals poorly, as the taste and quality of the meat are negatively impacted. Better-tasting meat is good for business. For their part, the reason why IPB's management team of Steve, Jeff, and Michelle are so enthusiastic about Black Angus beef is because of the "flavor profile." The meat is tender and juicy because of the marbled fat and corn-fed flesh. All three support the animal husbandry methods of the men and women whose cattle make their way to IPB. "We don't buy off of big feed yards like CAFOs," said Michelle. "We purchase our cattle from family farmers who take a great deal of pride in raising their animals, who feed their cattle the best corn, and who are passionate about their cattle." The trio set out, with the financial backing of their investors, to "change the landscape of Iowa feeders. To support family farms, and to give back to the community."

The religiously laced language of stewardship and words like "family," "caring," "faith," "blessed," and "fortunate" come through those in management as well as the line workers I interviewed at the plant. It is hard to determine the origins of the evangelically tinged language at the plant, but most certainly management team members use it, and it has stuck. All of the line workers I interviewed mentioned the high hourly wages in the same breath that they referred to gratitude, blessings/being blessed, and values of the company as primary reasons for their satisfaction at work. As anthropologist Karen Ho has written in her excellent ethnography of Wall Street, we should think of "the market" as "a set of daily, embodied practices and models" in "complex webs of social relations."[35] The marketplace of IPB is one of entangled and overlapping stewardship and a more humane vertical integration and treatment of the cattle and human workers alike. While the cattle and humans are expendable and fungible, they are treated better and are "valued" more. And workers who are treated better will stay at the plant longer and will recommend friends and family for the jobs that are difficult and dangerous.

All of the line workers and management team members with whom I talked expressed their pride in working for a company that had such "good values." Each of them brought up how management and the company at large "treats us like family." At several points during my weeklong immersion in the plant, line workers I talked with told me how much they appreciated "Mr. Johnson" coming down to say hello and ask them how they were doing. "That really means a lot to me, you know, that the head honcho will come down from his office to ask me how I am doing," one middle-aged Latino fabrication worker expressed. And I spoke at length with a former line worker, a middle-aged white non-Latino man who was injured on the job and who was given the job of janitor at the plant after he was no longer able to perform the same skills he had prior to his injury. He expressed his gratitude to IPB for not "canning" him altogether and for finding a job for him where he could earn a living. The lexicon of family-values-team is borne out in on-the-ground ways and gestures that to workers can mean a lot.

Neither Jeffrey, Steve, nor Michelle has said explicitly that IPB business is good for God or that IPB is a "religious" company. Yet if we take into consideration a more expansive definition and view of "religion," such as one that scholars of religion Charles Hirschkind and Brian Larkin have offered— that "religions are constituted through an architecture of circulation and representation, that in turn creates the pragmatic contexts for modes of practice and worship"—then perhaps we can say, at the very least, that religion is at work at Tyson, IPB, and the meatpacking industry.[36] Looking at the actions and language of the management is just as important as looking closely at what the line workers are doing and saying. Both "studying up," or focusing on those at the top of the means of power and production, and "studying down," or focusing on those who are nearer the bottom, are necessary for a more complete understanding of the dynamics of religion, migration, and

CHAPTER 6

In the Belly of the Beast

I T IS THE DEAD OF WINTER and the drive out to the rural Iowa beef processing plant is rather bleak. Gray-tinged snow hugs the highway as lone hawks and falcons hover in trees and on signs, waiting to catch their next meal. In many ways, this country-scape resembles an Ansel Adams photograph, a study in shades of black and white, a large tree standing tall here and there in a field. Rising in the midst of the frozen, cornstalk-dotted landscape is the cattle processing plant Iowa Premium Beef. The tractor trailers that camp outside the plant each morning have all been emptied of the cattle that have been herded together in the outdoor barn, if only for a short time. By the end of the workday, 1,100 head of Black Angus cattle will have entered the plant since the predawn hours of the day. They are never to leave the plant as living, breathing creatures. Rather, they will leave IPB carefully packaged as USDA choice and prime corn-fed Black Angus beef for discerning consumers across the United States and in forty-five global locations. The line that separates life and death is thin indeed.

There are many layers to the business of killing and producing meat that people eat, layers that I will examine in detail in this chapter. At Iowa Premium Beef in rural Tama, working-class white Americans of various Eastern and Western European backgrounds and Congolese, Somalian, Cambodian, Vietnamese, and Latino men and women work eight- to ten-hour shifts, five to six days a week, on "the line" to deliver choice and prime cuts of beef to millions of consumers. Their work is bloody, tiring, and difficult. Workers stand on their feet for long stretches at a time and use their bodies in ways that are repetitive, unrelenting, and graceful. They resemble meat ninja warriors— sawing, slicing, cutting, and packaging in precise, clean measures. Their work is an art form, and they are artists of the flesh. Their work is constantly supervised and monitored by IPB supervisors and USDA employees alike. What I discovered while shadowing at the plant is that the work that is done in this packing plant as well as in others, such as the Tyson plant in Columbus Junction, is so much more than what has derisively—and incorrectly—been called "unskilled work." This is highly skilled work. It is graceful and quick, efficient and seemingly effortless.

With permission from Iowa Premium Beef CEO Jeffrey Johnson and members of the plant's upper management, I spent a day touring and talking with workers at IPB and followed that visit up with a meeting with Jeffrey and Michelle Baumhover, IPB marketing director, to go over the details of my upcoming weeklong research visit.[1] I then spent a five-day workweek—fifty hours—shadowing workers in every department and division in the packing plant. The permission that Johnson and IPB granted was the first ever for an "outsider," and I am grateful for the trust they placed in me. They wanted me to tell the story of their company and of their employees, and I want to stay true to that vision in this chapter. They listened when I told them that I wanted to tell the plant's story because I thought that something important—and even bigger than the plant—was going on.

My goal was to understand this rural meatpacking plant, not so much to "expose" an industry but to provide readers and consumers with a deeper awareness and understanding of slaughterhouses. My aim in this chapter is not to explain away troubling aspects of the protein industry in which thousands upon thousands of animals are killed and processed each day but to take the reader through a day at a packing plant, highlighting what the average worker as well as the animals go through during a typical shift in various departments within the plant. The purpose of this chapter is to raise awareness both of the people who produce the food that feeds so many of us and of the animals whose lives are taken to feed us.

IPB is one of the most brutally honest workplaces I have ever experienced. To my surprise, I found it oddly refreshing, in spite of the blood, the odors, the noise, and the extreme temperatures. In order for this business to be successful, the women and men who work here must communicate clearly and concisely. Employees must speak to each other directly and work together to ensure their personal and collective safety. Their jobs are, in every sense of the word, on the line. They work alongside each other in tight spaces. Their limbs, which slice and cut massive quantities of meat during their shift, must remain limber as well as controlled. In front of the line of workers' bodies lies a conveyor belt on which chilled cattle carcass parts move to be further cut and inspected. Workers' and animals' bodies alike are lined up in neat and tight rows. Workers' lives are also "on the line," because if they are not paying attention to their task at hand or to the moving line of meat, they could put their body or their coworkers' bodies at risk.

The women and men who work at IPB and at meatpacking plants across the midwestern Corn Belt work six days a week, ten hours a day, in a physically and psychically demanding job that few of us could even imagine. Most white-collar professional women and men I know, including myself, would have a very difficult time performing the work that is done at plants like IPB. And many of us, if not most, would rather not think about the animal that was living before its life was taken as we purchase our tenderloin or sirloin at the grocery store. As anthropologist Timothy Pachirat has written of his own fieldwork in a packing plant, "In many of our meat dishes the animal form is so concealed and changed by the art of its preparation and carving that, while eating, one is scarcely reminded of its origin."[2]

But we must think about the entangled relationships between nonhuman animals and the humans who kill them if we are to appreciate the workers who are immersed in a killing industry and who put their bodies through stress, hardship, and danger to feed other humans. The humans who work in the U.S. slaughter industry are mostly brown and Black women and men who leave work exhausted and who must persevere and make dinner for their children and help with homework in the evenings. Refugees and whites who work the line in today's slaughterhouses are vulnerable people who enter churches and mosques to receive spiritual nourishment and fellowship outside of the plant. Let us consider how we rarely think about the women and men who kill, cut, and package the meat for us to eat. A lot happens between the time that the cattle are brought to the plant and when the red meat ends up on our plates.

During a shift at the packing plant, white, Latino, and African supervisors walk back and forth on the line, making sure their charges are doing quality work—work that is hidden and unknown to the vast majority of us, and it is to our detriment that we do not know. As Pachirat asserts, the work that meatpacking employees do is "a labor considered morally and physically repellent by the vast majority of society that is sequestered from view rather than eliminated or transformed."[3] When we do not see for ourselves, we do not know, we cannot empathize, and—most important—we cannot respect the hard work that these women and men do. They deserve our respect. We hear a lot about how migrants and refugees do the "dirty work" for the majority of Americans who simply cannot or will not do the kind of hard, labor-intensive work that is done at IPB.

One of the reasons for the lack of previous studies focusing on meatpacking plants and what goes on in them is the so-called ag-gag laws, which have been passed by states in response to undercover investigations of factory farms and factories. While pre-2011 laws were meant to protect damage to property from protesters, post-2011 ag-gag laws are more focused on "preventing economic damage to companies than to preventing physical harm," according to Alicia Prygoski of the Michigan State University College of Law.[4] They prohibit or restrict recording at industrialized farming operations. Ag-gag law proponents argue that they are a "safeguard to protect well-meaning farmers against animal protection organizations who present the footage in a misleading way," while opponents contend that "ag-gag laws are meant to hide animal abuse from the public and that these laws allow industrialized farming operations to put profit ahead of farmed animal welfare."[5] Iowa was the first state to impose ag-gag laws, followed by Utah, Missouri, Idaho, Wyoming, and North Carolina, and led the charge to impose criminal penalties on those in violation of the law.[6]

As an anthropologist with permission to be at the packing plant, I was like a "new hire" but not quite, for I wasn't able to actually work the line—though I was standing there watching closely, making mental notes and actual notes in my spiral notebook. My notebook was splattered with blood droplets by the end of the week.

My friendliness, whiteness, and no doubt my Hoosier heritage helped me gain entrance at the plant. My questions were patiently answered and my request to conduct fieldwork research at the plant was granted—a first for an "outsider," the company informed me. What I came away with is a deep understanding—*a story*—of an industry, its employees, and a business that provides hard, bloody work. This work is not for the fainthearted. It is work that literally requires blood and sweat and tears, for killing and processing 1,100 cattle a day is serious and solemn work. Whether we consume meat or not, we should know about the nature of the beast. We should know about the cattle processing industry and the women and men who make it work, because it is a story about what Americans want and about the people who provide it. We should also know more about the animals whose lives are cut short to feed humans. Here is the story of beef and about the people who kill, process, and package it for cookouts and dinners around the world. This is the backstory, the story behind the "Beef, it's what's for dinner" commercial.

Early Riser

It was 6:30 A.M., and I had been in the plant since 5:00 that morning. After I let myself in through the revolving doors with my visitor badge, I walked over to the main plant building and met Mikel "Mike" Gager, an army veteran in his sixties who is the food safety manager and supervisor for IPB's "hot side." We met in in his office on the third floor, and after some slurps of coffee, we suited up in our white frocks (which resemble hospital scrub tops), hairnets (plus a beard net for Mike), earplugs, and helmets. Once we reached the door that would take us "on the floor" of the plant, we sanitized our hands, dipped our boots in the requisite boot sanitizer station, and entered the "hot floor" or "hot side." (As with all businesses and companies, there is an insiders' language, and I had much to learn this week.) The hot floor is also called the slaughter floor, the kill floor, or the harvest or harvesting floor. In the end, the truth is that a live animal has recently been killed, and it is up to the 120 women and men who work on this floor to strip the beast of its hide and to prepare the carcass to be refrigerated for forty-eight hours. The offal, which includes intestines, kidneys, and other parts, will be removed here and cleaned and packaged for use. Intestines, for example, are cleaned and hand-processed by workers and become tripe for dishes like menudo, the popular Mexican stew.

Mike took me on a tour of the hot side before the killing had begun for the day. It was clean—spotless, even—and rather quiet as the employees had yet to filter in. Mike showed me each aspect of the kill floor and pointed out special features such as the self-sanitizing conveyor belt, which moved along primal parts of the meat, and the individual sanitizing stations, where 180-degree water was in constant supply to clean the workers' hooks, knives, and hands. Primal parts are pieces of meat that are separated from an animal's carcass during the slaughter process. Primal cuts of cattle include the chuck, rib, loin, and round. Processing a freshly killed animal is both a science and an art form. Hot side employees have their knives ready to perform their individual tasks, and once the hide is ripped off the body with a huge state-of-the-art machine, known simply as the "hide ripper," the tail is cut and loosened in what is called "bung dropping" and bellies are sliced open and the viscera removed. The blood and guts are washed off the carcass and the tables on a continual basis. Organs are removed and placed on hooks, and the carcass moves along on a specially designed self-sanitizing conveyor belt. The USDA employees on this line wear special white boots, which are designed to be worn on the table, where the employees literally walk around, inspecting the carcass parts.

Slaughter, a.k.a. Knocking

At the crack of dawn, they are brought in by the truckloads before the sun rises and throughout the day. They are dirty from the farms and tired from the journey. The hundreds of Black Angus cattle, both steers (males) and heifers (females) with their distinctive black tongues, will be unloaded into barns near the plant. These massive, powerful creatures are highly prized in the cattle industry for their marbled meat, in particular those that have been corn-fed, which industry insiders say provides the juiciest, most flavorful meat. These animals are expensive and priced according to market value. They will be fed, watered, and checked for any signs of illness by an on-site USDA inspector. There is a detailed and regulatory specific process known as an "ante-mortem inspection" (pre-death), which looks for signs of potential disease among the penned cattle at rest and in motion.[7] There is no place for sick, impaired, or injured cattle here, as the meat would be contaminated and not acceptable for food consumption. If an animal exhibits any signs of being a "downer," or not having the ability to get up or walk, then it will be euthanized, as this indicates illness, and will be sent to the landfill for processing. The cattle that are approved by the USDA inspector will enter into the plant sometime that workday and killed for consumption. The steers and heifers slaughtered on that day will be prepared to enter the massive cooler and will remain there for forty-eight hours, the required amount of time to allow the carcass to chill to prevent bacteria growth.

Most of us know that when we purchase meat and eat it that an animal has been killed. But many of us, especially the majority of us who grew up in urban areas and not around farm animals, don't really make the connection. We may have seen cattle at county or state fairs, but unless we were part of a 4-H club like many rural and small-town children, we lack the experience of growing up around large breed animals. And if we take our children to the grocery store and let them pick out bacon (my own son adores it) or hamburger patties, buying the prepackaged meat in a store far removed from the animal's place of origin inadvertently furthers the divide between animals and ourselves. We reinforce the message that meat is not only *in* the grocery store but that it is *of* it and *from* it. Our urban existences have cut us off from nature and where animals live, the ones that are raised to be consumed. If we eat meat or serve meat to our families and loved ones, then we should acknowledge and think about the fact that a living, breathing creature has given its life for us. If our children ask us about where the meat comes from, we should take the opportunity to explain to them that yes, a creature has died so that we can eat. If we fail to answer them honestly and forthrightly, we further our own and our children's cognitive dissonance between "us" and "them," the nonhuman animals.

Like the swine at Tyson, the cattle that make their way to IPB exist to feed humans. This is the core belief about animals in the protein industry, whether we are talking about chickens, turkeys, hogs, or cattle. Industry CEOs promote the belief that the animals who come to their plants are on earth to make the ultimate sacrifice: to maintain human existence. Protein industry heads like Dave Duncan, Jeffrey Johnson, and Steve Armstrong want to ensure that more humane methods such as knocking, or stunning, are used to kill the beasts, but they do not feel "sorry" that the animals are killed for human consumption, because "that is what their purpose is," as Mike, who led me around IPB's hot side, told me.

After the cattle are cleared by the USDA inspector, they are brought to the loading area that is connected to one end of the plant. This process starts at approximately 6:30 A.M. They are led, one by one, first down and then up a ramp that leads to the containment area. The cattle are in line and spaced apart from each other.

The ritual of killing is a solemn one. Raúl and Edith, the amazingly patient and generous Quality Assurance supervisors whom I shadowed on both the hot and cold sides during my week of observation, brought me up the ladder to the platform over the kill floor to watch. Our eyes met, and we all bowed our heads out of respect. It felt like a holy moment. I found myself whispering a soft prayer of thanks to this creature, whose life was being taken to feed people. Tears rolled down my face, and I felt my throat constrict out of sympathy and empathy for the animal. Its meat would end up on a plate somewhere, and I prayed that whoever tasted this steer's or heifer's meat would give thanks too.

The first thing that I heard when I entered the kill room, or knocking room, was the clicking and whooshing sound of rolling metal from the trolley system moving the cattle upward. The muffled, metallic-sounding "click click click click click click" is a lot like the sound of a rollercoaster, but softer, the metal and moving parts working in tandem to move something toward a destination. The clicking is muffled in accordance with the famous animal behaviorist Temple Grandin's recommendations and protocols for more humane killing of factory animals.

When I was up on the platform, I heard only the quiet moving of the hide against the metal walls around the animal's body. The smell was musky and fecal-tinged. There was no sound from the cow, no crying, just an audible shuffling of the body. Then, in the last seconds, the animal started moving a bit more quickly . . . its body told me, at least, that it *knew*. And that is when I began to cry softly, saying under my breath, "Oh, it knows, it *knows*." Then suddenly, it was over: the knocker "knocked" it in the center of its forehead and it fell over seconds later, on its side. The animals in this process are killed by a captive bolt gun, a pneumatic device that, as Mike informed me, "causes the cattle to be brain-dead and senseless" so that they do not feel any pain.[8]

The ritual knocking is very fast, taking only a matter of seconds. The creature I observed then slumped to the side and began to bleed out, what is called "exsanguination." The blood came from the hole in the animal's head and from its nose. As the now-dead animal moved along the trolley, its body pulsated with energy that was exiting the flesh as the remaining blood was pushed out of the body. The killing technique was also pioneered and championed by Temple Grandin, considered a celebrity at IPB, as many of the workers have met her personally and admire her for her knowledge and plain-spokenness about animals and humans.[9]

The blood ran down the floor and was squeegeed down a large drain by a kill floor worker. It would eventually make blood meal for farmers' fertilizer. The floor was slick with blood and was a dark, blackish red. By the time the carcass reached the end of the slaughter room line, mere minutes later, it was technically dead. A few moments later, another cow took the previous one's place, and the knocking went on all day, until all 1,100 cattle that were penned that morning were killed and were on their way to processing. An intricate process then ensued that transformed the whole, hided body into a hairless, red-and-white, fat-marbled carcass that hung by its Achilles tendon from a large hook. It was quite an engineering sight to behold: a thousand-pound carcass hanging from the strongest tendon in the body. I was told by hot side workers that the Achilles is the toughest tendon and can take the weight of the carcass.

I had never seen the execution of an animal in my life before this, and I can't say I am eager to repeat this experience. But I am grateful—yes, grateful—that I had the experience. I felt that witnessing the killing was a vital component of the research for this book. As difficult and heart-wrenching as it was for me, a vegetarian for the past thirty-plus years, I made myself watch it because I, too—like most of the readers of this book—am part of meat culture. I have made a personal choice to abstain from eating all meat, but I respect my loved ones' wishes to consume it.

Raúl and I talked later about watching the killing and how it affected us.

He asked me if I was "OK," and I said, "Yeah, but it was pretty intense." We talked about our sadness for the animals who were killed for their meat. Even though Raúl has watched cattle die many times at the plant and has been part of the cattle industry for over twenty-five years, it is still hard for him to observe and to process. I wondered aloud if the cattle knew what was going to happen to them. He nodded and said that yes, he thinks they do know. We both looked down, contemplative. He shared a story of growing up in Jalisco, Mexico, and being on his uncle's cattle ranch. "I used to be amazed because when my uncle would call each cow by name, she would run up to him. They know their names and are so smart. I have to think that they know what is happening to them when they are brought here. They are very smart animals."

Hot

It is called the "hot side" for a reason—it is *hot* in here. Damn hot—and steamy. During my visit, it felt like the upper eighties or lower nineties. And the smell was a pungent odor of hot, fresh blood mixed with scalding water. The recently killed, very large hanging animal carcasses were hot. The water used for cleaning and rinsing is always a USDA-mandated 180 degrees Fahrenheit. And the human labor required is very physical, and working bodies emit a lot of heat. While the entire business of slaughtering and boning meat is a very bloody one, the hot room is especially bloody. The carcass is fresh, and the women and men who work on the slaughter floor work amid blood for ten hours a day. It takes a certain kind of person to thrive in the environment, one who can handle a peculiar kind of intensity and massive amounts of blood, fat, and flesh in close quarters while moving at rapid speeds with saws, knives, and hooks.

According to Mike, who referred to himself interchangeably as "an old packinghouse veteran" at IPB, "an old kill floor slug," and "an old industry rat," "the bluntness and honesty on the kill floor is a good thing. We razz each other, yeah, but we have to be a tight-knit group. Kill floor people are definitely can-do people. They buck up and just do it. There's no crying or gnashing of the teeth here, and what we do is very direct." Mike insisted that we shouldn't feel sorry for the animals, because they are "very well treated" and "were born to be eaten." He feels good about this company and his job, because "everything we do is scientific and meets the highest safety standards in the industry."

Hot side workers have job titles that leave little to the imagination—jobs like "hide ripper," "head ripper," "belly ripper," "tongue ripper," "gutter," and "kidney popper." Each worker has a highly specialized job that she or he does day in and day out. And each body part is valuable, whether it is for human or nonhuman consumption.

Mike took me over to metal rows, like small bleachers, where the distinctive black tongues of the cattle are displayed, arched outward. They are highly prized in Japan and are vacuum-sealed and shipped overseas as part of an ever-growing global marketplace in which Iowa and other midwestern states such as Nebraska and Kansas represent the Corn Belt and Midwest in providing food to the world. As in all packing houses, an animal is disassembled into many parts, and companies like IPB strive to waste as little of it as possible. "We are a unique industry, really, because instead of putting something together, we take it apart," said IPB's chief safety officer, Sue, affectionately called "Safety Sue" by her coworkers. Indeed, what happens is a kind of bloody magic.

The hot side, also called the slaughter side and the kill floor, is an extreme place, and the workers there do not back down from the intensity. Sixtysomething Mike, for instance, is no stranger to situations deemed to be hard-core. He prides himself on being an "old industry guy" and sports tatted-up forearms and a nicotine-enhanced gravelly voice. He has seen a lot of the world and is no stranger to blood and violence. He is a proud veteran of "Nam," but he said he's seen a lot of things he wishes he could un-see. Mike unwinds from work and the grind of daily life by competing in rifle competitions. "I'm not bragging or anything, but I'm a pretty good shot." Turns out, Mike is a nationally ranked small-bore range shooter. He and his wife travel around the country for competitions. Mike said his youngest—whom he affectionately called "Tailpipe" "because she was the last one, you know. No more after her!"— is a naturally gifted shooter, but she hates competing.

As we stood outside the plant in the designated smoking area, sleet was starting to come down hard. But Mike is a lifelong smoker and needs his "nicotine diet" in order to keep going, so we stayed until his craving was satisfied. He quit once, in 2013, and stayed smoke-free for three months, but one day at a gas station he spotted his favorite cigarettes and bought a pack, thinking he could just stop at one. "Well, hell, by the middle of my drive I had smoked the whole damn pack!" he laughs. He soon stopped for another pack of his favorite Marlboro unfiltereds, also known as "one humps" because "well, hell, you know, there's just no going back from there." Mike loves the intensity of the unfiltereds and said that "there's nothing like it," but he rarely smokes them these days, opting for the filtereds because he knows the unfiltereds are "real, *real* bad for me."

So much for quitting, especially in this demanding industry where you need to be constantly alert. We ended up going outside for three smoke breaks that day, and he smoked another cigarette in the truck on our way to visit the water treatment center. After spending a week in the plant, I totally understood why one would smoke, and that's coming from someone who has never smoked a day in her life. The secondhand smoke I inhaled that day probably gave me the energy boost I needed to get through the day. And after the long week, I realized that I actually really like the smell of a just-lit cigarette. There is something about the smell of the tobacco and fire that is deeply appealing.

Some plant workers start work at 4:00 A.M. These are the employees who move the cold carcasses out of the chiller so that fresh carcasses can be moved in to chill for the required forty-eight hours. These workers— almost all men—use a chain system to move the heavy cold carcasses from the chiller directly to the USDA employee who grades the meat. After the carcass is graded with a purple stamp, the meat moves to the fabrication side, also called the cold side, where it will be deboned and cut into what are called "subprimal parts": the cut and packaged meat that we find in grocery stores and restaurants.

Women of the Hot Side

Mike told me he is quite proud of the fact that it is a group of younger women who rule the floor on the hot side. He hopes that by the time he retires, one of these will have his current job of hot side supervisor. "It's all about science," said Mike, who holds a B.S. in meat studies from Kansas State University. Kelsey, his right-hand food safety employee, is a recent Iowa State University graduate and has her B.S. in animal science. Like Mike, Kelsey has taken many chemistry courses and continues to take courses on food safety and hazard analysis in order to stay current with industry standards. IPB operates under the Global Food Safety System, and all of the food safety employees, like Mike and Kelsey, make sure to keep their credentials fresh by participating in continuing education seminars and courses online and at conferences. IPB is also part of the British Retail Consortium, and all of the eight food safety workers in Mike's department must be up to date on the requirements. "There's nine of us total, and we're a crackerjack crew. We work very hard, and we have to communicate regularly and directly for everything to run smoothly," said Mike. Each area of the kill floor has its own standard operating procedures (SOPs), and the food safety workers must know these standards and convey them to the line workers. The food safety workers must ensure that the live animal that comes in—covered in hair, dirt, and bacteria—is transformed into a bacteria-free and sterile carcass that is ready to be cut and packaged.

During my observation week, Kelsey walked the hot side, making sure that workers were following the SOPs for their division. As I shadowed her, we stood next to heads and tongues as they were cut off and out, and then we moved to the offal area, where carcass parts such as the tail were put in their respective bins. It was quite a sight to behold, as the individual tails quivered with the energy that remained in them. Large bins of mouths, recently re-moved with wizard knives, stood next to the tail bins. As I looked over to in-spect them, I saw that some of the lips also quivered with energy, as their tail counterparts did. It was surreal to contemplate the energy that resides in the animals' bodies. Hearts and livers, quite recently pulsating and beating with life, moved slowly by on large hooks, and some appeared to be moving, still full of energy from the formerly live animal that housed them. The tongues were cut out and cleaned and would be chilled overnight. The next day, they would be vacuum-sealed for a long shelf life.

On this day, it was Jessica's job to test bacteria levels each hour and to send the results to the IEH Laboratory and Consulting Group in the back of the plant. Throughout her shift, Jessica swabbed random hides, carcasses, and parts and sent the samples to the lab, where all of the information was entered into the computer system for analysis. Microbiological testing is industry standard, and Jessica is part of a cadre of workers who test for *E. coli* O157:H7 levels throughout each workday. While generic *Escherichia coli* (*E. coli*) bacte-ria are an essential but typically harmless element that exists within the diges-tive tract of healthy animals and humans, according to the North American Meat Institute, *E. coli* O157:H7 is a "virulent strain of the family of generic bacteria that is found in cattle, deer and other warm-blooded animals." Food safety protocols and technologies used in the meat industry today has proven to be highly effective, and *E. coli* 0157:H7 is removed during the processing and is "found in ground beef less than one third of one percent of the time."[10]

In addition to the carcasses, Jessica also tested the giant bins of beef trim-mings to make sure that the meat was safe and checked the water to make sure that it was at the industry-required 180 degrees Fahrenheit. "We actually run the water closer to 194 degrees, a little higher than industry standards," Mike told me later. IPB must be obsessed with food safety, as contaminated meat would ruin the company. Concentrated chlorinated water is at each knife station for line workers to dip their knives into, and they rinse their blades in the scalding water. The water is recycled in the plant and is kept at the requisite temperature, thanks to the two boilers that continuously run.

Jessica told me that she is engaged in what is called "process monitoring," a system in which various checkpoints are visited and tested throughout the day. "So we take a sterile sponge with a buffer solution and we swipe the carcass with the hide on and with the hide off at various points during the day. We want to give ourselves snapshots of the bacterial reduction." Jessica and Kelsey stressed how much science goes into what they do and how important it is to ensure the safety of the food product and the safety of the consumer who will eat the product. A minimum of sixty surface samples are taken each day, a number that is deemed "scientifically relevant." The lab will enrich the samples using a system called PCR, polymer chain reaction. "Basically, if there's bacteria there, we want to verify that it is there, and if it is there, we will kill it. It is all about the pH and making the surface of whatever it is—meat, knife, etcetera, inhospitable to bacteria."

During my time on the hot side, one of the boilers went out, and the line was shut down for just under fifteen minutes. Once it was fixed and checked by a qualified technician, the plant was up and running again. To ensure that the raw meat was thoroughly bacteria-free, USDA-approved lactic acid was sprayed on the meat as it went through the line toward its destination in the chiller. As Jessica walked quickly through the hot side on her rounds checking for bacteria, Kelsey inspected each station and made sure that the individual SOPs were being followed. She checked off boxes on her worksheet, which she would enter into the computer system later. As I stood next to her, we watched the hides being ripped from the still-hot carcasses, "like a banana being peeled," she observed out loud. This part of the line is called the "skinny line," and it is where the carcass hangs by an Achilles tendon, the "toughest ligament in its body," I was told by several workers.

Eloida, a young and vivacious young Latina in her early twenties, is the plant's main dentician. Her job is to inspect the teeth of each carcass to rule out bovine spongiform encephalopathy (BSE), also known as mad cow disease. Cattle that are over thirty months old are more susceptible to BSE, and a telltale sign, in addition to lethargy when it is alive, is three front teeth on top instead of two. If three teeth are detected, the carcass is deemed unfit for human consumption and is marked for incineration at the landfill. As I watched, Eloida, wearing blue latex gloves, expertly and deftly swiped the inside of each carcass's mouth. After each mouth swipe, she managed to gracefully do a 180-degree turn and wash her hands off in the hot running water, ready to inspect the next head. I was fascinated with her grace and precision. I was told by Kelsey that Eloida did not start at the plant as a dentician but that she is "the best" and has a perfect record so far. Like Kelsey and Jessica, Eloida is petite, and I marveled at her resilience and strength. Her job, like all jobs here on the kill floor, is hot, bloody, and invasive. For hours on end, Eloida stands and inspects the insides of carcasses' mouths for disease, and she must be efficient as well as careful. Mike said she is "one of the best" he's ever seen and that she is "a natural" at the job, much better than her predecessor.

Eloida patiently showed me the intricacies of her job. I followed her over to the carcass, whose mouth was open. I was amazed by how deftly and quickly she worked. There is no wasted time, no lag time for her. As she waits for each carcass to reach her work area, she washes her hands thoroughly. When it arrives, she checks the mouth of each and every carcass. Eloida plays a key role in ruling out any and all carcasses that might be carriers of the dreaded and deadly BSE virus. She spends a little extra time on the ones that are marked as "30 plus," as older steers tend to exhibit the disease at higher rates.

Cattle thirty months or older are treated with special care and discernment. The carcass's backbone is spray-painted a bright pink to indicate that it is a "30 plus" animal and that specific parts are to be removed and disposed of. Even if there are no detected issues with the teeth, the entire skull (including the brain), eyes, spinal cord, vertebral column, backbone, ganglia, and trigeminal ganglia are all removed and incinerated, as BSE can live in these parts. I learned that the tonsils are removed from all cattle, regardless of their age. The company errs on the side of caution, as detection of BSE would ruin the company and put all of the employees out of work.

If Eloida detects a carcass with BSE, she stamps it with a bright purple "MC," for "Mad Cow," stamp. During my time shadowing her, she did not detect any BSE. I marveled at this young woman who carried so much responsibility. Eloida seemed completely unfazed by her job, a difficult and grotesque task. She constantly washed her hands, wiped her face with paper towels that are in ample supply, and smiled. I was amazed at how unruffled she appeared, in her bright emoji-printed bandanna tucked neatly under her hard hat. For next to her work area was a large drain through which blood, flesh, hair, and teeth flowed. She and the other workers around her seemed impervious to the carnage that was all around them.

Mike and his kill-floor food-safety staff touch base throughout the day, meeting several times to go over the day's results. For his part, Mike checks the USDA website regularly, looking for notifications and any changes in directives. "There's just a ton of regulations, and we absolutely have to be on top of them. It is a continual process, that is for sure, and my job is to make sure we are always in compliance. We are in communication with each other all the time. Communication is really the number one thing here. We have to talk *to* and *with* our employees—not *at* them—and I believe that what you do matters, not just what you say, you know?" Mike drove home the importance of each and every worker: "Each job and each person is vital to the functioning of our business and what we are trying to achieve, whether we are talking about Mr. Johnson or the worker who cleans the drains in the basement."

The kill floor is a hive of activity. Mostly African and Latino men and women work alongside each other, mindful of their own task but also of their coworkers next to them. The work is careful, meticulous, and quick. I watched for hours and gained an appreciation for the craft of working on the slaughter floor. The women and men on this side must ensure that the recently killed animal is de-hided, gutted, beheaded, cut in half, and eviscerated before the carcass can enter the blast chiller for two days. Most of the work is done by skilled hands, but some is done by machines. The hide ripping is done by machines, but it is not always done perfectly. When I was on the floor, I saw several hides that were partially ripped, and workers had to cut and remove the rest by hand. Sometimes the horns did not come off, and a few times the hide was left on the head. It is up to the highly skilled employees to quickly and efficiently remove the remaining hide and horns—whatever was missed by the errant machines.

One sight that will stay with me was the four individuals who used electric saws to cut the carcasses in half. They moved gracefully, up and down, to a rhythmic beat. One of the four was a tiny Sudanese woman, beautiful and strong, wearing a colorful kente cloth head wrap underneath her helmet. Our eyes met, and I smiled at her slightly. I tried hard to show respect and appreciation for her and for what she was doing. I found myself amazed by the work that she did. Her arms were muscled, chiseled, like the arms of the three men who worked with her. She was the lone woman in this part of the kill floor, and she held her own. In my fieldnotes I had jotted "badass" next to my observations.

In an age when many of us are being told to stand more and sit less at work, the women and men on the hot side are ahead of the game. They take only short breaks throughout the day to rest their limbs and exchange soiled work garb for clean smocks and gloves after breaks. I found myself wondering how many steps an average worker would take during a typical shift on the kill floor. 20,000? 30,000? All of the workers appeared to be physically fit.

So much blood. It ran down the animals' bodies, out of their mouths, and onto the floor that was already covered in running blood. So much water. The water washed away the blood, out of the mouths, off the bodies, onto the floor, and down the drain, where it flowed to the basement. I wondered what it was like in the basement—and soon found out. It felt like descending into a kind of hell. All of the animal waste was pushed from the various drains down a giant chute to the basement. It smelled like nothing I had ever smelled before, a terrible mixture of excrement, intestines, blood, hair, flesh. This was the first time I felt like throwing up, but I kept it together and willed myself to not get sick. We were in what Mike called "the bowels of the plant." Literally. I felt as though I was in a giant toilet. It was worse than anything I have smelled in my life.

Safety First

She is known as "Safety Sue" to her coworkers. Susan Munhusen has been with the plant since its opening, and her job is to ensure that the plant is operating according to Occupational Safety and Health Administration, or OSHA, standards. She started in the meat industry at the age of sixteen, when she worked in the receiving part of a packing plant, where farmers brought carcasses to be processed. After she graduated from high school, Sue attended Iowa State University and graduated with a B.S. in meat science. Like others on the management team, Sue started on the floor and worked her way up. Sue referred to IPB as "the start-up of all start-ups." "When the company first opened, we had 100 employees, and now we have, just a little over three years later, 880 employees!" Sue is proud to have been there from the beginning and takes great pride in her work.

Unlike other meatpacking plants that have a parent company, IPB, she pointed out, is "on its own." "We have models for how we want to be like Creekstone, but unlike most packing plants, we have no sister company to call to consult if and when something goes wrong or we need advice." Being a start-up has its advantages, too, but in the early days, Sue said she and everyone else "pretty much lived at work." While most workers' jobs are focused on one or two skilled tasks that they hone through hours upon hours of work, Sue's job is multifaceted. She makes sure that all of the new hires are properly trained in food safety and worker safety, which means that she spends a lot of time each week with them. She typically works eighty hours a week, something she doesn't bat an eye at, she said, because she has done it for so long that anything less seems strange.

Sue, now in her midfifties, reflected on the realities and challenges of gender and work, especially for women. She told me that she had been raised with the belief that "women can do it all" but that in many ways, this belief had hurt her. "I mean, here I was, working eighty-plus hours a week when my kids were young, and one day I just turned to my husband in tears and said, 'Why did we even have kids?' I mean, they were being raised by a nanny. We were never around because all we did was work." So Sue made the decision to work from home as a consultant while her children were in school. It was the best solution for the time, she said, because she was able to keep contributing financially to the family and also be there for her kids more. Like many women of that generation, her own mother had been a stay-at-home mom. "She was able to cook, clean, take care of the children. She could really focus and do all of those things well. I tried to do all of that—cooking homemade meals, cleaning, being there for my kids—while working the hours I was working, and it just wasn't possible to do it all." Sue considers herself a feminist but said that women have to be realistic and not put so much pressure on themselves to be and do everything. She said she felt let down by the feminist movement, which she thinks "kind of lied" to women by telling them they could do it all.

Sue is an open and direct speaker and draws upon these skills to address the new hires frankly about the realities of their new jobs. She told me that she wants to be "completely up front" about the dangers of the job and about how workers can keep themselves and their coworkers safe. During the orientation that I participated in, Sue instructed us to always use the handrails, wear nonslip boots, make sure cuts are properly cleaned at the nurse's office, and to report all injuries, no matter how small. "Even a small cut can get infected and turn into sepsis if you do not report it and have it treated right away." She told our group of new hires, "I would rather write someone up or fire them for violating safety standards than have to call their family and tell them you are not coming home."

Sue trained us to use a fire extinguisher properly and schooled us in the acronym LOTO, short for "lock out, tag out." We were shown a video with proper LOTO technique, and Sue handed us Jolly Ranchers to make sure we were awake and paying attention. The sugar rush was intentional, and we all popped the hard sour-sweet candies into our mouths. As we watched the short instructional film and listened to Sue's explanations, it was clear to the group that in the event of a machine malfunction or breakdown, we were to notify our supervisors and have the impaired machine tagged so that it would not be used until it was properly fixed. Sue said she doesn't like to tell "horror stories," as she called them, but she did share one story of an employee at another plant where she previously worked who did not follow proper LOTO procedure and was electrocuted. "He tried to take a shortcut, and he died. Please don't take any shortcuts!" Sue told us that IPB had gone through six managers who did not follow LOTO procedures. "We are strict here, but it is the best policy because we want our workers safe and alive. The machines are dangerous, and we need to acknowledge that." She briefly referred to a safety-related fatality at IPB in 2014, when a worker disregarded proper operating procedure and fell into an auger. "He died instantly," she told us, letting it sink in for effect.

We learned all about the fluids that make the plant run. We were taught the intricacies of anhydrous ammonia usage and why it is preferred for cooling carcasses in cold storage and for keeping the raw meat cold in fabrication on the cold side. IPB's entire cooling stem runs on anhydrous ammonia, and so far, it has never leaked. Sue told us that when the plant was purchased and renovated for IPB's use and ownership, all of the pipes were replaced. But she told us the warning signs of an ammonia leak: watering eyes, tingling skin, and a strong odor. "Get out" if any of those symptoms arise, she said. There had never been a leak in the plant's short history, but she wanted to prepare all workers just in case.

Sue also went over PPE, personal protective equipment. All employees are to inspect their equipment each day and to make sure they are clean and properly functioning. All workers are required to wear one of three types of hearing protection: foam earplugs, rubber earplugs, or earmuffs (which look like Beats headphones). The rubber earplugs edge out the foam by a few decibels as the best in ear protection. As Sue passed out our earplugs, I asked for a pair of purple rubber plugs. We were also shown some ergonomic and stretching exercises to do with our hands, to keep them limber and strong. "Our goal is to make the job fit the person so that you, the worker, can stay in a neutral position," Sue told us.

Sue told me when we talked during a break that this is a good company and a good job but that "it is not perfect." She told me that her husband had quit the week earlier but didn't share any details. He had been the head of the international floor, where meat is processed and packaged for special orders. What she did share was that "it was time for a change. He is currently exploring other options." She wanted to talk more, but we did not have much private space or time to talk. She said that if she could change something about the plant, it would be the distribution center, which she thinks is "far too close" to the plant.

Kelsey was my intrepid guide for a good part of a day at the plant. Kelsey was confident and assured on the floor, and I watched as she navigated the blood, carcasses, and many moving parts on the hot side. I did my best to follow in her footsteps, quite literally. I felt clunky by comparison, my new Caterpillar steel-toed boots heavy and slow.

Kelsey is at the plant six days a week, from 7:00 to 5:30. She lives a fifteen-minute drive away in a home she and her husband recently purchased. Currently, Kelsey told me, 150 head of cattle are processed each hour, and she and Mike have put in a request for one more USDA person to be on the hot side so they can push production to 160 head an hour. There are currently seven USDA women and men on the line, and this would put them at eight USDA employees to oversee the kill floor. Kelsey took me through the intricacies of the kill floor, where I watched the hide ripping, gut ripping, tongue cutting, head cutting, and the sawing in half of carcasses. The work on the hot side is intense, and workers must move quickly to inhibit bacterial growth. At the end of the hot side line is a carcass that has been deboned, gutted, and prepared for the chiller, where it will remain for two days, after which it's moved to the cold side.

As we stood next to each other and watched the complex and multipart process, Kelsey pointed out the sweetbreads, which are removed from the neck and are considered a delicacy. During my visit, Kelsey was preparing for a plant-wide audit. She had a lot of paperwork to do and a lot of monitoring. During the audit, a third party will inspect all of the paperwork and will watch employees while they work—kind of like what I was doing in my role as an ethnographer, I thought.

Cold

The motto on the fabrication floor, also called fab, the cold floor, boning, or just plain old "cold," is "first in, first out." What this means is that the carcasses that have been chilling in the thirty-four-degree cooler for forty-eight hours must be moved out when the fab floor workers start their shift at 4:15 each morning. Once the chilled carcasses are moved out of the massive cooler, the live cattle that are waiting outside the plant in the barn pens can begin to be moved in for the knocking/stunning/killing/slaughtering.

Iowa Premium Beef purchases cattle from 350 family farms in Iowa and surrounding Corn Belt states. A day on the cold side involves moving carcasses from the giant cooler, also known as the blast chiller, carcass cooler, or hot box, to a worker who wields a saw and cuts through the side of the carcass to expose the thirteenth rib, which is the area the USDA inspector checks to grade the meat. Another worker checks the rib cut and trims it a bit more if the marbling needs to be exposed more. Roger Verhoesen, a meat industry veteran of over thirty years, runs this part of the plant's production and told me that the point of all of this is to get the meat color to "bloom"—to get that nice red coloring—and for the fat to be seen by the USDA inspector. Like everyone else I met and talked with at IPB, Roger is a big fan of Black Angus meat. "Corn-fed Black Angus beef is simply the best source of protein out there," Roger told me as we stood in the hot box watching the giant carcasses move by us on the trolley system. Roger waxed poetic about the various cuts of meat that would be cut in fabrication: ribeye strip from the hindquarters; filet mignon, which lies encased in fat up against the backbone. Filet mignon is particularly tender because it is the least used muscle, he told me. Roger loves his job and is proud of the work that he oversees at the plant. "We have high quality materials here. We break it into amazing parts, and we sell the best beef in the country. We also provide stable jobs to a lot of people." Each morning, six days a week, Roger gets up at 3:00 A.M., drives to work, and is on the line supervising at 4:15.

I learned that fat is good, but it has to be the right kind of fat in the meat. It's all about the marbling and where the marbling is in relation to the flesh. A fattened-up steer or heifer doesn't always produce the best meat, as what matters is fat on the inside, not the outside, of the animal's carcass. It is the inside fat, the marbled fat within the meat, that is considered good fat. The bad fat is the kind that just adds weight to the cattle for purposes of sale—akin to what humans might call "love handles" or a "muffin top." Roger wanted to make sure that I understand good fat versus bad fat in cuts of meat: "Some farmers, you see, they try to fatten up their cattle to get the best market price, but all of that fat is trimmed away and is basically expensive fat that we waste and that we paid for and then have to pass on that cost to our consumer. Consumers don't want to purchase a fatty cut of meat. What they want is the fat marbling that is inside the cut, because that is the fat that gives the meat the tender, flavorful taste we love."

I asked Roger whether they can determine if cattle have been deliberately fattened up, and he chuckled and said, "No, but I wish we had a way to non-invasively see inside the cattle to determine where the fat is . . . on the outside or inside." If the company determines that cattle from a particular farm has been fattened up, the farmer will be approached and told that his cattle will be discounted the next purchase time because the fat was outside layer fat and not inside marbling fat.

During my observation week, I was able to get up close and personal with the hanging carcasses in the USDA inspection area and to see how one of the USDA employees works. Brent has been a USDA inspector for forty years, and to say that he is highly skilled at his job is an understatement. I watched as he examined the thirteenth rib area and determined what grade the meat was. He then stamped the carcass, in purple ink, with the designation choice, prime, or select. I found out that what determines the grade is the pattern of marbling inside the meat. I watched closely as Brent rolled the stamp onto the carcass to see how he assigned it to one of the three main categories. He was a very good teacher, and after an hour or so shadowing him, I thought I had the hang of it. My determinations were pretty darn close to what Brent's were, give or take a choice for a prime and prime for a choice here and there. Brent said that even though a USDA meat grades chart hangs on the wall behind him, he doesn't need to consult it anymore because he's been doing his job for so long that he knows the cut after looking at it for a few seconds.

Brent is a Kansas State graduate and grew up on a cattle ranch in western Kansas. He had planned on taking over the family business, but when the market crashed in 1973, he decided to work in the "other side" of the beef industry. He starts his work each day at 4:00 A.M. and doesn't stop until the last carcass is graded and stamped. It is a long day of standing in the cold, looking at carcasses, and grading them for the market.

Each carcass is tagged with its "hot weight" before it enters the cooler. Inside the cooler, the carcass will shrink and lose some weight, and in order to keep the meat from getting a bit dry, cold water is applied to it. Cold water brings down the temperature of the carcass and minimizes bacteria growth. The carcasses are organized in rows: prime in one row; Est8, IPB's boutique brand sold to restaurants, in another; choice in another line. I saw all men in the hot box, white, African, and Latino. Roger told me that the harder jobs are done by younger men. These jobs also pay more, he said, and "a lot of these guys have families, so it works out well for them."

When we walked out of the cooler to the line, Roger pointed out the "black hats," men who wear black helmets that indicate they have the hardest jobs. Roger has worked most jobs on the line. He started working in the packing industry, like most of his management coworkers, on the floor. I asked Roger what his favorite job in the line was and why, and he instantly responded, "Boning chucks and ribs—it is actually fun to do. I know that sounds weird, but I really enjoyed both jobs."

As Roger surveyed the cold floor, he talked about how important it is to be transparent with me so that I can convey the company's practices to the public, "because today's generation wants to know where their food comes from.

We want to highlight our practices, which we believe are the best in the industry, from start to finish. We stand on a platform where we can view the fabrication lines and the workers busily cutting and trimming various cuts of meat." Roger pointed out the Quality Control employees, the "orange hats," who, like the Quality Control workers on the hot side, scanned the cuts of meat with experienced eyes. They hooked the cuts that needed more trimming or that did not look up to the company's standard. As the cuts went by on the line, Roger gave me an explanation of what they were and where the market is for the cut. The beef short plate cut is an export item, popular in South Korea, Hong Kong, Japan, and China. The rib eyes, prime rib, and chuck tenders are popular in the United States, as they are "center of the plate" meats. As we watched the red meat move below us, Roger provided a comparative analysis of American tastes and Pacific Rim countries' tastes. "In the United States, meat eaters tend to have meat at the center of the meal. Everything else is a complement or a condiment to the meat. In Pacific Rim countries, rice is at the center of the diet, and the meat is a complement to the rice. It is among other complementary foods to the rice. We also eat more meat in the U.S. In Japan, for example, the average citizen eats much less meat than we do, and the cuts themselves are smaller."

I saw how technology aids the processing of meat. At every stage, from live animal to packaged and boxed meat, the meat is weighed. The company is able to see how much is wasted at each phase. From the live weight to the hot weight, the cold weight, and the packaged weight, the carcass is gauged for waste, and the goal is to maximize use of the animal. Even the offal is calculated. Everything is computerized, and it is Roger's job each morning to go over the previous day's yields. Management meetings occur each morning and at intervals throughout the day, as it is important to the success of the company for its management to be "on the same page," as Roger put it.

At each stage, supervisors watch the workers as they hook, cut, and slice, and they intervene when they see that the meat is not being cut properly. The goal is worker safety, food safety, and a premium product. As we stood over the fab line, Roger pointed out a too-fatty cut of meat and said that because the outer fat wasn't cut close enough to the flesh on the hot side, the fab side worker must now do the extra work and slow down his productivity as well as the line's flow. What is clear is that each worker is an important part of the overall running and functioning of the line. Workers must do their jobs quickly and effectively so that they keep the line moving. And sometimes, because they are working at a quick pace, they miss all of the fat that someone else down the line has to fix.

Roger, who has worked in the pork industry as well, said pork processing is "much more automated" than is the beef industry, where most everything is done by hand. My tours of both pork and beef plants confirmed his observation and analysis. "What we have here in the plant are highly skilled butchers. Almost everything, save for the vacuum-sealed packaging, is done by hand, and even then, it is workers' hands that make sure the packaging goes smoothly." Like Mike on the hot side, Roger is proud to be overseeing a talented crew of workers.

As we moved into the round area, where round steaks are cut, something happened that stopped the line. As the Latino worker cut into the meat with his saw, a hidden abscess was struck, and yellowish ooze sprayed onto the floor. I was amazed by how much fluid emitted from the carcass. The workers' reactions were swift and professional. Roger jumped in to supervise, and immediately the carcass was removed and all of the equipment—saws, knives, hooks—and the floor were hosed off with scalding water. Workers hosed off their heavy plastic frock covers and boots. Gloves were exchanged for disinfected ones. From my outside observer's perspective, the situation seemed to be handled effectively.

Yet as I took notes, which I had been given explicit permission to do, Roger looked over to me and said, "I don't think you want that in your book, do you?" I looked up, surprised. I held my pen in midair, not quite knowing what to do. I nodded and stopped writing. I realized that despite my assurances that I was not intending to write an exposé of the meat industry, the fact was that I was seeing everything in the plant. My presence put folks on edge, and despite their friendliness and helpfulness, it hit me that I could be a danger to them and to the other workers. Folks here were understandably worried about my angle. Yet if consumers of meat want to know where their meat comes from, they should know that abscesses in meat happen. Roger admitted that it is impossible to catch everything all the time, but when a problem emerges, workers take care of it right away. Animals' bodies are prone to disease and decay, like all flesh and blood.

In this case and in this plant, the emergency situation was handled swiftly and effectively. Safety and order were maintained. I had been told for the past two days during orientation that IPB operates under strict USDA and OSHA guidelines and is ever mindful of them, and I saw this in action. The fact that this plant is considered a small one is to the workers' and consumers' benefit. Those in management are proud of being small, as it provides them with what they see as higher levels of quality control. The management team get to know the workers, and the line supervisors know all of the employees who work for them. The small size of the plant, coupled with the low worker-to-management ratio, is a recipe for a safe plant and product. This is the theory and, from what I observed all week, a reality. At several points in our time spent together, Roger turned to me and spoke very highly of the refugees. "With the refugees, their work ethic is ingrained in them. They work hard for good pay, and they are happy to make a good living working here." He said that what he does at the plant is far less important than what the line workers—mostly Latino and African—do, because what they do is the most important job of all.

CHAPTER 7

Fulfilling Dreams

P LACE MATTERS. What makes a place a home—a house? A yard for children to play in? A church to attend? For the 76 Township Catholics, the women and men who continue to work to ensure that their Irish Catholic legacy lives on in Ardon, Iowa, place matters very much. While St. Malachy parish was decommissioned by the diocese many years ago and is no longer technically a "church," what matters to the rural township's settler families is that the memory lives on and that the parish is maintained. The building is cleaned and lovingly maintained by members of the St. Malachy Preservation Society. Former members of the parish mow the lawn, weed the flower beds, and polish the pews each spring. The annual steeplechase run provides funds for the physical maintenance, and the Christmas service attracts hundreds of people. Though decommissioned, it will remain a living, sacred place for as long as it is remembered and maintained. It is the heart of an Irish Catholic community that is still very much alive. And it represents the perseverance and tenacity of hardworking farmers, a rural people.

We may read a lot about the virtues of white Europeans who settled the "New World" after making their transatlantic voyages and leaving their countries of origin. While the vast majority remained in the urban milieus in which they landed, others ventured into the country and less-populated places in territories that became the states of Iowa, Nebraska, Kansas, and Illinois. These Irish, Czech, German, and Bohemian women and men farmed, brewed beer, went to church, and raised their families. They were ministered to by their priests and pastors, and they were buried in cemeteries near their churches. They made their homes in the Corn Belt and defined the "heartland" from the late nineteenth century to the mid-twentieth century. They

were entrepreneurial and made their homes in sparsely populated rural locales that dotted the midwestern frontier. And importantly, these folks were
not just passing through; they literally put down their roots, and in many
cases, their great-grandchildren today farm the land they first tilled years ago.

America's story of migration, settlement, and making new homes can
be seen afresh today when we look at recent arrivals to the Corn Belt. The
story of Latinos—primarily women and men of Mexican descent, the first
non-European migrants to move to the Corn Belt from Mexico and Central
America in the mid-twentieth century—is remarkably similar to that of white
ethnics in regard to the factors pushing and pulling them to migrate. Like
their white ethnic counterparts of the late nineteenth century, Latinos who
came to the Midwest, and who continue to come, left economic uncertainty
at best and poverty and violence at worst to come to a place where jobs ex-
isted and opportunities beckoned. While many white Europeans planted
crops and churches, Latinos came to work as agricultural workers and in the
meatpacking plants that continue to dot the rural landscape. The midwestern
Corn Belt region has welcomed these newer immigrant groups and families,
and most are opting to stay. Making a home for their families is the number
one priority for the Latino, Chin Burmese, and African refugees who came
to the Corn Belt for work. The Midwest is the answer to the dream of owning
a house, having a grass-filled yard for their kids, and a stable job. For some,
this new home in the Corn Belt also means a church or mosque that attends
to spiritual and religious needs.

While the meatpacking plants were the primary economic pull factor for
the majority of immigrants and refugees who came to places like Iowa, Illinois, Nebraska, and Kansas, some immigrants and their families are able
to break the cycle of working at packing plants. Some open their own businesses; others become the first in their families to attend college and pursue
a job *not* at the town's packing plant. Women and men like Brenda, José, and
Adela are challenging the stereotypes of Latinos and are adding their talents
to America's long history of entrepreneurs. They are here to stay.

Brenda: Future Immigration Lawyer

She is a devout Catholic and young mother of two little girls, ages one and two
at the time we met for lunch at the Marshalltown, Iowa, Perkins restaurant.
Brenda is the first person in her extended Mexican-descent family to graduate from college. She is also one of the first "to not have to," in her words,
work at the local pork processing plant, JBS, formerly known as Swift. Brenda

graduated in May 2018 with a major in political science and minors in history and Latin American studies. When we met, she planned on taking some time off to work for a local law firm that specializes in immigration law and hoped to attend law school at either Drake University or the University of Iowa within a few years.

Born in Watsonville, California, to undocumented Mexican parents, Brenda is the second of five children. Her mother, Yolanda, hails from Nayarit, near the tourist destination of Guadalajara, and crossed over to the States to work in agriculture and restaurants—whatever work she could find. For Yolanda, sending money home each month to her own mother was important to help her raise Brenda's older sister, who was born in California and who spent her first eight years in Mexico with her *abuela*. Yolanda would return to see her mother and daughter as often as possible, but it was risky, given her immigration status. She sent money regularly and worked as many hours as she could physically work. She met Javier, the man who would become Brenda's and her younger brother's father, and when the children were toddlers, they talked about moving from the increasingly expensive California valley. Yolanda desperately wanted to be with her older daughter and to bring her to the States from Mexico, and so they decided that the family of five would move to rural Iowa, a state neither Yolanda nor Javier had been to. They had heard of it from Javier's brother, who was living in a small town called Marshalltown and working with his wife at the local pork plant. For most Latinos in Iowa, neither the state nor the Midwest is the first place of entry in the United States. It is often the second or third location of residence, and this is almost always because of work.

For Brenda's parents, Marshalltown was their second U.S. home, and they moved there to work at the Swift pork processing plant, which was hiring in the late 1990s. Brenda was a toddler when the family moved to rural Iowa in 1999. While Brenda's memories of her life pre-Iowa are almost nonexistent, she said, her memories of Iowa begin with the "big green house" the family moved into. It was her uncle's home, her father's brother, and in total there were ten individuals, two families, living in the house. "I remember this house as a huge house. It was green, and there was a large, very green backyard. My parents, brother, sister, and I lived in the small part of the house that was an add-on, and my uncle and his family lived in the main part. I have very happy memories of living in this house, my first Iowa home."

Within a few years, her parents had saved enough money from their jobs at Swift to purchase a home near the plant, in a Latino-majority neighborhood known as "Woodbury." They could see the plant from their home, and her parents could walk to work. Brenda remembers lots and lots of white clothes that her mother washed each week at the laundromat; they were the smocks from Swift, which employees were responsible for washing and bringing back to work each week. Her parents were both line workers, and each night her mom would bring out her work knife and sharpen it. "She was very conscientious about keeping that knife sharp, and she said her job was easier with a very sharp knife." Brenda also recalled the trucks that would come in and out of the plant all day long. "I remember the trucks and the terrible smell. That area smells so bad, and it still does today."

As we ate our lunch, Brenda reflected on the hard work her parents did at the plant. "My mom always used to tell us kids, 'I work here so that you do not have to.'" As she talked about her mother, Brenda got choked up and wiped away tears. She paused for a moment and said, "My mother has always worked so hard for us. She has sacrificed so much in her life, and she has never complained. I love her so much and am committed to taking care of her as she gets older."

The stresses of work, providing for three young children, and living in a foreign country was too much for Javier, though, and he left the family and returned to central Mexico, where he lives today. Somehow, Yolanda was able to provide for her children on her Swift wages. She went on to have two more children, with little to no assistance from their fathers. Not long after Javier left, Yolanda quit her job at Swift for a waitressing job at a popular local Mexican restaurant. She was starting to worry about the company's increased scrutiny of background checks and feared that her undocumented status would be discovered. When she was offered a job at the restaurant she jumped at the chance and was able to make a decent living for her young family, said Brenda. "When we were little my mom would bring us to work with her at the restaurant because we had no babysitter. We would draw, color, and fold napkins for her when she was working her shift. I liked going to work with her, and saw myself as going to work, too." She has fond memories of summer days when she and her brother would eat lunch at their mom's restaurant and walk down the street to the library, where she would read, help the librarian translate for Spanish-speaking patrons, and, as she grew older, catalog books.

Brenda credits her mom for being an incredible role model. "I saw how hard she worked each and every day. She wanted us to study and work hard at school so we could go to college and not have to work hard jobs like her." Brenda reflected on Latino parents who labor and whose children tend to be in the after-school programs. "When I was growing up, most of the kids who were in the after-school programs were Latinos, because our parents worked.

After their shifts were over at Swift or at the restaurants, they'd come pick us up." Like most of the Latino kids of her generation, Brenda said, she went to the public school because the Catholic school was just too expensive. "I think if my mom could have afforded to have sent us kids to Catholic school she would have, but we have gotten a good education in the public schools. And today my youngest sibling, my brother, is thirteen and has some learning disabilities. The public school has services and programs for him that private schools just cannot provide."

Yolanda's ethics of sacrifice and determination greatly impacted Brenda, who received a full-ride scholarship to the University of Iowa. She enjoyed her first few years on campus and made a best friend in her fellow Mexican American roommate, Corenna, currently an accountant at a major midwestern urban hub.

Brenda's life took a turn for the unexpected when she discovered she was pregnant midway during her sophomore year of college. She and her now-husband Miguel had been dating for several years, and "getting pregnant was, well, not planned, but in the end, it was a happy surprise." Brenda met with her advisor and found out that she could finish her major almost exclusively online. During her junior and senior years, she drove to campus twice a week for her other classes, which she said was "not so bad, really."

Her mother, husband, and Catholic faith have given Brenda strength to manage her life as a young mother and a first-generation Latina university student studying immigration law. Brenda says it was la Virgen María who watched over her, ensuring her success in school. When she was pregnant with her first child, Miguel brought her back a beautiful statue of the Virgin of Guadalupe, which she placed at the center of their mantel. While Brenda attends Mass, for her, Mass is not the only part of her identity as a Catholic. Brenda considers Catholicism a cultural, family-centered faith. "My Catholicism has really given me a faith foundation. I love what having faith has done for me and my family. It gives us an identity as a people, and it is cultural for sure. I love to pray the rosary, and I love all of the parts of the religion that have to do with children." Part of Mexican Catholic culture involves a third birthday *presentación* for little girls, which is their "coming out" to the church. "It is kind of like a mini-quinceañera, and the little girls wear a pretty dress and there is cake after the Mass."

Brenda loves Miguel, and they have two beautiful girls, who are the center of Brenda's life now. She can't wait until her own girls' *presentaciónes* at church and is currently planning their baptisms on Easter Sunday, as most of her family members can get the day off of work to attend the big event. Husband

Miguel works as a cook at a local restaurant and has been able to arrange his schedule so that he can care for their daughters while Brenda prepares for her classes and exams. Brenda said she "couldn't have done it" without the help of her husband. "He always encourages me to study, and he really supports me. When I look like I am falling asleep at night over my books, he says to me, 'You can do it; you just have a little more to go, right?' He is so supportive of my career goals to be an immigration lawyer." Brenda's goal of becoming an immigration lawyer has been informed by her loved ones' undocumented status. Worried that her mother or her husband could be deported, Brenda has reached out to a local immigration lawyer, and the family is receiving counsel. She knows firsthand what families go through, families where "people work so hard to provide for their children and are good people, good members of society."

When we met, Brenda was excited about her then-impending spring 2018 graduation from the University of Iowa and planned on inviting the many members of her extended family in Iowa. She said that "everyone is so excited that I am graduating, and yeah, I guess it is a big deal, because I am the first in my entire family to get a bachelor's degree. I had to tell everyone about the date several months ago so that they can request off work. My mom and Miguel have already put in for the day off." And her best friend from college will be there to cheer on her friend, a first-generation Latina who birthed two babies, got married, and graduated with a major and two minors.

José: Reinvigorating a Downtown

It is safe to say that José is one of the most recognizable figures in Columbus Junction, Iowa. He seems to be everywhere, all the time, whether it is at the public school, coaching kids in track and field, at his downtown Take 2 Video Store and Burgers, at the local laundromat he owns and maintains, or at the homes he rents out in town. José describes himself as Catholic but is more private with his faith and rarely attends Mass. He is always working. And when he is not working or attending one of his teenage sons' sporting or school events or coaching, he is running. José is a marathon runner and averages two marathons each year, plus the numerous 10Ks and half marathons he runs for training purposes.

But even though he is not sitting in the pews save for Christmas and Easter, José considers himself "*católico* through and through." His video and burger shop is a shrine to la Virgen María and her throng of saints, running, and *fútbol*—what white Americans call, he said with a grimace, "soccer." The

Mexican colors of red, green, and white adorn the walls, and it is easy to imagine myself in Mexico when sitting and eating the cheese quesadilla, frijoles, and arroz that José put in front of me. As I sipped my Coke and ate the delicious food he made, José shared his story of hard work and "building something I can pass on to my kids." José is proud of what he has accomplished in Columbus Junction, and his business is an important center where Columbus Junction Latinos gather to get some food, rent a movie, and catch up on community news and information.

Getting up each morning at five to run with his teenage son Mark is all in a day's work for José, who prides himself on a having a strong work ethic. Running has been his passion for many years, and he works with the high school cross-country team as a pacer. When we met in the spring of 2018, he was training for a fall marathon and hoped to log 600 miles before the race. José's goal is to qualify for the Boston Marathon one day. Recognizing a fellow running enthusiast in me, José talked at length about running forms and shoes. Since reading the book *Born to Run*, about the Tarahumara Indians and their culture of running barefoot, José runs barefoot on his treadmill, and when he is outside, he wears thin-soled shoes. "I read the book and at first I thought it was just nonsense to run barefoot or without a lot of padding in your shoes. But I kept going, inspired by the Tarahumaras, and it completely changed the way I run. I can run faster, longer, and better than I used to." He felt so strong and confident that he was hoping to train for his first ultramarathon in the upcoming years.

As we sat and talked, José had to get up to greet and serve his many customers, who trickled in throughout the day. Patrons ranged from NAPA workers who came in wearing their hard hats to order lunch, to at-home moms wanting to get lunch and rent a movie, to tenants who dropped in for a bite and to catch up. The NAPA workers ordered their chicken patty sandwiches "with everything," fries, bottles of water, and large Cokes. Ever the host and conversationalist, José tried talking with his customers, asking them how they were doing, what they were working on that day, and the like. The NAPA guys weren't too interested in small talk, and José took the hint. He focused on making their food and started talking to Frank, a fellow running enthusiast, who came in to see how José did in last weekend's Des Moines marathon.

"You're upright!" Frank exclaimed when he walks into the store.

"Yeah, man, feeling all right but a little tired today." José chuckled. The men talked about running for several minutes while José finished preparing the NAPA guys' orders and took them their baskets of food. After José and Frank finished discussing their mutual dislike of running in cold, rainy weather,

Frank said he had come in to ask José for a donation for the upcoming Swinging Bridge Festival, an annual event in Columbus Junction celebrating the town's landmark and bringing members of the community together. José's ready response was "Yes, sign me up," and he wrote a check and gave it to Frank.

As I sat and observed the comings and goings in José's shop, I was amazed by all of the linguistic and cultural code-switching he did and by how quickly and efficiently he accomplished it. When white non-Latinos came in to order food, he talked to them in English, writing down their order and ringing them up as he answered the landline in Spanish and responded to a question about a VHS cassette in Spanish. José is a master of multitasking and code-switching, moving swiftly from English to Spanish, cooking and serving food, and suggesting movies customers might be interested in watching.

José said he has always worked hard and has been a "hustler," working and taking advantage of opportunities to succeed in his life. "I've always wanted to make myself noticeable, because that is how you get things done for your people." He migrated from Mexico City to Brooklyn, New York, in 1988, when he was a teenager, with his older brother. His parents worked all the time, he said, and he and his brother were "getting into trouble," so his mom and dad sent the boys to New York to live with extended family. Like most Latinos who wound up in Iowa and the larger Corn Belt region, José first migrated somewhere else—in his case, New York City—and made his way to the Midwest as his secondary residence to work. Specifically, he came to Columbus Junction in 1997 to work at Tyson and has lived in Columbus Junction for twenty-five years. He and his wife have also been married for that long and have three children, two teenage sons and a daughter in her junior year at the University of Iowa.

During my visit with him, José had an easy rapport with the dozens of individuals who came in during the day to talk, order food, and to hear about his most recent marathon. The Illinois marathon was "flatter than Chicago's course" but had a "killer hill around mile twenty-four." Running, the high school boys' soccer team, and the politics of the current school board dominated the afternoon's conversations. It was clear that his customers come to him for information and advice. Several customers talked with him about the high school soccer team, which was at the time ranked fourth in the state of Iowa. José was very proud of his son Mark, a starter on the team, but he empathized with the team they'd played the other day because it was a blowout: "I wish that the guys had let them score a goal," he said. "It was pretty tough for the other team to get beat ten to zero."

An elderly white couple, Jim and Carol, walked in, Carol with the aid of a cane, to order lunch and to tell José that their grandson had placed fifteenth in a recent road race. José beamed and said, "Aww, that is just great. You tell him congratulations for me. Tell him that all of this hard work will make him a better person." After Jim ordered hamburgers and fries for himself and his wife Carol, he hesitated for a moment and then said to José, "I hate to tell you this, but there is some leaking in the living room." The retired couple rented one of José's downtown apartments. José told him, "Don't worry, I'll go down and fix it in a little bit. I will go in and apply some foam spray." He later told me that the place had some roof issues and that he would probably have to replace the entire roof in the late spring or early summer.

As Jim brought her a burger basket, Carol asked, "José, do you think you will run the Boston sometime?" Smiling, José answered, "Yeah, I'd love to, but I have to qualify first!" While he'd run a good pace at last weekend's race, he was "still a little too slow" to qualify for Boston, so his goal was to shave off some minutes and try to qualify in the fall.

After Carol and Jim said their good-byes, José and Bob, a white male patron, got into what became a heated discussion about the school board and the status of the local schools. José knew Bob well and wasted no time in soliciting his opinion on the school board and the quality of education in the town's schools, the salaries of the coaches, and life in Columbus Junction. Bob told José that he thought they needed to start looking for a new head football coach as the team had gone through a "terrible" season. The riff on the coach and the poorly performing team led to a sustained conversation on the "terrible" quality of education in the town. Bob said, "I pulled my kids out of Columbus Junction's school and they go to Winfield. We drive them to and from school each day, but man, it is worth it. You know Winfield schools have a 4–5 score. Columbus Junction has a 1." José pressed him a bit, asking him, "Have you ever run a school with 70 percent Latinos, and many of them who are recent arrivals and who speak little to no English?" Bob shook his head no. José continued, "And you know, the teachers are poorly paid, and the ESL program is a joke. A total joke. And they just let go the outreach coordinator who was in charge of home visits. They let her go, the main outreach to poor Latino families who speak little English, but they keep building." Bob interjected and nodded affirmatively. "Yeah, man, they need to quit building. I mean, why build a shed for trash? It is a ridiculous waste of money." José expressed his profound worry for the local youth, who he said are "not being prepared for college. I mean, they go for a semester or two and then drop out and move back home. Our kids, especially the Spanish-speaking Latino kids, are being left behind."

The men continued their discussion amicably, and it turned out that they agreed on most issues. They both thought that the school board needed "all new people" and that the school should to do a better job reaching out to Latino and Burmese kids. They agreed that the football coach needed to go and that "maybe the soccer coach [could] also coach the football team." The men talked about what they saw as the inevitable demise of the NFL and American football, and the rise of soccer (*fútbol*). Bob's reasoning focused on the economics of the sports, not necessarily the problem of chronic traumatic encephalopathy in American football.

"Man, I really think that NASCAR and the NFL are both going down. They are too expensive. People can't afford to buy tickets. You can't raise ticket prices from a hundred dollars to three hundred dollars when no one is getting raises and the economy is not getting any better." José nodded in agreement.

And on the topic of money, the men returned to the high school football team and expressed their frustration that the "terrible" football coach was being paid so much. Bob said, "That guy, he is getting a big fat paycheck for doing nothing. Nothing. I went to one game and that was enough for me. I won't go again until they get a new coach and start winning some games."

Bob finished his fries, drank the rest of his Coke, and told José that he would be racing his car that weekend at the CJ Speedway in Vinton, Iowa, the southeastern Iowa racetrack whose slogan is "The racers make the show and the fans make them go." José shook Bob's his hand and told him that he would "try to make it out" to watch him race. After Bob left, there was a rare lull in the day, and José sat down again to talk. On the topic of race relations in the town, José shook his head and said that there is "so much racism" in Columbus Junction. He referred back to his conversation with Bob and the poor quality of the local schools. "The school was great once, when it was all white kids and white families were invested in their success. Now that you have a Latino-majority student body, the commitment to excellence in education has really waned. School board members and white parents have literally blamed Latinos and their families for the decline in the quality. I have told them, 'It is your fault. You aren't reaching out to them. You have given up on them.'" José brought up the community outreach school employee who made home visits and who is fluent in Spanish. "They fired her. I mean, she wasn't paid that much, and she was the only one who did home visits. She translated for families and was their lifeline to the school. So what did they do? They fired her, citing budget concerns. Yet they keep building, like Bob pointed out."

José continued to talk about racism in his town and didn't mince words: "The school and school board is run by white privileged people. They do not understand the issues that Latino and Burmese families have in their lives. They don't know about and don't want to know about a single Mexican mom who is supporting a family of four or five because her husband was deported. I don't think anyone in the school knows about . . . or cares about her and her family."

When I asked him if he would consider running for the school board, he chuckled and said he was "way too passionate" to do so. He has chosen to direct his efforts toward other grassroots organizing areas that he thinks have direct and positive impacts on Columbus Junction's immigrant and refugee communities. He was the founder of the local League of United Latin American Citizens and remains the chapter leader. He works on organizing Latinos and Burmese and has been involved in the "get out and vote" campaign to register documented Latinos to vote in local, state, and national elections. "The worst thing we can do is to not get involved. I run my businesses, coach the kids with running, raise awareness of the issues facing Latinos through LULAC . . . and I include Burmese too in our local chapter . . . and I try to motivate younger Latinos to be involved." José said he has realized "that I can't be everything, but I can be something. I want to make my mark on my community. I want to show my kids and their friends that you can accomplish a lot when you are passionate and when you organize. Organizing is everything, because together we can accomplish a lot." He founded a local chapter of GEAR UP (Gaining Early Awareness and Readiness for Undergraduate Programs) for Columbus Junction Latino eighth graders. It is one of twelve chapters in the state of Iowa. The youth have to raise $2,000 apiece for the trip to Washington, D.C., which is focused on getting the teens ready for high school and success in life. The trip to the nation's capital in the summer before their freshman year is meant to get them excited about their future and about building what José referred to as a "college-going culture" to help them envision success.

José is known for his youth advocacy and for his commitment to Columbus Junction. He wants his town to prosper, and he knows that in order for this to happen, the local youth need to be empowered. José draws on his resources and contacts as a local businessman to help young adults succeed. He is close to his priest, Father Joseph Sia, who he said "understands me and knows what I believe. He knows that I will fight for my people. Father and I are both doing something important for our community, and there is a mutual respect there. We work together and trust each other. We both want the

Latinos and Burmese in our community to thrive, and we will continue to work for them."

José turned and nodded his head toward the statue of the Virgin of Guadalupe on the shelf. "For me and so many Mexican people, Guadalupe is not really so much about the church but about our Mexican heritage. She came to us to tell us that she loved us, and she was responsible for healing so many people in Mexico. I think that she talked to God and told him stop the diseases in Mexico City. That is the miracle—that she appeared to a poor Indian and that she protected poor Indians and mestizos." José said that Guadalupe is "in my DNA. It is in the DNA of Mexican people, and we just have devotion." Seeing devotion to the Virgin as a biological trait as much as a cultural characteristic, José is grateful that she introduced monotheism and "got rid of all the other gods and turned attention to her and to her son." José doesn't feel as though he needs to go to church to "be Catholic." He is an activist for his community and lives out his commitment to the poor and to social justice in his daily work. He sees himself as a connector, and as a business owner he takes pride in knowing many members of his community: Latino, Burmese, and white.

José also takes pride in bringing his Mexican heritage to "all people in Columbus Junction." He noted that el Día de los Muertos is celebrated in Mexico but not so much in the United States' Midwest. He chuckled as he talked about his efforts to "get Día de los Muertos to Columbus Junction. "My *abuela* had an *ofrenda* [a home altar] in Mexico. She had photos of family members who had died and they were spread out on the altar. She had foods that my *abuelo* liked set out on the altar. You know that the ancestors come back for the Days of the Dead, and my grandmother made an impression on me. . . . Well, when I set up an *ofrenda* in my shop a couple of times, people would come in and be like, 'What?!' I explained it to them the reasons why Mexicans set up *ofrendas* and what Día de los Muertos means, but it hasn't really gone over that well here. But I'll keep trying to introduce it and will keep explaining why it is important to do."

José said he would continue to be an advocate for Latino youth and for Latinos and all immigrants. "I myself went through many hardships. I came to the United States as a young person without my parents, who stayed behind. The reason why we all come here, to the U.S., is for a better life. That's nature, you know, to want to be in the best situation you can be in. That's what we want for ourselves and for our children. We are all the same in wanting that—it ties us together." He continued, "In reality, we are all so much more alike than we are different. Yet we as a country and as individuals put borders on our cities, our country. I will continue to work to break down those borders that we have put up that divides us from each other, because I really believe that we are one people. And what I do in my job each day is to try to bring people together and to be a role model for our young people."

Adela: Providing Food and *Cultura*

Adela, like her friend and fellow downtown small business owner José, came to Columbus Junction to work at the Tyson pork processing plant. And like José, she left her job at the plant after working there for many years to open her own small business, and she has never looked back. Adela loves being her own boss. She works hard and is at her store each day for most of the day, but she loves it, she told me, and would never go back to Tyson.

A tiny woman, Adela is always moving. Indeed, her beautiful long hair piled artfully on top of her head is probably more than half her body weight. When I spent part of the day at her shop, it was, like every day, all hustle and bustle. A young employee was busy stocking shelves with canned and glass jar items imported from Mexico. When he was done neatly arranging the many cans and bottles, he moved over to the small fresh produce area and began stacking limes, lemons, and chiles. Within minutes of my arrival, women and men flooded the shop. They had just gotten off their shift at Tyson and were coming in to purchase tomatillos, avocados, chiles, and limes that Adela imports from the motherland. They bought prepaid phone cards to use to call family in Mexico. Several men purchased hats, and a couple of women bought shawls as well as piñatas for their children's birthday parties.

Adela said it makes her happy to provide the things that her friends need. While she doesn't miss working at Tyson, she missed working alongside her "hermanas y hermanos," but owning and running her store allows her to see them each week and to stay in touch with their lives. Like most of the Latino-owned downtown businesses, Adela caters to Tyson workers, most of whom are Mexican-descent Latinos. As I sat on a stool she provided for me, Adela walked over to the women and men who entered her store and hugged each of them individually, asking them, *en español*, how their family was. She chatted with a group of women who held plastic bags of chiles that they would be using in their dinner preparations, and she grabbed a bag of corn tortillas for her friend who asked for them.

The women and men who come to her store are all Guatemalans and Mexicanos, Latino men and women who work long, hard shifts at Tyson and who savor the opportunity to purchase foods and items they could find at home in Mexico. While she is only about a mile away from her former employer, she said it feels like millions of miles away. She is in her own space now, in charge of her destiny. Adela said that when she was employed at Tyson as a line worker, her hands would hurt all of the time and her back would ache. She worked there for several years and it was good pay, but she just couldn't handle hurting any longer. So she quit and opened up her New York Dollar Store. She is the primary employee but does pay a young Mexican man for part-time work. She is getting older and needs help unloading the truck that brings the produce, cans and jars of food, and other specialty goods like candles. For Adela, it is her faith and love of la Virgen de Guadalupe, whose image is everywhere in her tienda, that has gotten her to the place she is today: a small business owner, free of the demands and challenges of the meatpacking plant, free to run her own business. "I tell you, it was la Virgen, and her alone, who helped me leave the plant and to run my own tienda. I am forever grateful to her and light a *vela* for her each night. God and la Virgen are good and watch over those of us who are poor and who need them the most."

CHAPTER 8

Reyna

STAYING FOR THE DREAM

REYNA MISSES THE LUSH greenery of Santa Eulalia, her birthplace in rural western Guatemala. It is her home and will always be home; she thinks of it each day. When her children are tucked in and asleep at night, she lets down her guard and cries for the land, the smells, the sounds. She aches out of loneliness for her husband, who was deported two years ago. She misses her mother and extended family. When she closes her eyes, she can see the majestic Cuchumatanes mountains and the thousands of trees whose fragrances and colors bring her joy. She likes to talk about the many herbs and greens she grew in her family's small garden, the rooster and hens that ran around the yard, pecking at anything that got in their way, and the sunsets that took her breath away.

Reyna was eager to share her Q'anjob'al heritage with me, and as we talked at my home in Spanish, a second language for both of us, she scrolled through dozens of photos on her cell phone. She played YouTube videos of her Mayan foodways, clothing, and village celebrations. She showed me a gorgeous photo of her and her daughter, then a toddler, now six, in their colorful native dresses that Reyna and her mother wove on their family loom. Reyna has always felt proud to be Q'anjob'al. Her people and primary language are Q'anjob'al, spoken by 140,000 people in Guatemala and just under 10,000 outside of the country.

Since migrating to the United States, however, Reyna has come to rely on her oldest son, now twelve, who is fluent in Q'anjob'al, Spanish, and English. She is self-conscious about her lack of fluency in Spanish and English, and throughout our conversations, Alejandro Jr. helped translate from Q'anjob'al to Spanish and English for me, as Reyna is most comfortable speaking in her native tongue to her eldest, who is a gifted linguist and translator. Q'anjob'al, Reyna's native language, is understood and spoken by her sons; her daughter, who left Guatemala when she was a toddler, understands but is not a fluent speaker.

As we walked over to look at my husband Steve's backyard garden, she pointed to what he and I had thought was a weed and exclaimed that it was *yierba mora*, an herb used for medicinal purposes and known for reducing fevers. She pulled up an image of the herb, scientifically known as *Solanum nigrum*, on YouTube. From now on we will harvest them for Reyna, as she wants to make batches of soup to stave off COVID-19 and whatever other viruses might come her family's way. I told her we would love to try some of the soup.

Later that night, before I drove her and the kids back to their apartment, my husband helped her with packing bags of various greens and herbs for her to take home. I got several texts from her later that night with photos of her preparing the Guatemalan tamales that she makes using the leaves of swiss chard and spinach. The photos show her hands filling the leaves with the homemade corn masa, rolling them, and presenting them on plates next to the bowls of homemade salsa. For our next dinner together, Reyna said she will show us how to make her homemade tamales and salsas.

Like Rosa, whose story introduced the book, Reyna has endured an arduous journey from west-central Guatemala with her two youngest children. Her dream has always been, she said, for her three children to have a better life than she did. One day she looked around and decided that she no longer wanted to live in dire poverty. While she loved the greenness of Huehuetenango, the abundance of trees, and the open land for her children to run and play in, she reached a point where she could not see a future for her children. Gangs, chronic unemployment, and a lack of education was not a future she wanted for her kids.

Reyna said her children were not getting an adequate education, and they were very poor, "muy, muy pobres." Her husband Alejandro had been saving up to hire a coyote, who ended up taking him and their eldest child, Alejandro Jr., then seven, across the border in south Texas. Their journey was a successful one, and Alejandro Sr. and Jr. were able to cross undetected and make their way to central Iowa, where they had extended family waiting. The two moved in with relatives in their already cramped two-bedroom apartment, and Alejandro Sr. secured a job, enrolled Alejandro Jr. in school, and saved up to hire a coyote to bring Reyna and the two younger children over. Roughly a year later, Reyna crossed in the middle of the night with then six-year-old

Mario and two-year-old Sofía. She shared bits and pieces of the journey with me, but it is difficult for her to talk about it. It was dangerous, exhausting, and something she never wants to experience again. She was physically assaulted but kept her children from being hurt physically, she said.

The family of five was grateful to be reunited and vowed to always be together. Alejandro and Reyna felt as though they could finally plan for their children's futures. The local schools were excellent, and the services for migrant families were better than they had hoped for. They lived with extended family and were on their way to afford renting an apartment of their own in the same complex.

But the family's happiness and sense of security was short-lived. While her husband had crossed as an undocumented person and decided not to fill out the paperwork to be granted asylum in the United States, Reyna decided she did not want to live under the specter of deportation and all of the stresses associated with it. She made arrangements for relatives to pick the children up for school one morning while she and Alejandro left early to drive to Omaha, Nebraska, where she planned to apply for asylum and a work permit. The couple enjoyed the long ride together, able to talk—just the two of them—for the first time in a long time. They stopped at McDonald's for lunch on the way, a real treat for them. Yet once they arrived at the ICE check-in site, things started to unravel. When Reyna was inside the building speaking to a translator, an ICE agent noticed Alejandro inside the car, resting with his eyes shut. He was promptly arrested for entering the country illegally, detained, and deported within weeks. Reyna was devastated—as were their children. She had wanted to "do the right thing" for her family by filling out the paperwork, and the next thing she knew her husband had been deported and she was left behind with three young children and no income. And she now realized that her oldest child, Alejandro Jr., had a particularly tenuous immigration status because he had crossed with his father and had not had the proper immigration papers filled out and filed. He is fluent in four languages—his father's Acateco, his mother's Q'anjob'al, Spanish, and English. He has been the family's translator and lifeline in their adopted country, and he shifts between languages with ease. Overnight, the family's situation changed dramatically. Without her husband's income, Reyna had to rely on the goodwill of friends and family, and because she had not yet been granted her work permit, she had to wear an ankle monitor and was not allowed to work for months.

The bright spot in the story is that a circle of well-meaning white Iowans and Latinos alike have come to her aid. The Iowa City Center for Worker Justice got involved in assisting Reyna, and funds were given for her to hire an immigration lawyer. For a year, a retired white woman named Pat, an active member of Iowa City's United Church of Christ, gave her children rides to school and drove Alejandro Jr. to his weekly orchestra practices. Pat spoke to her church congregation about allocating $100 a month for Reyna's rent until she had her work permit and began to draw paychecks. Moreover, several upper-middle-class white women affiliated with the Unitarian Universalist community in town also helped out with grocery money, gently used clothing, and toiletries like shampoo, toothpaste, and deodorant. Retired Spanish teachers have met with Reyna to help her improve both her Spanish and English. Other well-meaning white women affiliated with the Church of Christ, Catholic Church, Catholic Worker House, and Unitarian Universalist organizations have stepped in to help with rides to the grocery store, to city-sponsored activities for children, and to parks for playdates. Catholic workers such as Emily Sinnwell have repeatedly stepped up as translators, dealing with apartment building supervisors to ensure that appliances are fixed and running. Emily consistently makes sure that bus passes are given out for Reyna and her sister-in law, brother-in-law, and younger sister to take the bus to their jobs at McDonald's, to Walmart, and to the mall—a favorite of the family. And I, too, have become a friend to the family and give rides to the mall, grocery store, and pre-COVID-19 city-sponsored family activities.

For the past five years, white religious women have stepped up to take Reyna and the children shopping for clothes, shoes, and backpacks for school. The network of care and support is a story that needs to be told, as there are many citizens who believe that making America great is by being good neighbors and showing love and concern for newcomers to the United States. Yet while Reyna has received an outpouring of support by local organizations and individuals alike, she has also endured many setbacks and heartaches. For the first year after her husband's deportation, they spoke regularly on the phone, and he vowed to save up money to find his way back to his family. As we would drive around in the car, she would hold up her phone gleefully, with the camera facing outward, taking videos of the green landscape, stores, and schools that we passed. At that time Reyna and her husband were hopeful, despite the distance that separated them, and the kids missed their papa very much. Yet time dragged on, and the realities of their reunion looked to be insurmountable. Much to Reyna's anguish and horror, there is very little chance that she will see her husband again. The financial cost is burdensome, and he is fearful of risking deportation a second time. Right now, there is no work to be had in southwestern Guatemala, and even if there was, it would take several years to save the money to try to cross the border again—and it would be especially risky a second time.

In the weeks and months that followed her husband's deportation, Reyna was lonely, depressed, and in anguish over her separation from her husband. What keeps her going and from falling into complete despair, she told me, is her children. She has to get up in the morning to take care of them, to send them to school, and to go to work at McDonald's, the job she was able to secure. Her love for her children and her hopes of their reunion with Alejandro motivate her.

While she has been, and continues to be, "sick with sadness," Reyna has persevered. She thanks God each day for her children and lives for them, she said. She takes them to a Pentecostal church, a church whose congregation is full of Mayans and other asylum-seeking Central Americans from the Northern Triangle. It feels like home each Sunday, and Reyna and the kids can eat foods of their native land and village. Since receiving her work permit in January 2019, Reyna has worked as many hours as possible at the local McDonald's franchise, which is a short ten-minute walk from her apartment. She locates free family events for the weekends and is not afraid to ask for rides so that her children can enjoy events and take a break from the stresses that accompany their everyday lives.

Reyna is a woman who loves her children and who hustles each and every day for them. She is not ashamed of who she is and where she is from and is proud of her Guatemalan heritage. Her work ethic is boundless, and she is grateful for the opportunities to make money for her family. Reyna's children go to "una escuela muy buena," a very good school, and Sofía was enrolled in a Head Start program before she entered kindergarten and has thrived. Reyna's younger sister, who arrived more recently, is attending the local high school and works a part-time job after school at another McDonald's in town. She hopes to be able to transfer to the same store where her older sister works but said she is glad to have a job so she can contribute to the family's resources. Sofía, her brothers, and her cousin Maricella eat their breakfast and lunch at school along with white Iowan families benefiting from the federal free and reduced lunch program. The school PTA ensures that the children go home on Fridays with a backpack full of easy-to-heat-and-eat foods so that they do not go hungry during non-school days. Moreover, during COVID-19, the family was able to pick up breakfast and lunch at the local high school during the week and are able to secure food during the week from the school's summer breakfast and lunch program.

While refugee families like Reyna's have experienced an abundance of support from concerned white Iowans, the sadness and longing for her husband and for Santa Eulalia that Reyna feels is palpable. While she does not miss the poverty and her village's lack of opportunities, she misses her *familia* and *cultura* deeply. She showed me photos on her phone of the traditional dress that she and María wore. When she scrolls through images of her husband and large, extended family, as well as her roosters and hens, they make her happy but also "tear at her heart."

Despite her sadness and longing for her *familia*, Reyna is determined to stay in the United States. She is thrilled that her children are gaining fluency in English and that they are making friends. She is proud to wear her McDonald's work uniform and to provide for her family. She loves her church community and has formed close friendships with other women. The church is her second home. She never misses Sunday services, and her kids look forward to the good food, singing, and friendships that they have formed at this special place. Fellow churchgoers give Reyna and the kids a ride there and back each Sunday, and it is her favorite part of the week. She showed me her earrings and best blouse and pants that she reserves just for church. In pre-COVID times, she and the kids spent most of the day worshipping, eating familiar foods, and connecting with other asylum seekers and immigrants. For the better part of one day each week, Reyna and her children are surrounded by women, men, and children who look like her and speak a similar dialect. She now looks to her future and to her children's futures. She is here to work, live, and stay. For all of the assistance she has received, Reyna said with emotion, "Me siento muy bendecido": I feel very blessed.

COVID-19, Meatpacking, and Refugees

Reyna and many of the women and men I have worked with during the research and writing of this book have been hit hard by COVID-19 since the virus made its appearance in Iowa in March 2020. Her hours at McDonald's have been cut back, but she is relieved to still have steady work to pay her bills and to try to save up some money for a used car. Like all of the refugee families I met with, Reyna's family members have pooled their money and resources for food, shelter, and clothing. The public schools' free breakfast and lunch program that continued after the schools shut down has helped Reyna tremendously, and she is grateful her kids have two guaranteed meals a day. While it is harder to pay the bills, she is still able to do it. Reyna is a survivor.

The meatpacking plant employees I interviewed for this book have been deeply affected by President Trump's May 2020 executive order forcing U.S. meatpacking plants to remain open despite the continuing spread of COVID-19. A couple of my interlocutors who work at the plants have been infected by COVID-19 and have thankfully recovered. Others refuse to go back to the plant and are looking for other work, which is difficult in this economy. By invoking the Defense Production Act, Trump laid bare the consistent anti-refugee stance of his administration and of those politicians who support him. The order says nothing about how packing plant workers will be protected, a reality Trump tacitly acknowledged when describing the "liability" issues that are sure to emerge when workers sicken and die. Trump's iteration of the 1950s wartime act puts profits over people and is one more instance of how his administration has championed corporations over working people's lives. The executive order is one more act that exposes the ongoing precarity of refugees' status in the United States.

As we have learned, meatpacking plants and workers once had strong union representation, starting with the turn-of-the-twentieth-century Amalgamated Meat Cutters and Butcher Workmen of North America and the United Packinghouse Workers of America. Yet beginning in the 1980s, packing plants and their unions were shuttered and reopened as "right-to-work" plants in the Midwest. Packing plants moved from urban hubs to rural areas decimated by the farm crisis. White and Black union employees, once guaranteed an hourly wage of twenty-five dollars per hour, saw the plants reopen at wages starting at thirteen dollars per hour, topping out at eighteen dollars per hour. Corporations such as Tyson, Smithfield, Agriprocessors, and JBS turned largely to undocumented migrants.

From 2005 to 2008, sweeping ICE raids transformed the workforce yet again. In the wake of the raids, the protein industry turned to documented refugees, people from Burma, various Central African states, and Thailand. Meatpacking towns such as Columbus Junction, Iowa, or Guymon, Oklahoma, are now some of the most diverse communities in the United States. These are the frontline workers on whom meat-eaters depend. Trump's May 2020 executive order signals that their lives do not matter to this administration. Their lives are viewed as fungible. What matters to this administration is putting meat on tables for the people whose lives are deemed to matter most; and the lives of certain people—refugees—are not as important as the pork chops they produce. And yet refugees who work at the packing plants are grateful for the work and the economic status that their hard and dangerous labor affords them.

In this second Gilded Age of U.S. meatpacking, the tug of war between corporations and workers has steadily moved in corporations' favor. The odds have not been in workers' favor because the deck has increasingly been stacked against them—even with sympathetic plant managers and line supervisors who incorporate the language of care and concern for their workers. At the Tyson hog-processing plant in Columbus Junction, which has become a hotspot for COVID-19 cases, employees stopped showing up after coworkers started getting sick. They are Chin Burmese families who live in multigenerational homes and French Congolese families who live ten per household and whose grandparents help raise their grandbabies. They fled a hellish existence to come to the United States, and they are not willing to risk their lives and the lives of their loved ones for a paycheck.

According to one of my friends at the Columbus Junction plant, when the number of COVID-19 cases began to creep upward, two-thirds of the workers stayed home out of fear and anxiety. They forced the Tyson plant to shut down for two weeks. Joe Blay, the Tyson plant chaplain, said "something drastic had to happen" after employees stopped showing up as COVID-19 spread through the workforce. Even in this right-to-work state with weakened union representation, workers are refusing to show up for work—a trend seen across the nation in other packing plants. According to Joe, during the closure, the plant managers and executives took action and installed safety measures such as partitions between line workers' workspaces and implemented line slow-downs. In the cafeteria, plexiglass was installed down the middle of the tables, and markings were put in place so diners could eat six feet apart. Testing kits, face masks, and face shields were secured for all workers.

Yet not all employees have returned, because they are scared, according to my interlocutor at the plant, who wished not to be named for fear of reprisal. They know about Trump's executive order requiring the plants to remain open, but they fear for their health and the health of their families. According to my friend, "No one, I mean no one, is going to tell the workers that they have to return to work. The executive order is utter nonsense. If people are sick or scared of getting sick, they won't come to work. Period." My Tyson plant interviewee called Trump "clueless"—"He doesn't care about lives, and he doesn't grasp the issue"—and added that they closed the plant because people were not coming to work—two-thirds of the workforce stayed home. "You know, these workers are not going to sacrifice their lives for money. They went through so much trauma to come here, and they are not going to risk dying from a virus."

My friend and I talked at length about the anti-immigrant, anti-refugee language and actions coming out of the White House and how it is not pro-life but anti-life. He pointed out that the administration makes it clear that some people's lives—white evangelical Christians, mostly—matter to the Trump administration, and that there is a deeply embedded irony in the administration's stance toward refugees. "These people, whose lives do not matter to the administration, are the ones providing food and sustenance for others' lives." We also talked at length about the embedded ironies in the administration's pro-life platform and theology, supported by a majority of white Christian evangelicals. My friend, a deeply religious man, is perplexed by what he views as an inconsistent pro-life belief system and platform of white evangelicals and the Trump administration. "I really don't understand white evangelicals. They are telling refugees—meatpacking workers—that their lives are not valuable. The fact that these evangelicals believe and say that Trump is God-sent and pro-life reminds me of the Sadducees in Jesus's time. As long as they were close to power, they're happy. They enjoy power and special privileges, and they have sold out."

I hope that in its own small way, this book has drawn attention not only to the precarity of refugees' existence here in the United States but also to what the women and men featured here want, and that is the opportunity to live, to provide for their families, and to experience some joy. These women, men, and their children are resilient. The refugees in this book have dreams similar to the ones of white Americans in the book. They don't want us to feel "sorry" for them. They work hard and expect fair treatment. They are proud of the hard work that they do at McDonald's, Tyson, and Iowa Premium Beef and want to be treated with respect. They are willing to continue doing the work that they do, but they want to be protected at work and to know that their lives matter to their employers. They are not asking for extras, just the right to work and to not die from their work. If we consume meat, it is important for us to understand that what we grill for our families more than likely was harvested and processed by women and men who buy light-up shoes for their daughters and who belong to faith communities, individuals who contribute to our society and to the American values we claim to uphold.

Additionally, I hope that refugees who process our meat, cook our burgers, and perform countless essential jobs for the United States and the world through their labor can feel and experience the United States as home. Further, I fervently hope, as a white American anthropologist, mother, wife, and friend to many of the refugees featured in this book, that we are able to come to a point in our country where whites become not merely tolerant or even comfortable with the new demographic realities but accepting of the new American pluralism and all of the beauty and joy it brings to our

ACKNOWLEDGMENTS

MANY INDIVIDUALS have supported this project and have shared their insights that helped shape this book. I am incredibly lucky to have such brilliant, generous, supportive people in my life. I want to start by thanking one person in particular, my best friend and spouse, Stephen Andrew Warren, for his unwavering faith in this project and in me. He has never once doubted me in all of our years together, and his love and encouragement have helped get me through these many years in academia. My academic journey has not always been an easy one, but Steve always—*always*—supported me. My life and my work are far more fulfilling and beautiful because he is with me. I love him so very much.

I am grateful to the many refugees who took the time to talk with me and to share their experiences. I am humbled by them and by the strength they show each and every day. They entrusted me with their stories, which moved me to tears and kindled a fire within me. I admire them for their perseverance, resilience, and commitment to their families. It is my hope that in its small way, this book helps amplify their voices and that readers come away with greater empathy as well as with a desire to engage in actions that help lead to some societal and structural changes that have positive impacts on refugees' lives.

I am also grateful to my white interlocutors who took the time to have coffee, talk, and share their stories of work and faith. I admire them for their fortitude, work ethic, and deep devotion to place. Spending time with them helped me understand that what we see and hear in the news can be surface-level, and their stories give depth to this project.

My friend Father Joseph Sia showed ongoing enthusiasm for this book and helped connect me to many of the individuals whose stories fill its pages. His support has really meant a lot to me. Bishop Thomas Zinkula and Catholic Charities director Kent Ferris have also been big supporters, and I thank them for their friendship and encouragement along the way. Emily Sinnwell and David Goodner, friends and co-founders of the Iowa City Catholic Worker House, have encouraged and cheered me on the past several years. Their ongoing commitment to works of mercy and accompaniment of refugees inspires me.

Questions and observations from colleagues across the country have absolutely made this book better than it would have been. A 2017–2018 Career Development Award from the University of Iowa, along with a 2017–2018 Sabbatical Grant for Researchers from the Louisville Institute, afforded me a year away from teaching and service at the University of Iowa so that I could focus on my research and writing. A book subvention award from the University of Iowa's Office of the Vice President for Research and Economic Development and the Department of Religious Studies allowed me to hire a professional indexer. The support I received from the Louisville Institute gave me the time to not only write a first draft of the book but also gain valuable feedback from my colleagues at our working group sessions. A heartfelt thanks is due the institute's staff—Ed Aponte, Don Richter, Keri Leichty, Pam Collins, and Jessica Bowman—who made the weekend-long gathering as collegial as it was productive. And a warm thanks goes to my Louisville Institute working group cohort, especially Kyle Brooks, Robert Chao Romero, Hannah Waits, Chris Tirres, Jaisy Joseph, and Jon Calvillo, for careful reading of what was then a work in progress. I hope that they are able to see some of the fruits of our spirited dialogue. Their own research inspires me, and I am proud to know them and learn from them.

I am indebted to the many colleagues and their institutions who invited me to share my work at various stages of research and writing. It has been a humbling experience to receive feedback on my research as it has developed, from the earliest to the final stages. I am indeed a lucky scholar to be part of such a vibrant and supportive village.

Marie Griffith and Leigh Schmidt of the Danforth Center, Washington University–St. Louis, invited me to share my perspective on Latino Catholicism at the Danforth Center's 2016 "American Catholicism, American Politics Reconsidered" event. My fellow panelists Tim Matovina, Eugene McCarraher, and Leslie Woodcock Tentler asked excellent questions that prompted me to consider the political climate of the Corn Belt and the repercussions for Latinos in the workplace and in their communities. As part of the University of Southern California's American Parish Project, I was able to learn from my sociologist colleagues who are all doing fantastic work on American parishes. Warm thanks go to Tricia Mein Bruce, Gary Adler, Brian Starks, Tia Pratt, Brett Hoover, Nancy Ammerman, Kathleen Garces-Foley, April Manalang, and the late and dear Mary Ellen Koneiczny for their generative feedback on the fieldwork I shared as part of the American Parish Project working group.

My friend Felipe Hinojosa, a brilliant leader in Latino religious studies and history, has consistently provided me with excellent advice and criticism regarding my work. I am grateful to him for inviting me out to Texas A&M in 2017 to share my research and for encouraging me to dig more deeply into the many layers of racial politics in the Corn Belt. I am glad that he served as one of the outside reviewers of this book and am grateful for his openness. Felipe and his wonderful graduate students, along with Donnalee Dox in religious studies and performance studies, provided the kind of critical feedback that absolutely made the book better.

Colleagues at the University of Virginia provided the space for a wonderfully fruitful discussion at the Religious Movement(s): Migration and Belief in the Americas conference, hosted by the University of Virginia Centro de las Américas/Americas Center in 2018. I am especially grateful to Matt Hedstrom and Jalane Smith for bringing together scholars of American religion, race, and migration and for giving us the space to share our scholarship. A warm thank-you goes out to Matt and Jalane for hosting this three-day gathering, along with co-presenters Emily Clark, Brett Hendrickson, Sylvester Johnson, Andrew Chestnut, Elaine Peña, Paul Johnson, Jennifer Scheper Hughes, Tom Tweed, Liza McAlister, Angela Tarango, Brent Crosson, Tony Tian-Ren Lin, and Roberto Lint Sagarena. I came away from the conference in awe of the work that they are all doing, as well as with an affirmation that amplifying the voices of our interlocutors matters.

I thank Saint Louis University friends and colleagues Rachel Lindsey, Pauline Lee, and Samantha Arten, who organized and hosted the Lived Religion in the Digital Age conference in the fall of 2019. This was a collegial, intellectually stimulating gathering where I was able to share some of my research as well as thoughts on what it means to take a lived religion orientation in our work. I was honored to be among brilliant, generative colleagues including Marla Frederick, Katie Holscher, Mike Pasquier, Teresa Smallwood, Jolyon Baraka Thomas, Lincoln Mullen, Kijan Bloomfield, Mary Dunn, Nancy Ammerman, Marie Griffith, and John Turner. I appreciate their feedback and encouragement.

One of the aspects of my job that I love the most is having the opportunity to present my work on Catholicism to Catholics out in the community. I always find that laymen and laywomen bring their enthusiasm, fascinating lived religious histories, and excellent questions to these talks. I am grateful to Dean Sonja Fritzche of Michigan State University and Arthur Versluvius, chair of religious studies at MSU, who worked with St. John Church and Catholic Student Center Oversight Committee on American Catholic Thought and Culture, for inviting me to share my findings on midwestern Catholicism in the fall of 2019. During my time at MSU, I was able to see my good friend and colleague Amy DeRogatis, who always provides a model of excellent scholarship, teaching, and parenting. A highlight of this trip was breakfast with Amy and Shreena Ghandi, as well as a post-talk pub hangout with Amy and Sara Moslener at HopCat. I am so lucky to have colleagues who are also friends and who live full, rich lives.

A visit to Princeton to present my research to faculty and graduate students in the winter of 2019 at the Religion in the Americas workshop was a wonderful way to round off several years of sharing my work and learning from my colleagues and friends. A special thank-you goes to religious studies Ph.D. student Madeline Gambino, who provided a brilliant response to the book chapter draft that had pre-circulated. I came away from this experience deeply impressed with the work that graduate student colleagues in American religion are doing and thank Madeline and her graduate student cohort Michael Baysa, Mélena Laudig, William Stell, and Andrew Walker-Cornetta for their astute questions and insights.

My faculty colleagues at Princeton provided, as I expected, brilliant feedback. I thank Judith Weisenfeld, Anthony Petro, Jenny Wiley-Legath, and Heath Carter for their generous as well as generative comments and criticism. The Religion in the Americas workshop was a model of collegiality and gave me hope—as did all of the workshops and working groups in which I was a participant—for the future of American religious studies.

Many colleagues here at the University of Iowa have been supportive and interested in the work that I have been doing since arriving here in the fall of 2012. I am especially grateful to Iowa colleagues-friends Rachel Marie-Crane Williams, Maurine Neiman, Christopher Rasheem-McMillan, Teresa Mangum, Lina Murillo, Jennifer New, Naomi Greyser, Leslie Schwalm, Steve Warren, Glenn Penny, Nick Yablon, and Joe Kearney. My Gender, Women's, and Sexuality Studies colleagues' social justice–oriented pedagogy and research always inspires. Colleagues in Religious Studies and in the Division of Interdisciplinary Programs have shown support and encouragement. A special shout-out of gratitude is in order for three Iowa colleagues: Associate Vice President for Research and Development Anne Ricketts, Research Support Coordinator Cheryl Ridgeway, and Grants Administrator Ann Knudson. All three of these women have demonstrated their support of my research in tangible ways, and for this I am deeply grateful.

One of the reasons I love working and living in Iowa is the opportunity to teach and to learn from both undergraduate students and graduate students. I have had the honor and privilege to mentor and work with Drs. Jennifer Stone, Stephanie Grossnickle-Batterton, Kayla Wheeler, Gwendolyn

Gillson, and Iva Patel, brilliant women who are contributing their many gifts and talents to their students and colleagues. I am so proud of them. My current doctoral students Emma Rifai, John Sheridan, and Carlos Ruíz Martínez continually impress me with their teaching and research, and it is an honor to work with them and learn from them. I remain indebted to my mentor Bob Orsi and to John Corrigan, Carol Greenhouse, Michael D. Jackson, and David Haberman, whose mentoring, scholarship, and commitment to the people they write about speaks volumes.

What has mattered so much over the years are the meals, conversations, and drinks shared with colleagues who have become dear friends. I am incredibly fortunate to have a wide circle of academic friends who live their lives with integrity and purpose. A huge group hug goes out to my tribe of fierce, brilliant women friends-colleagues: Kathy Cummings, Catherine Brekus, Judith Weisenfeld, Heather Curtis, Julie Byrne, Amy Koehlinger, Sue B. Ridgely, Amy DeRogatis, Tricia Mein Bruce, Brenna Moore, Emily Clark, Katie Holscher, Sara Williams, Susan Reynolds, Sarah McFarland Taylor, Nicole Renée Phillips, Kate Dugan, Stephanie Brehm, Ariel Schwartz, Samira Mehta, and Amanda Baugh. They have shown me love and concern over the years and know me and honor me as a whole person. And my Iowa City friends Jennifer "Yohnnie" Juhlin, Maurine Neiman, Anna Blaedel, M. Barclay, Mary Landon, Beth Fettweis, Julie Kearney, Pam Nims, Becky Pitman, and Kecia Leary got me to laugh, drink a glass of wine, and be present and grateful for the moment. My neighbor and friend Kyle Vogel likewise showed friendship and appreciation for the book research. Kyle always wanted to make sure there was love and romance in the book for broad appeal—and I hope that he is happy with the results. And not to leave out my nonhuman companion, my sweet and feisty Vizsla pup, Rosie, deserves a special shout-out for making me get out and power walk each day. Her snuggles helped me set the tone for my day and kept me grounded.

Indeed, I brought my whole person to the research and writing of this book. When I met with my interlocutors and they spoke of their love for their children, I felt a warm love for my own children. When mothers wept with worry for their children's futures and shared their great joys, I felt deep compassion and love for them. When I was away on research trips and giving talks, I missed my children and longed to be with them. It can be very challenging to be a devoted mother, partner, scholar, and teacher. It is joyful and fulfilling, but it is hard, and we need to acknowledge that in all its wonderfulness and messiness.

A huge and heartfelt thank-you goes out to my incredible editor, Elaine

Maisner, of UNC Press. Working with Elaine has been one of the great joys of my academic career. Elaine is encouraging, exacting, and wise—and always helps me hone my ideas and arguments into something better. Indeed, the entire staff of professionals at UNC Press is amazing, and I want to thank Erin Granville, UNC Press senior project editor; Dino Battista, UNC Press senior director of marketing and digital business development; Liz Orange, UNC Press marketing assistant; Sonya Bonczek, director of publicity; and Julie Bush, who copyedited *Meatpacking America* and whose talents are reflected in each page. And a warm thank-you goes out to my friend Lois Mincks, whom I first met at St. Joseph parish, Columbus Junction, in 2013, and whose photographic talents are featured in this book. Thank you, Lois, for spending countless hours poring through your hundreds of photographs and making special trips to take new photos for the book. I appreciate you and am so fortunate to know you and your family.

I want to end by focusing on my children, whom I love more than I could ever express: Cormac, who will be eighteen when the book is published; Declan, who will be fifteen; and Josie, twelve. You three are the light and joy of my life and were always understanding when I had to take research trips and hole up in my office to write. You asked questions about what I was up to and were always supportive. As you begin to think about what you would like to do in your lives and about what paths you might take, I hope that I have shown you and will continue to show you that a life well lived includes doing what you love. You are my greatest gift, and I wish for you lives that are deeply fulfilling and full of love. It is because of you three that I was able to connect with the women and men whose stories fill the pages of this book. Cormac, Declan, and Josie—you have made my heart whole and complete. It is the greatest blessing of my life to be your mama.

NOTES

Preface

1. The technical terminology designates an *asylum seeker* as someone who is seeking international protection but whose claim for refugee status has not yet been determined. A *refugee* is someone who has been recognized as such under the UN's 1951 Refugee Convention. In *Meatpacking America*, I will refer to all of the women and men I interviewed and worked with as refugees, whether or not they have obtained the legal status and designation as such. The simple fact is that all of them are seeking legal protection and safety under U.S. law.

In the August 27, 2019, Iowa Public Radio news special on refugees in eastern Iowa, the reporter Kate Payne highlighted the growing number of African refugees, in particular, who are moving to Iowa as part of a larger movement of secondary migration within the country. Iowa is an increasingly popular destination as its lush greenery, abundance of land, and slower pace of life appeal to families originally from Burundi who are moving from Illinois, New Jersey, California, Tennessee, and Georgia to live and work. As more native-born Iowans are leaving the state, refugees and immigrants are replacing them. And houses of worship like St. Paul's United Methodist Church in Cedar Rapids are embracing these newcomers to the state. As one Central African refugee, Nifasha Verariya, a member of St. Paul's, commented, "My dad always said, I am going to take you to a beautiful place. I'm going to take you to a place where you will have good schooling, you're going to have a good life, you're going to learn how to drive and have your own car. And it's happening! I drive now and I'm finished with school. Most of the stuff he said came true." Kate Payne, "Refugee Communities Seek Out Iowa to Put Down Roots," *Iowa Public Radio News*, August 27, 2019, https://www.iowapublicradio.org/post/refugee-communities-seek -out-iowa-put-down-roots.

2. In this book I adhere to the definitions of *migrant*, *refugee*, and *asylum seeker* laid out by the Council on Foreign Relations, or CFR. The CFR is an excellent, peer-reviewed resource and is continually updating its reports. According to the CFR, *migrant* is an umbrella term for asylum seekers, refugees, and economic migrants; *asylum seekers* are people fleeing persecution or conflict; and *economic migrants* are people who leave home to look for work. As the CFR explains, in the United States system, *refugees* are seeking entry from a third country, and asylum seekers follow a different protocol from those applying for refugee status. Asylum seekers meet criteria for refugee status but apply from within the United States or at ports of entry to the United States. Refugees are entitled to rights and protections

spelled out in international treaties. Economic migrants, however, are not entitled to the same protections as refugees under international law. Claire Felter and James McBride, "How Does the U.S. Refugee System Work?," Council of Foreign Relations, October 10, 2018, https://www.cfr.org/backgrounder/how-does-us-refugee-system -work.

3. The Trump administration has made it nearly impossible for Central American refugees to gain entrance to the United States, and asylum-seeking refugees are being sent back to dangerous, unstable countries for further "processing." The Northern Triangle is one of the most dangerous regions in the world to live. Nicole Narea, "Trump's Agreements in Central America Are Dismantling the Asylum System as We Know It," *Vox*, November 20, 2019, https://www.vox.com/2019/9/26/20870768 /trump-agreement-honduras-guatemala-el-salvador-explained.

4. Felter and McBride, "How Does the U.S. Refugee System Work?"

5. Jeffrey Hallock, Ariel G. Ruiz Soto, and Michael Fix, "In Search of Safety, Grow- ing Numbers of Women Flee Central America," Migration Policy Institute, May 30, 2018, https://www.migrationpolicy.org/article/search-safety-growing-numbers -women-flee-central-america.

6. See Kenneth M. Quinn, "Inside Robert D. Ray's Extraordinary Humanitarian Legacy," *Des Moines Register*, July 10, 2018, https://www.desmoinesregister.com /story/opinion/columnists/iowa-view/2018/07/10/iowa-governor-bob-ray-legacy -refugees-tai-dam-boat-people-cambodia-vietnam/768706002/; Daniel E. Slotnik, "Robert D. Ray, Centrist G. O. P. Governor of Iowa, Dies at 89," *New York Times*, July 10, 2018, https://www.nytimes.com/2018/07/10/obituaries/robert-d-ray-centrist -gop-governor-of-iowa-dies-at-89.html.

7. Sarah Smarsh, "Something Special Is Happening in Rural America," *New York Times*, September 17, 2019.

8. Sarah Smarsh, *Heartland: A Memoir of Working Hard and Being Broke in the Richest Country on Earth* (New York: Scribner, 2018), 123.

9. The farm crisis of the 1980s hit midwestern farmers particularly hard. For a clear and well-researched explanation of the farm crisis, see "1980s Farm Crisis," Market to Market Classroom, Iowa PBS, http://www.iowapbs.org/mtom/classroom/module /13999/farm-crisis; and for a look into how farmers are continuing to respond and learn from the crisis, see Nathanael Johnson, "What One Farmer Learned from Surviving the '80s Farm Crisis," *Grist*, April 21, 2015, https://grist.org/food/what-one -farmer-learned-from-surviving-the-80s-farm-crisis/.

10. "1980s Farm Crisis."

11. See Mayra Rodriguez Vallardes, "Trump's Trade Wars Are Hurting Midwest- ern Farmers, Banks, and State Coffers," *Forbes*, August 12, 2019; Chris Clayton, "Ag Policy Blog: Surveying Midwest Crop Farmers on China Tariffs," *Progressive Farmer*, November 4, 2019, https://www.dtnpf.com/agriculture/web/ag/blogs/ag-policy -blog/blog-post/2019/11/04/surveying-midwest-crop-farmers-china; Associated Press, "Trump Agricultural Policies Roil Midwest Farmers," *Courthouse News Service*, August 29, 2019, https://www.courthousenews.com/midwest-farmers-roiled-at -trump-ag-policies/; P. J. Huffstutter and Tom Polansek, "Many US Farmers Fume

at Washington, Not Trump, over Biofuel, Trade Policies," *Reuters*, September 10, 2019, https://www.reuters.com/article/us-usa-election-farmers/many-u-s-farmers -fume-at-washington-not-trump-over-biofuel-trade-policies-idUSKCN1VV11U; Ed Zwirn, "US Meat Industry Concerned about China Response to New Tariffs," *Food Navigator-USA*, May 10, 2019, https://www.globalmeatnews.com/Article/2019/05/10 /US-meat-industry-concerned-about-China-response-to-new-tariffs; Keegan Elmer and Liz Crampton, "Trump Tariffs Crush US Pig Farmers," *Politico*, June 19, 2019, https://www.politico.com/story/2019/06/19/trump-tariffs-us-pig-farmers-1538546; and Nyshka Chandran and Everett Rosenfeld, "China Announces It's Imposing New Tariffs on 128 US Products," *CNBC*, April 1, 2018, https://www.cnbc.com/2018/04/01 /china-announces-new-tariffs-on-us-meat-and-fruit-amid-trade-war-fears.html.

12. Erik Sherman, "Here's the Crushing Truth about American Farmers under Trump's Trade War," *Forbes*, December 27, 2019, https://www.forbes.com/sites /eriksherman/2019/12/27/trump-china-tariffs-farmers-subsidies/#18e3d5575b39.

13. I thank my colleague and friend Felipe Hinojosa for his astute observations and for pushing me to focus on the palpable feelings of not belonging and uncertainty that whites and refugees share in Iowa and rural America. Felipe's own work is a model of scholarly excellence, and my work has greatly benefited from his.

Introduction

1. See the preface for information on the interviewees and the locations where the interviews and conversations took place.

2. Shannon Speed, *Incarcerated Stories: Indigenous Women Migrants and Violence in the Settler-Capitalist State* (Chapel Hill: University of North Carolina Press, 2019).

3. Speed, 3.

4. Speed, 3.

5. The only thing that is not "real" about the undocumented individuals with whom I spoke and spent time is their names, to safeguard their identities. The names of some of the women and men featured in the book do reflect their given, birth names. They are documented citizens and refugees and want their names to be shared and their stories told to enlighten the readers of this book.

6. In addition to his many newspaper articles, see Art Cullen, *Storm Lake: A Chronicle of Change, Resilience, and Hope from a Heartland Newspaper* (New York: Viking, 2018).

7. Tyson Foods CEO Noel White issued a statement on Tyson's blog in March 2020 to announce the company's strategy to educate and take care of hourly workers, referred to as "team members": "Since information is the best tool for combatting the spread of COVID-19, we've been diligent about educating team members about the virus and ways to avoid catching it." The company created an "internal coronavirus page with access to videos and information about the virus, as well as the company's efforts to address it." In addition, White announced measures taken to ensure team members are not penalized for their illness, which include these: "relaxing attendance policies in our plants by eliminating any punitive effect for missing work due to

illness"; "waiving the 5 consecutive day waiting period for Short Term Disability benefits"; "waiving the co-pay, co-insurance and deductible for doctor visits for COVID-19 testing as well as eliminating pre-approval or preauthorization step"; "waiving co-pays for the use of telemedicine"; and "relaxing refill limits for 30 day prescriptions of maintenance medication." Noel White, "Protecting Team Members and Our Company; Ensuring Business Continuity," *The Feed Blog*, March 13, 2020, https://thefeed.blog/2020/03/13/protecting-team-members-and-our-company -ensuring-business-continuity/.

8. Robert Wuthnow, *The Left Behind: Decline and Rage in Rural America* (Princeton: Princeton University Press, 2018), 4.

9. Bethany Moreton, *To Serve God and Wal-Mart: The Making of Christian Free Enterprise* (Cambridge: Harvard University Press, 2010); Nicole Kirk, *Wannamaker's Temple: The Business of Religion in an Iconic Department Store* (New York: New York University Press, 2018).

10. Darren E. Grem, *The Blessings of Business: How Corporations Shaped Conservative Christianity* (New York: Oxford University Press, 2016).

11. Ayumi Takenaka, "Secondary Migration: Who Re-migrates and Why These Migrants Matter," Migration Policy Institute, https://www.migrationpolicy.org /article/secondary-migration-who-re-migrates-and-why-these-migrants-matter.

12. Alicia Schmidt Camacho, *Migrant Imaginaries: Latino Cultural Politics in the U.S.-Mexico Borderlands* (New York: New York University Press, 2008), 286.

13. Nicole Novak, "Immigration Raids Are Human-Made Disasters—and Iowans Know How to Respond," *Des Moines Register*, May 8, 2019, https://www.desmoines register.com/story/opinion/columnists/iowa-view/2019/05/08/mt-pleasant-ice-raid -disaster-but-many-stepped-up-help-immigration-recovery/1139465001/.

14. There is indeed fear among many whites in the Corn Belt, the same fear that we see throughout America: fear of change. But in the course of my own research I have not discovered a widespread rage of the kind that is portrayed in sociologist Robert Wuthnow's *The Left Behind: Decline and Rage in Rural America*. What I have found is that while there is some rage, for the most part there is fear and uncertainty, as many white rural midwesterners have not encountered a lot of ethnic and racial difference. But as they do, they see what the newer arrivals are contributing to their towns and communities. For some of these white native-born Americans, the fear morphs into what has been called the "alt-right," but for the vast majority—and these are the folks I have spent time with and interviewed—it is far too simplistic and, in the end, uninformed to call them "racist," "right-wingers," and/or "alt-right."

What I have discovered in my research is that while many white Americans struggle with what they perceive as rapidly changing demographics in America, they are usually not the racist tropes we find depicted in the media. Indeed, numerous white rural Americans are struggling with demographic changes in their communities. Many of these women and men are senior citizens living on Social Security and small pensions, and they receive most of their news from television. But the story gets more complicated as these white native-born Americans are cared for by Latinas, Vietnamese, and Chin Burmese female caregivers and are grateful for their help. They have developed friendships with some of their caregivers and have formed relationships that defy "angry white man/woman" stereotypes. White Iowans see their Latino and refugee neighbors shopping downtown, at work, and at church. They smile and exchange pleasantries but oftentimes do not engage in deep dialogue because of a language barrier. White Americans' preponderance toward monolingualism is indeed a major barrier toward cross-cultural dialogue and meaningful interactions with Spanish-speaking Latinos and is one of the biggest barriers to lessening cultural and linguistic divides.

15. For revisionist histories of the American Midwest, see Andrew R. Cayton, *The Midwest and the Nation: Rethinking the History of an American Region* (Bloomington: Indiana University Press, 1990); Andrew R. Cayton and Susan Grey, eds., *The Identity of the American Midwest: Essays on Regional History* (Bloomington: Indiana University Press, 2007); and Kristin L. Hoganson, *The Heartland: An American Story* (New York: Penguin Press, 2019). The Hoganson quote is from p. xxii.

16. Julianne Couch, *The Small-Town Midwest: Resilience and Hope in the Twenty-First Century* (Iowa City: University of Iowa Press, 2016).

17. For news stories on the Spencer–Storm Lake basketball game of January 2018, see Dana Larsen, "Racist Chants Reported at Storm Lake, Spencer High School Basketball Games," *Globe Gazette*, January 25, 2018, updated December 20, 2018, https://globegazette.com/news/iowa/racist-chants-reported-at-storm-lake-spencer -high-school-basketball-games/article_2a173cf5-c2af-5323-b5d8-5ca5bf979d8f.html. For another source on racism in Iowa's small towns and in sports, see Kyle Munson, "He's a Black High School Quarterback. 5 of His Teammates Were Pictured in White Hoods. It May Get Worse," *Des Moines Register*, September 8, 2017, updated September 11, 2017, https://www.desmoinesregister.com/story/news/local/columnists /kyle-munson/2017/09/08/black-high-school-quarterback-teammates-pictured -white-hoods-cross-burning-kkk-confederate-flag/644784001/.

18. The majority of white non-Latino Iowans with whom I have spoken, broken bread, and laughed and cried are more hopeful than afraid. They love America and admire those newcomers who display their own love for the Stars and Stripes. Deep down in their bones they know, and sometimes acknowledge, that their towns would be shuttered or significantly diminished were it not for the recent migrants and refugee arrivals. But fears and concerns exist and can and do manifest themselves in ethnocentric and racist comments and actions. If stoked and left unchallenged, they can burn out of control and will negatively impact a community. It is my hope, more than anything, that this book in its small way can help prevent the flames of xenophobia from being started in the first place.

Chapter 1

1. Linda Gordon, *The Second Coming of the KKK: The Ku Klux Klan of the 1920s and the American Political Tradition* (New York: Liveright Books, 2018), 4.

2. Jo Ann Manfra, "Hometown Politics and the American Protective Association, 1887–1890," *Annals of Iowa* 55, no 2 (Spring 1996): 138–66.

3. Manfra, 166.

4. Carol Bodensteiner, *Growing Up Country: Memories of an Iowa Farm Girl* (Des Moines: Rising Sun Press, 2008), 80–81.

5. Bodensteiner, 52.

6. Paula Kane, introduction to *Gender Identities in American Catholicism*, ed. Paula M. Kane, Karen Kennelly, and James Kenneally (New York: Orbis Books, 2001), xxvi.

7. Lisa Lynn Ossian, "The Home Fronts of Iowa, 1940–1945" (Ph.D. diss., Iowa State University, 1998), 4.

8. The *St. Malachy's Church of Ardon, Iowa, Cookbook* (Audubon, Iowa: Jumbo Jack's Cookbook Co., 1988), http://iagenweb.org/muscatine/Societies/stmalachy.htm, gives this bit of history:

> These immigrants and other Catholic families in the area established the parish of St. Malachy's of Ardon in 1856, a brick church built 1 ½ miles west of the village of Ardon on present day X-43 north of the existing 76 township hall. Bartholomew Cashman donated one acre of land for the structure with the construction done mainly by the parishioners, the brick being fired in a kiln ¼ mile north of the church. Ten acres of timber land across the road were given by the Thomas Kelly family for fuel. The new church was named after a twelfth century Bishop of Ireland, St. Malachy. Because of the shortage of priests in this area, Bishop Loras of the Diocese of Dubuque (the Davenport Diocese was created in 1881) designated St. Malachy's an out-mission to be served when a priest was available.

9. Barb Arland-Fye, "Judge Closes Bankruptcy Case against Diocese of Daven-port," *Catholic News Service*, July 5, 2012, https://www.catholicnews.com/services /englishnews/2012/judge-closes-bankruptcy-case-against-diocese-of-davenport.cfm.

10. Stefan Farrar, "Iowa Diocese to Close Nearly Half of Parishes," *Church Militant*, January 17, 2017, https://www.churchmilitant.com/news/article/iowa-diocese -planning-to-close-45-of-parishes.

11. Hillary Kaell, "Seeing the Invisible: Ambient Catholicism on the Side of the Road," *Journal of the American Academy of Religion* 85 (March 2017): 136–37.

12. Janet Weaver, "Iowa Migrant Workers," Migration Is Beautiful, Iowa Women's Archives, University of Iowa Libraries, 2016, https://migration.lib.uiowa.edu/exhibits /show/activism/iowa-migrant-workers.

13. W. K. Barger and Ernesto M. Reza, *The Farm Labor Movement in the Midwest: Social Change and Adaptation among Migrant Farmworkers in the Midwest* (Austin: University of Texas Press, 1994), 35.

14. For a more detailed history of the city of Muscatine and of Mexicans and Puerto Ricans who worked for Heinz and braceros, see Micheal Hutchinson, "River of Steel, River of Sweat: Early Mexican American Community in Muscatine, Iowa," Migration Is Beautiful, Iowa Women's Archives, University of Iowa Libraries, 2016, http://migration.lib.uiowa.edu/exhibits/show/barrio-settlements/muscatine.

15. It saddens me to have to write this endnote. Mike lost his battle with cancer in June 2020 as I was revising the book for publication. He will be missed.

16. *Saint Joseph's Catholic Church: Sesquicentennial Past and Present Celebrating 150 Years, 1853–2003* (Columbus Junction, Iowa: St. Joseph's Catholic Church, 2003), 4.

17. The modest population growth of 3 percent throughout Iowa in the 1940s and 1950s was due to a postwar baby boom rather than in-migration from other states and places. See Paul J. Jehlik and Ray E. Wakeley, "Rural-Urban Migration in Iowa, 1940–5," *IAHEES Research Bulletin* 31, no. 407 (April 1954): 779–835, 781.

18. Samuel Mazzuchelli, *The Memoirs of Father Samuel Mazzuchelli, OP* (Chicago: Priory Press, 1967), 321.

19. Current boosterism and telling the story of Columbus Junction, Iowa, focus on more recent refugees and migrants to the city. When religion is mentioned, the Catholic past and present tend to not be included. The online series Exploring the Renewal of the Heartland, for example, credits the Methodist church in Columbus Junction for its outreach and work with Chin Burmese but doesn't mention long-standing Catholic outreach to Latino migrants. "Columbus Junction, Iowa," Exploring the Renewal of the Heartland, Ewing Marion Kaufmann Foundation, accessed December 12, 2020, https://www.kauffman.org/eship-city/columbus -junction/.

20. Sadly, this was the last time I was to talk with Bob, who passed away several months later.

21. Helen B. Shaffer, "Mixed Marriage," in *Editorial Research Reports 1961*, vol. 1 (Washington, D.C.: CQ Press, 1961), 379–98, https://library.cqpress.com/cqresearcher /document.php?id=cqresrre1961052400#H2_2. The rise of interfaith marriages in postwar America has been called a "different sort of civil religion" by the historian Erika B. Seamon, "An Era of Interreligious Marriage: Societal Doors Open in the Twentieth Century," in *Interfaith Marriage in America* (New York: Palgrave Macmillan, 2012), 71–91.

Chapter 2

1. Gary Schnitkey in the Department of Consumer Culture and Economics at the University of Illinois asserts that there is "remarkable stability in shares of planted corn acres across states." The six states with the most acres of corn are Iowa, with 14.6 million acres; Illinois, with 12.5 million acres; Nebraska, with 10.3 million acres; Minnesota, with 8.7 million acres; Indiana, with 6.1 million acres; and South Dakota, with 5.5 million acres. Gary Schnitkey, "Little Change in Where Corn Is Planted in the United States," *FarmDoc Daily*, April 3, 2012, https://farmdocdaily.illinois.edu /2012/04/little-change-in-where-corn-is.html.

2. Iowa has forty-two ethanol plants and produces 25 percent of ethanol in the United States. See "Ethanol Plants," Iowa Corn, accessed December 13, 2020, http:// www.iowacorn.org/en/ethanol/iowa_ethanol_plants/.

3. Robert Wuthnow, *The Left Behind: Decline and Rage in Rural America* (Princeton: Princeton University Press, 2018), 143–44. Wuthnow's recent books focusing on rural white America are based on qualitative and quantitative sociological research and are important works that delve into the sociological role of religion in rural America. See

Wuthnow, *In the Blood: Understanding America's Farm Families* (Princeton: Princeton University Press, 2015); *Red State Religion: Faith and Politics in America's Heartland* (Princeton: Princeton University Press, 2012); and *Small-Town America: Finding Community, Shaping the Future* (Princeton: Princeton University Press, 2013). For other excellent monographs on economic challenges and decline in the Midwest and in small-town and rural America in particular, see Chad Broughton, *Boom, Bust, Exodus: The Rust Belt, the Maquilas, and a Tale of Two Cities* (Oxford: Oxford University Press, 2015); Patrick J. Carr and Maria J. Kefalas, *Hollowing Out the Middle: The Rural Brain Drain and What It Means for America* (Boston: Beacon Press, 2009); and Cynthia M. Duncan, *Worlds Apart: Poverty and Politics in Rural America* (New Haven: Yale University Press, 2014).

4. Wuthnow, *Left Behind*, 144.

5. Louis Mendoza, "Conversations across 'Our America,'" in *The Latina/o Midwest Reader*, ed. Omar Valerio-Jiménez, Santiago Vaquera-Vásquez, and Claire Fox (Urbana: University of Illinois Press, 2017), 31.

6. Wuthnow, *Left Behind*, 4.

7. Sujey Vega, *Latino Heartland: Of Borders and Belonging in the Midwest* (New York: New York University Press, 2015), 179. Vega's excellent work is part of a new wave of revisionist scholarship that focuses on Latinos in the Midwest. Fine examples of this work include Teresa Delgadillo, *Latina Lives in Milwaukee* (Urbana: University of Illinois Press, 2015); Michael Innis-Jiménez, *Steel Barrio: The Great Mexican Migration to South Chicago, 1915–1940* (New York: New York University Press, 2013); Lilia Fernández, *Brown in the Windy City: Mexicans and Puerto Ricans in Postwar Chicago* (Chicago: University of Chicago Press, 2012); Ann V. Millard and Jorge Chapa, *Apple Pie and Enchiladas: Latino Newcomers in the Rural Midwest* (Austin: University of Texas Press, 2001); Rubén O. Martinez, ed., *Latinos in the Midwest* (East Lansing: Michigan State University Press, 2011); Omar Valerio-Jiménez, Santiago Vaquera-Vásquez, and Claire F. Fox, eds., *The Latina/o Midwest Reader* (Urbana: University of Illinois Press, 2017); and Deborah Kanter, *Chicago Católico: Making Catholic Parishes Mexican* (Urbana: University of Illinois Press, 2019). While the scholarship on Latinos in the Midwest is expanding, we still need more on Latinos and religion in the Midwest. In the past, many histories of Latinos have overlooked or downplayed the role of religion and spirituality. While we are most certainly seeing a new focus on the religious and spiritual lives of Latinos in the Midwest, it is my hope that humanists and social scientists alike will pay greater attention to religion and spirituality and how they impact people and their communities. Felipe Hinojosa in *Latino Mennonites: Civil Rights, Faith, and Evangelical Culture* (Baltimore: Johns Hopkins University Press, 2014) includes the Midwest in his sweeping study of how Latino Mennonites combined evangelical fervor with a call for civil rights. Deborah Kanter's recently published *Chicago Católico* is an excellent example of a historical study that takes into account the intersectionalities of migration, settlement, religion, and society.

8. As the historian Mildred Throne has pointed out, agriculture in the state of Iowa

underwent radical changes from the mid-nineteenth century to the early twentieth century. First-wave migrants to the state were subsistence farmers, but by the end of the nineteenth century, the shift to commercial agriculture—which would dramatically change the culture and landscape of the state—had begun. Corinne and Urban were part of the last generation of subsistence farmers and saw agriculture shift from what Throne calls a "way of life" to a business. Mildred Throne, "Southern Iowa Agriculture, 1833–1890: The Process from Subsistence to Commercial Corn-Belt Farming," *Agricultural History* 23, no. 2 (April 1949), 124–30.

9. "By the Numbers—Iowa Latino Facts—State of Iowa," League of United Latin American Citizens Council #307, accessed January 12, 2021, http://latinovoteiowa .org/about-us/iowa-map/.

10. Wuthnow, *Left Behind*, 144.

11. Deborah Fink, *Cutting into the Meatpacking Line: Workers and Change in the Rural Midwest* (Chapel Hill: University of North Carolina Press, 1998), 1.

12. Fink, 1.

13. For an excellent study of urban working-class labor and the role of progressive religion, see Heath Carter's *Union Made: Working People and the Rise of Social Christianity in Chicago* (Oxford: Oxford University Press, 2015).

14. See Tricia Mein Bruce, *Parish and Place: Making Room for Diversity in the American Catholic Church* (New York: Oxford University Press, 2017); Brett Hoover, *The Shared Parish: Latinos, Anglos, and the Future of U.S. Catholicism* (New York: NYU Press, 2014).

15. Human Rights Watch has reported that sending deportees home to violent countries results in sexual violence, other forms of violence, and in some cases death. See "At Least 138 Salvadorans Deported by U.S. Were Killed, Report Says," *Time*, February 6, 2020, https://time.com/5778851/el-salvador-deportation-killed-u-s -refugees/; and Sarah Stillman, "When Deportation Is a Death Sentence," *New Yorker*, January 15, 2018, https://www.newyorker.com/magazine/2018/01/15/when-deportation -is-a-death-sentence.

16. Camila Kirtzman, "Domestic and Gang Violence Victims Become Ineligible for Asylum," Children's Defense Fund—New York, August 2018, https://www .childrensdefense.org/cdfny/wp-content/uploads/sites/3/2018/08/Domestic-Gang -Violence-Report-with-GRAPHIC.pdf.

17. Moreover, some Latinos are on a temporary H-2A work visa program for agricultural workers, and others who work in the meatpacking plants that dot the Midwest are on an H-2B visa for temporary nonagricultural workers.

18. According to a 2012 Pew Research Center study, the vast majority of U.S. Latinos claim affiliation with Roman Catholicism, at 62 percent; 19 percent claim affiliation with Protestant evangelicals and 13 percent with mainline Protestants. The high rates of Latino affiliation with Roman Catholicism contrast sharply with the general population, which in 2012 was 23 percent Catholic and 50 percent Protestant (white evangelical, 18 percent; white mainline, 17 percent; Black Protestant, 9 percent; other, 6 percent). Paul Taylor, Mark Hugo Lopez, Jessica Martínez, and Gabriel

Velasco, "Part V: Politics, Values, and Religion," in *When Labels Don't Fit: Hispanics and Their Views of Identity*, April 4, 2012, https://www.pewresearch.org/hispanic/2012/04/04/v-politics-values-and-religion/.

19. State Data Center of Iowa and the Office of Latino Affairs, *Latinos in Iowa, 2020*, September 2020, https://www.iowadatacenter.org/Publications/latinos2020.pdf.

20. The Latino population has grown in all midwestern Corn Belt states and continues to rise. In Ohio, Indiana, Illinois, Wisconsin, Michigan, Iowa, Nebraska, and Kansas, the Latino population has experienced rapid growth since 2000. Lydia R. Anderson, "Hispanics in the Midwest," *Ohio Population News*, Center for Family and Demographic Research, April 2016, https://www.bgsu.edu/content/dam/BGSU/college-of-arts-and-sciences/center-for-family-and-demographic-research/documents/OPN/Ohio-Population-News-2016-Hispanics-in-the-Midwest.pdf. The Latino population continues to grow across the United States by way of migration, in-migration from other states, and births. In 2017, the states that experienced the largest Latino population growth included Wyoming, Maryland, Hawai'i, Oklahoma, Nebraska, Massachusetts, Kansas, Idaho, Washington, Oregon, Utah, and Rhode Island. Elliott Davis, "13 States with Recent Hispanic Population Growth," *U.S. News & World Report*, February 25, 2020, https://www.usnews.com/news/best-states/slideshows/13-states-with-recent-hispanic-population-growth.

21. Courtney Crowder and MacKenzie Elmer, "A Decade after a Massive Raid Nabbed 400 Undocumented Workers, a Tiny Town Fights to Reclaim Its Identity," *Des Moines Register*, May 17, 2018, https://www.desmoinesregister.com/story/news/investigations/2018/05/10/postville-immigration-raid-10-year-anniversary-town-reclaims-identity/587995002/.

22. According to the Tyson Fresh Meats official website, Tyson Foods, Inc., pays its employees an average of $15.63 an hour. Hourly pay at Tyson Foods ranges from $11.24 to $23.52 an hour. Tyson Foods employees with the job title Ammonia Refrigeration Technician make the most, with an average hourly rate of $21.66, while employees with the title Laborer make the least. At the Columbus Junction plant, there are ample opportunities to move up the pay scale and to apply for new positions, as I learned during my fieldwork there. According to the 2020 Cost of Living Calculator, the cost of living in Columbus Junction, Iowa, rates a 77.7 on a scale of 100, which means that anything below 100 is cheaper than the U.S. average. "2020 Cost of Living Calculator: Columbus Junction, Iowa vs Branson, Colorado," Best Places, accessed December 13, 2020, https://www.bestplaces.net/cost-of-living/columbus-junction-ia/branson-co/50000.

23. Father Joseph Sia, homily, St. Joseph parish, Columbus Junction, Iowa, February 2016.

24. Mary Jo Bane, "A House Divided," in *American Parishes: Remaking Local Catholicism*, ed. Gary Adler, Tricia Bruce, and Brian Starks (New York: Fordham University Press, July 2019), 153–72.

25. "Older Iowans: 2018," State Data Center of Iowa and the Iowa Department on Aging, May 2018, http://publications.iowa.gov/28014/1/older2018.pdf.

26. Sujey Vega, *Latino Heartland: Of Borders and Belonging in the Midwest* (New York: New York University Press, 2015).

27. Sharon R. Ennis, Merarys Rios-Vargas, and Nora G. Albert, *The Hispanic Population: 2010*, 2010 Census Briefs, C2010BR-04, U.S. Census Bureau, May 2011, https://www.census.gov/prod/cen2010/briefs/c2010br-04.pdf.

28. The U.S. Census reported in August 2019 that there were 59.9 million Latinos in the United States, at 18.3 percent of the total U.S. population. "Hispanic Heritage Month 2019," United States Census Bureau, August 20, 2019, https://www.census .gov/newsroom/facts-for-features/2019/hispanic-heritage-month.html.

29. Michael J. Broadway, "Meatpacking," *Encyclopedia of the Great Plains* (Lincoln: University of Nebraska Press, 2011), accessed September 15, 2018, http://plains humanities.unl.edu/encyclopedia/doc/egp.ind.038.xml.

30. Fink, *Cutting into the Meatpacking Line*. In their book *The Mayans among Us: Migrant Women and Meatpacking on the Great Plains*, Ann Sittig and Martha González offer compelling stories of faith and work and of Mayans' invisibility to most Americans (Lincoln, Neb.: Bison Books, 2016).

31. Melissa Regennitter, "Labor Pains: Migrant Workers in Conesville Say They've Been Left Stranded," *Muscatine Journal*, August 8, 2008, https://muscatinejournal .com/news/local/labor-pains-migrant-workers-in-conesville-say-they-ve-been /article_b0f6cf72–7c4c-5a35–955f-076db72529aa.html.

32. See the following essay on migrant farmworkers and the cycle of low wages and exploitation: Brian Barth, "The High Cost of Cheap Labor," *Modern Farmer*, February 21, 2017, http://modernfarmer.com/2017/02/migrant-farm-workers-the -high-cost-of-cheap-labor/.

33. Regennitter, "Labor Pains."

34. Regennitter, "Labor Pains."

35. Regennitter, "Labor Pains."

36. "Migrant Health," Proteus, accessed December 13, 2020, https://www .proteusinc.net/programs/iowa/health/.

37. Nathaniel Otjen, "Latino Immigrant Gardeners in Iowa: Local Knowledge and the Cultivation of a Twenty-First-Century Environmental Consciousness" (bachelor's honors thesis, University of Iowa, 2016).

38. See *The Harvest/La Cosecha*, directed by U. Roberto Romano (Cinema Libre Studio, 2011).

Chapter 3

1. "Fr. Bernie Celebrates 25 Years in Priesthood," June 15, 2011, *Albia Newspapers* https://www.albianews.com/news/article_9afadc5e-9760-11e0-8c19-001cc4c002e0 .html.

2. Robert R. Dykstra, "Iowans and the Politics of Race," in *Iowa History Reader*, ed. Marvin Bergman (Iowa City: University of Iowa Press, 1996), 129–57, 131.

3. Shirley Ragsdale, "Serious Problems Await New Bishop," *Des Moines Register*, October 13, 2006.

4. Jessica Martínez, "Among Catholics, Fewer Latinos Than Whites Seek Changes to the Church," Pew Research Center, September 21, 2015, https://www.pewresearch .org/fact-tank/2015/09/21/latino-catholics-white-catholics-changes-to-church/.

5. Since our interviews, Father Greg has left St. Joseph and is now a hospital chaplain at University of Iowa hospitals, Iowa City. Father Guillermo Treviño is his replacement as parish priest.

6. "Boards Making a Difference: Dual Language Programs," Iowa Association of School Boards, accessed September 15, 2018, https://www.ia-sb.org/Main /Newsroom/Boards_Making_a_Difference/Dual_Language_Programs.aspx.

7. A renewed sociology of the parish will lead us to reconceptualize American Catholic Studies as both an urban phenomenon *and* an agrarian one. For their part, sociologists have offered some useful frameworks for understanding contemporary American Catholicisms, and these have included magnet parishes, territorial parishes, flagship parishes, and national parishes. As Brett Hoover notes, sociologists tend to use the terminology "parallel congregations," while pastoral leaders have leaned toward the designation "multicultural parishes," "mixed parishes," or "integrated parish." Brett Hoover, *The Shared Parish: Latinos, Anglos, and the Future of American Catholicism* (New York: New York University Press, 2014).

Chapter 4

1. James Merchant and David Osterberg, "Iowans Want Action Limiting CAFOs," *Iowa Press Citizen*, February 19, 2020, 7A.

2. Jim Caufield, "Group Says DNR Fails in Oversight, Enforcement of Manure Laws," *Perry News*, November 5, 2015, https://theperrynews.com/group-says-dnr -fails-in-oversight-enforcement-of-manure-laws/.

3. Jamie Konopacky and Soren Rundquist, "EWG Mapping and Study Show Large CAFOs in Iowa Up Fivefold since 1990," EWG, January 21, 2020, https://www.ewg .org/interactive-maps/2020-iowa-cafos/.

4. Caufield, "DNR Fails in Oversight."

5. Donnelle Eller, "Shades of Brown: Iowa Ranks No. 1 in, Ahem, No. 2, UI Researcher Calculates," *Des Moines Register*, June 10, 2019, https://www.desmoines register.com/story/money/agriculture/2019/06/10/iowa-leads-nation-poop -manure-university-iowa-livestock-clean-water-pollution-shades-brown-waste /1379973001/.

6. William Cronon, *Nature's Metropolis: Chicago and the Great West* (New York: W. W. Norton, 1992), 226.

7. "How Much Is Iowa Getting Pooped On?," Raygun (blog), accessed September 10, 2017, https://www.raygunsite.com/blogs/news/how-much-is-iowa -getting-pooped-on.

8. See Darren E. Grem, *The Blessings of Business: How Corporations Shaped Conservative Christianity* (New York: Oxford University Press, 2016).

9. Upton Sinclair, *The Jungle* (New York: Dover, 1906), 21.

10. My strategy for the day was to breathe through my mouth, and I used my

nostrils to push out all of the smells. The mantras I repeated to myself over and over were, "I can do this," and this was a "very important part of the book research." As I walked through the plant, I took mental and written notes so that readers could see the same sights, smell the smells, and know what workers do there. As I took the tour, I knew that I needed to see the bowels of the plant, quite literally, if I was to convey the realities of a meat processing plant. I think of the current negative sentiments against immigrants and about how they supposedly take away jobs from "Americans." This was my sacrifice as an anthropologist of religion, however small, to portray a truth, a reality of the hard, bloody, and dangerous labor that immigrants and refugees do each day. It is labor that feeds native-born American families and families across the world.

11. For an insightful history of Henry Ford and his impact on American business and the work ethic, see Richard Snow, *I Invented the Modern Age: The Rise of Henry Ford* (New York: Scribner, 2014).

12. Frederick Winslow Taylor, *Scientific Management* (New York: Harper, 1947).

13. For more details on the U.S. Diversity Lottery program, see the U.S. Department of State website Travel.State.Gov: https://travel.state.gov/content/travel/en/us-visas/immigrate/diversity-visa-program-entry.html.

14. Emma Green, "Finding Jesus at Work," *The Atlantic*, February 17, 2016, https://www.theatlantic.com/business/archive/2016/02/work-secularization-chaplaincies/462987/.

15. For an excellent source on Don Tyson and the rise of chicken in America, see Steve Striffler, *Chicken: The Dangerous Transformation of America's Favorite Food* (New Haven: Yale University Press, 2005). For the go-to source on S. Truett Cathy, Chick-fil-A, and the broader Faith at Work movement in the United States, see Grem, *Blessings of Business.*

16. Miller and Tarvin quoted in Green, "Finding Jesus at Work."

17. "Tyson Foods Appoints Karen Diefendorf as Director of Chaplain Services" (press release), Tyson Foods, March 15, 2017, https://www.tysonfoods.com/news/news-releases/2017/3/tyson-foods-appoints-karen-diefendorf-director-chaplain-services.

18. Diefendorf earned her bachelor of arts in Christian education from Lincoln Christian College in Lincoln, Illinois; her master of divinity from Lincoln Christian Seminary in Lincoln; and her master of sacred theology from Yale University.

19. "Tyson Foods Appoints."

20. "Tyson Foods Appoints."

21. David W. Miller, *God at Work: The History and Promise of the Faith at Work Movement* (Oxford: University of Oxford Press, 2007), 74.

22. C. S. Lewis, *The Four Loves* (New York: Harcourt, Brace, Jovanovich, 1960), 169–70.

23. Ruth Behar, *The Vulnerable Observer: Anthropology That Breaks Your Heart* (Boston: Beacon Press, 1996).

24. Alex Blanchette, in his recent and excellent ethnography of workers at a vertically integrated hog slaughterhouse, draws the reader's attention to the

industrialized animal-human bonds that are formed and the emotions involved in the work. See *Porkopolis: American Animality, Standardized Life, and the Factory Farm* (Durham: Duke University Press, 2020). See also other recent scholarship by anthropologists on meatpacking, migration, and rural and small-town America: Clement Loo, ed., *Invisible Sacrifices: How Industrial Food Production Obscures Bodies and Lives in Interdisciplinary Perspectives on Participation and Food Justice* (Fayetteville: University of Arkansas Press, forthcoming 2021); Cristina Ortiz, "Newcomers in a Small Town: The Challenges of Being an Immigrant in Rural Minnesota," Center for Rural Policy and Development, accessed January 14, 2021, https://www.ruralmn.org/publications/letters-to-the-new-governor-of-minnesota/issue-01/newcomers-in-a-small-town/; and Angela Stuesse, *Scratching Out a Living: Latinos, Race, and Work in the Deep South* (Berkeley: University of California Press, 2016). Joanna Siercks Smith's Ph.D. dissertation, "Prohibition, Transgression, and the Configuration of Bodies at the Modern Slaughterhouse" (Chapel Hill: University of North Carolina Press, forthcoming 2021), examines meatpacking in North Carolina, social stratification, and what Siercks Smith calls "negative sacred space."

25. Sociologist of religion Wade Clark Roof, in his essay "Blood in the Barbecue?," makes the argument that pigs and the rituals around southern barbecue are sacred symbols and acts (in *God in the Details: American Religion in Popular Culture*, ed. Eric Mazur and Kate McCarthy, 2nd ed. [New York: Routledge, 2011], 108–19). One could reasonably extend Roof's argument and apply it to *Meatpacking America* and the centrality of pork in Iowa and surrounding Corn Belt states.

26. World Health Organization, *Global Tuberculosis Report 2020* (Geneva: World Health Organization), https://apps.who.int/iris/bitstream/handle/10665/336069/9789240013131-eng.pdf. Current and archived WHO reports on tuberculosis are available at the Institutional Repository for Information Sharing, https://apps.who.int/iris/. The WHO's *Global Tuberculosis Report 2020* reports that "the COVID-19 pandemic threatens to reverse recent progress in reducing the global burden of TB disease" and offers this sobering prognosis: "The global number of TB deaths could increase by around 0.2–0.4 million in 2020 alone, if health services are disrupted to the extent that the number of people with TB who are detected and treated falls by 25–50% over a period of 3 months." World Health Organization, *Global Tuberculosis Report 2020*, xvi.

27. According to Dr. Hornick, companies like Tyson are not required to screen workers/employees.

28. "Side Effects," TB Alert, accessed August 15, 2018, https://www.tbalert.org/about-tb/global-tb-challenges/side-effects/.

29. Ed Raber, "Washington's Heidi Vittetoe Named '2011 Woman in Agriculture' by Iowa Farm Bureau," December 12, 2011, https://www.thegazette.com/2011/12/12/washingtons-heidi-vittetoe-named-2011-woman-in-agriculture-by-iowa-farm-bureau.

30. For a short and concise overview of the causes and fallout of the 1980s farm crisis, see Kurt Lawton, "Taking a Look Back at the 1980s Farm Crisis and Its

Impacts," *Corn and Soybean Digest*, August 22, 2016, http://www.cornandsoybean digest.com/marketing/taking-look-back-1980s-farm-crisis-and-its-impacts. For a more detailed history and analysis of the crisis, see Sue Ann Atkinson, "The Farm Crisis of the 1980s in Iowa: Its Roots and Its Inner Workings" (master's thesis, Iowa State University, 1999), https://lib.dr.iastate.edu/cgi/viewcontent.cgi?article=17848 &context=rtd.

31. Jacob Bunge and Jesse Newman, "To Stay on the Land, Farmers Add Extra Jobs," *Wall Street Journal*, February 25, 2018, https://www.wsj.com/articles/to-stay -on-the-land-american-farmers-add-extra-jobs-1519582071. According to a recent Iowa State University Ag Extension report, one in three farmers today has a job outside of farming where he or she works more than 200 days. William Edwards, "New Census of Agriculture Reveals Much About Iowa Farms," Iowa State University Extension and Outreach, September 2019, https://www.extension.iastate.edu /agdm/articles/edwards/EdwSept19.html.

Chapter 5

1. According to JW.org, the church-sponsored organization and website, Jehovah's Witnesses have had a presence in the Congo since the 1930s. Currently, there are close to 178,000 Jehovah's Witnesses in the Congo and over 3,200 congregations. See the Congo page at JW.org: https://www.jw.org/en/jehovahs-witnesses/worldwide /CD/.

Jehovah's Witnesses have sponsored language programs and classes at the Tongo-gara refugee camp, the same camp where James and his family lived prior to coming to the United States. "Jehovah's Witnesses Conventions Kick into High Gear," *Newsday*, July 5, 2019, https://www.newsday.co.zw/2019/07/jehovahs-witnesses -conventions-kick-into-high-gear/.

2. For detailed information on the hiring process of refugees in Iowa, see Bureau of Refugee Services, "Hiring Refugees," Iowa Department of Human Services, https://dhs.iowa.gov/Consumers/RefugeeServices/Employment/HiringRefugees.

3. IPB was purchased by the Omaha, Nebraska-based National Beef Packing on June 10, 2019.

4. Creekstone Farms' branding of itself as a company dedicated to stewardship of land and animals was appealing to the heads of IPB. The upper-management team at IPB has worked hard to follow Creekstone Farms' example of telling a story of encouraging farm-to-table eating, supporting family farms, and integrating faith into their business. See the company website at https://www.creekstonefarms.com.

5. George Ford, "Tama Approves Tax Breaks for Idled Beef Processing Plant," *The Gazette*, July 6, 2013, http://www.thegazette.com/2013/07/06/tama-approves-tax -breaks-for-idled-beef-processing-plant.

6. Colin Gordon, *Stolen Chances: Low-Wage Work and Wage Theft in Iowa*, Iowa Policy Project, September 2, 2015, https://www.iowapolicyproject.org/2015Research /150902-wagetheft.html. Gordon provides sobering data from a study of 300 Iowa

workers that includes the following statistics: 25 percent of the respondents reported wage theft in the previous year; 20 percent of the respondents reported not having received overtime pay, to a total of almost $40,000 in unpaid wages; nearly 20 percent of the surveyed worked reported late or unpaid wages, to a total of $20,000; and 20 percent of the workers surveyed reported not being paid at all for some of the hours worked.

7. Courtney Crowder and MacKenzie Elmer, "Postville Raid Anniversary: A Timeline of Events in One of America's Largest Illegal Immigration Campaigns," *Des Moines Register*, May 10, 2018, https://www.desmoinesregister.com/story/news /investigations/2018/05/10/postville-raid-anniversary-timeline-aaron-rubashkin -agriprocessors-postville-iowa-immigration-raid/588025002/.

8. James Sherk, "Right-to-Work Laws: Myth vs. Fact," The Heritage Foundation, December 12, 2014, https://www.heritage.org/jobs-and-labor/report/right-work -laws-myth-vs-fact.

9. Ryan Erickson and Karla Walter, "Right to Work Would Harm All Americans," Center for American Progress Action Fund, May 18, 2017, https://www.american progressaction.org/issues/economy/reports/2017/05/18/167539/right-work-harm -americans/.

10. The Center for American Progress also asserts that "opponents of unions frequently claim that workers who decline to join a union are still legally required to support that union's political activities. In reality, however, these fees exclude the costs of political activities." Erickson and Walter, "Right to Work Would Harm All Americans."

11. Jimmy M. Skaggs, *Prime Cut: Livestock Raising and Meatpacking in the United States, 1607–1983* (College Station: Texas A&M University Press, 2000), 190.

12. Steve Striffler, *Chicken: The Dangerous Transformation of America's Favorite Food* (New Haven: Yale University Press, 2005), 39.

13. Striffler, 72.

14. Skaggs, *Prime Cut*, 191.

15. Skaggs, 191.

16. Skaggs, 191.

17. Brenda's brothers were target for gang recruitment during a rise in gang activity and involvement in Greeley and surrounding Colorado towns. See Mike Peters, "The Gangs," *Greeley Tribune*, November 12, 2004, https://www.greeleytribune.com/news /local/the-gangs/; and Peters, "Gangs in Greeley," *Greeley Tribune*, April 24, 2005, https://www.greeleytribune.com/news/gangs-in-greeley-riding-into-the-dark-side/.

18. Amanda Porterfield, Darren E. Grem, and John Corrigan, eds., *The Business Turn in American Religious History* (Oxford: Oxford University Press, 2017), 13.

19. Porterfield, Grem, and Corrigan, 13–14.

20. Porterfield, Grem, and Corrigan, 13.

21. Bethany Moreton, *To Serve God and Wal-Mart: The Making of Christian Free Enterprise* (Cambridge, Mass.: Harvard University Press, 2010).

22. Robert Wright, preface to *The Business Turn in American Religious History*, ed.

Amanda Porterfield, Darren E. Grem, and John Corrigan (Oxford: Oxford University Press, 2017), x.

23. Porterfield, Grem, and Corrigan, *Business Turn*, 4–5.

24. Joe Blay, email to me, Tuesday, February 13, 2018.

25. "New 100% Halal Beef Processing Plant Opening in Tama, Iowa," *Halal Transactions* (blog), Halal Transactions of Omaha, June 24, 2014, https://halaltransactions .wordpress.com/2014/06/24/new-0-halal-beef-slaughtering-plant-opening-in -tama-ia/.

26. According to the Halal Food Authority guidelines,

> To make meat halal or permissible, an animal or poultry has to be slaughtered in a ritual way known as Zibah or Zabihah. To make it readily comprehended halal is somewhat like Jewish kosher and, Zibah is with some exception similar to Shechita. The Qur'an gives following underlined injunctions in chapter al-Maida 5:3 that:
>
> • Zabihah require animals to be alive and healthy at the time of slaughter, since carrion is forbidden and, jugular vein, carotid artery and windpipe have to be severed by a razor sharp knife by a single swipe, to incur as less a pain as possible. Here the only difference is that a rabbi will read what is required by his faith and, a Muslim will recite tasmiya or shahada, which fulfills the requirement of dedication. The question of how to overcome the issue of recitation of shahada on individual bird whence we now have poultry being slaughtered at a rate of six to nine thousand per hour, has already been addressed. A Muslim is commanded to commence all his deeds in the name of Allah.
> • All the flowing blood (al- An'am 6:145) must be drained out of the carcass, as blood is forbidden.
> • Swine flesh is also forbidden, and it is repeated in few other places in the Qur'an.
> • Forbidden is an animal that has been killed by strangling or by a violent blow, or by a headlong fall.

"Definition of Halal," Halal Food Authority, accessed May 15, 2018, https://www .halalfoodauthority.com/definition-of-halal.

27. "Definition of Halal."

28. Porterfield, Grem, and Corrigan, *Business Turn*, 10.

29. "New 100% Halal."

30. "New 100% Halal."

31. People for the Ethical Treatment of Animals alleges that there were "botched stunning incidents" at the Tama Iowa Premium Beef plant on at least four separate occasions: May 10 and August 1, 7, and 8, 2018. "PETA Calls for Criminal Charges vs. Iowa Premium, Employees," *Tama-Toledo (IA) News Chronicle*, September 15, 2018, https://www.tamatoledonews.com/news/business/2018/09/15/p-e-t-a-calls-for -criminal-charges-vs-iowa-premium-employees/.

32. Temple Grandin, "Euthanasia and Slaughter of Livestock," *Journal of Animal Veterinary Medical Association* 204 (1994): 1355.

33. Nathanael Johnson, "Livestock Expert Temple Grandin on What's Wrong—and Right—with Factory Farming Today," *Vox*, August 12, 2015, https://www.vox.com/2015/8/12/9132717/temple-grandin.

34. Daisy Freund, "How Animal Welfare Leads to Better Meat: A Lesson from Spain," *The Atlantic*, August 25, 2011, https://www.theatlantic.com/health/archive/2011/08/how-animal-welfare-leads-to-better-meat-a-lesson-from-spain/244127/.

35. Karen Ho, *Liquidated: An Ethnography of Wall Street* (Durham: Duke University Press, 2009), 29–30.

36. Charles Hirschkind and Brian Larkin, "Introduction: Media and the Political Forms of Religion," *Social Text* 26, no. 3 (2008): 1.

Chapter 6

1. Since the time of my fieldwork, IPB has been purchased by National Beef, a Kansas-City based company. Ryan McCarthy and Kimberlie Clyma, "National Beef Acquires Iowa Premium," *Meat + Poultry*, March 12, 2019, https://www.meatpoultry.com/articles/21002-national-beef-acquires-iowa-premium.

2. Timothy Pachirat, *Every Twelve Seconds: Industrialized Slaughter and the Politics of Sight* (New Haven: Yale University Press, 2011), 10.

3. Pachirat, 11.

4. Alicia Prygoski, "Brief Summary of Ag-Gag Laws," Michigan State University College of Law, 2015, https://www.animallaw.info/article/brief-summary-of-ag-gag-laws.

5. Prygoski, "Brief Summary of Ag-Gag Laws."

6. Prygoski, "Brief Summary of Ag-Gag Laws." While Iowa, Utah, Missouri, Idaho, and Wyoming impose criminal penalties on those parties in violation of their state's ag-gag laws, North Carolina imposes civil sanctions on those ruled in violation of the ag-gag laws.

7. All animals that are scheduled to be slaughtered in a U.S. facility must receive an ante-mortem inspection. The USDA has clear guidelines for ante-mortem inspections. See "Ante Mortem Inspection," Food Safety and Inspection Service, U.S. Department of Agriculture, December 16, 2014, https://www.fsis.usda.gov/wps/wcm/connect/521b3568-3e3e-4289-8852-37e6ce806867/LSIT_AnteMortem.pdf?MOD=AJPERES.

8. Temple Grandin, "Recommended Captive Bolt Stunning Techniques for Cattle," Dr. Temple Grandin's website, February 2020, https://www.grandin.com/humane/cap.bolt.tips.html.

9. "Meet Mary Temple Grandin, an Autistic Professor and Engineering Hero," *Interesting Engineering*, December 5, 2016, https://interestingengineering.com/meet-temple-grandin-autistic-professor-named-hero-time.

10. Foundation for Meat and Poultry Research Association, "*E. coli* O157:H7," accessed January 11, 2021, http://www.meatpoultryfoundation.org/fact-sheets/e-coli-0157h7.

INDEX

Note: Page numbers in italics refer to illustrative matter.

Abby, 62, 65

Adela, 196, 207–8

Afghan refugees, xii

African American populations: in Iowa towns, 73–74, 76, 109; in meatpacking jobs, 89, 139; racism against, 11–12, 73–74; religious faith of, 107, 108, 113, 233n18; work of, 173, 215. *See also* racism

African Methodist Episcopal Church (AME), 107, 108, 113. *See also* Christianity; Methodists

African refugees, xii; death of, 152–53; languages and, 138, 143, 152, 239n1; in meatpacking jobs, 50, 51, 66, 138, 139, 146, 152–53, 171; workplace religion of, 113, 165–66. *See also names of specific African nations; names of specific persons*

ag-gag laws, 174, 242n6. *See also* animal welfare

agricultural workers: bracero program of, 28; on ethnic white family farms, 11, 17, *18*, 22–23, 30–32, 35–37, 41, 130–34; H-2A visa system for, 47, 67, 233n17; health insurance for, 103, 146, 156–58, 164; health services for, 4, 69, 85–86, 238n26; housing for, 67, 68, 71; job satisfaction of, 142–47, 169, 190; of Latino populations, 27–29, 45, 47–51, 67–68; wages and benefits of, 67, 95, 103, 146; wage theft of, 144–45; workplace religion of, 96–97, 107–21. *See also* health and safety of agricultural workers; meatpacking and processing; migrant populations

Agriprocessors plant, 56, 57, 138, 145, 215

air pollution, 90, 92–94, 96, 142

Alain, 89–91

Alejandro, 209, 210–11, 212–13

All Nations Baptist Church, 105–6, 113

Altar and Rosary Society, 34, 35, 63

Amalgamated Meat Cutters and Butcher Workmen of North America, 147, 215

American Catholicism. *See* Catholicism

American Protective Association, 12

Amos, Martin, 80, 81

angry white racist trope, xvi, 7, 229n14. *See also* racism

animal welfare, 167–68, 174, 177, 241n31. *See also* awareness of animals; slaughter of animals

Ann, 21

anxiety, 54–55, 79, 124, 216

Ardon, Iowa, 11–23, 195. *See also* 76 Township, Iowa

Arkansas, 49, 110

Armstrong, Steve, 140–41, 145, 163, 165

art, 80–81, 132, 133

asylum-seekers/asylees: federal policies on, xi, xi–xii, 225n2, 226n3; as term, 225n1. *See also* migrant populations; refugee populations

autism, 168

awareness of animals, 168, 177–79, 236n24. *See also* animal welfare

Bane, Mary Jo, 62

Baptist Church, 105

Barger, W. K., 28

Batubenga, Maurice, 119

Baumhover, Michelle, 138, 141, 145

beef production: Black Angus cattle, 140–42, 167, 168, 171, 176, 190; CAFOs for, 48, 49; labor conditions in, 171. *See also* Iowa Premium Beef (IPB), Tama, Iowa; meatpacking and processing

Behar, Ruth, 117

Bell, Tom, 68–69

Bell's Melons and Detasseling, 68–69

belonging, 4–5, 25, 50–51, 61–62, 213–14. *See also* citizenship; inclusivity

benefits. *See* wages and benefits

Benita, 101–7

Bhutanese refugees, xii

bilingualism, 59–60, 61–62, 84, 152, 202. *See also* language; Spanish language

Black Americans. *See* African American populations

Black Angus cattle, 140–42, 167, 168, 171, 176, 190. *See also* beef production

Blanchette, Alex, 236n24

Blay, Joe, 96, 107–9, 111, 113–21, 164, 216

blessings, as term, 120, 137, 143, 169, 214

Blessings of Business, The (Grem), 6

"Blood in the Barbecue" (Roof), 238n25

Bodensteiner, Carol, 12–13, 41

bovine spongiform encephalopathy (BSE), 183–84

bracero program, 28. *See also* agricultural workers; H-2A visa system

Brenda, 150–52, 157–58, 196–200

Burmese refugees, xii, 228n14, 231n19; Catholic parishioners of, 59; in Columbus Junction, Iowa, 204–5; health of, 128; housing of, 71; in meatpacking jobs, 50, 58, 138, 139

Burundi refugees, 225n1

business values and service messaging, 111, 112–13, 148, 161–65. *See also* paternalism; stewardship, language of

CAFOs (confined animal feeding operations), xiv, 48–49, 59, 92–93, 142. *See also* beef production; hog production; meatpacking and processing; poultry production; slaughter of animals

California, 225n1

Cambodia, 143

Cambodian refugees, 143, 153, 171

captive bolt gun, 167, 168, 177

Cargill, 52, 145

Carol, 21

carpooling, 104, 138, 146

Carter, Jimmy, xiii, xvii

Cashman, Bartholomew, 19

Catalina, 123–27

Catholic Church Charities, 137

Catholicism, 233n18, 236n7; of Brenda, 196, 199; of Hargrafen family, 11–23, 31–34; of Hook family, 35–36; of Jenny, 132–33; of Joe, 144; of José, 200, 206; of Kieswetter family, 158–61; language and, 47–48, 50–51, 59–65, 78–79, 81, 125, 133; of Lois Mincks, 41, 43; missionaries, 33, 75; parish closures, 19–20, 24–25; in Parnell, Iowa, 23–24; of Rodriguez family, 47, 68–69; of Rosa, 1–3; of Stoller family, 38–40; Vatican II, 14, 75; in Wapello, Iowa, 20, 24–26. *See also* religious faith, overview; Virgen de Guadalupe; workplace religion

Catholic priests, 85–87; Bishop Martin Amos, 80, 81; Bishop Thomas Zinkula, 82; Father Bernie Weir, 52, 53–54, 73–80; Father Greg Steckel, 52, 53, 82–87; Father Joseph Sia, xx, 47, 49, 52, 53, 56–61, 79; Father Rudy Juarez, 52, 53, 80–81. *See also* Catholicism; Latino populations; religious leaders

Cathy, S. Truett, 110

Cati, 1–3

cattle. *See* beef production

Center for American Progress, 147, 240n10

Central African Republic, 128. *See also* African refugees

chicken. *See* poultry production

Chicken (Striffler), 147–48

Chick-fil-A, 110, 113

Chin Burmese refugees, 50, 196, 228n14, 231n19. *See also* Burmese refugees

Christianity: of African refugees, 105–6; AME chaplain Joe Blay, 107–9, 111, 113–21; evangelical Protestants, 6, 55, 97, 101, 110–12, 115, 217, 233n18; Jehovah's Witnesses, xx, 135, 138, 165, 239n1; Lutherans, 12–13, 34; Methodists, xx, 34, 35, 38, 55; Mormons, 55; Muslims relations, 43; Pentecostals, 55, 57, 59, 213; Presbyterians, 34; servant leadership rhetoric of, 161–65. *See also* paternalism; religious faith, overview; workplace religion

Christmas celebrations and rituals, 15

citizenship, xi, 54, 70, 71. *See also* belonging; deportations; vulnerability

Clark, Maura, 75

cognitive dissonance, xvi, 176–77

cold side, 153, 157, 181, 188, 189–94. *See also* meatpacking and processing

collective effervescence, 118

Colonnese, Michael, 24

Colorado, 150–51, 240n17

Columbus Junction, Iowa, xiii, 91, 231n19; economy of, 58–59; education in, 203–5; establishment of, 33; population groups in, xviii, 66, 76–77, 78–79, 215; religious community in, 31–37, 231n19

communitas, 118

compartmentalization, 113, 115, 141–42

ConAgra, 52

condensation position, 138. *See also* meatpacking and processing

Conesville, Iowa, 67–70

confined animal feeding operations. *See* CAFOs

Congolese refugees: Alain, 89–91; death of, 152–53; family structure of, 216; James, 135–38, 142–43, 152; in meatpacking jobs, 144, 146, 152–53, 171. *See also* African refugees; Democratic Republic of the Congo

corn production, 48, 50, 231n1

coronavirus. *See* COVID-19

corporate paternalism, 111, 112, 115–16, 146, 148, 163

Corrigan, John, 162

Council on Foreign Relations (CFR), 225n2

COVID-19, 4, 210, 214–17, 227n7, 238n26

Crazy Horse, 30

Creekstone Farms, 140, 166, 239n4

Cronon, William, 94, 96

Cuban refugees, 144–46

Cullen, Art, 3, 9

Daryl, 153, 155

Defense Production Act, 215

Democratic Republic of the Congo, 128, 135, 138, 143, 165, 239n1. *See also* Congolese refugees

Denison, Iowa, 66, 67. *See also* Iowa Beef Packers, Denison, Iowa

dentician position, 183–84

deportations, 8, 54–58, 138, 209, 211, 233n15. *See also* citizenship

Día de los Muertos, 206

Diefendorf, Karen, 110, 237n18

diet, 69, 105, 110, 127, 175, 176, 192

disease: bovine spongiform encephalopathy (BSE), 183–84; COVID-19, 4, 210, 214–17, 227n7, 238n26; *E. coli* bacteria and, 93, 182; tuberculosis, 127–28, 238n26. *See also* food safety protocols and compliance; health and safety of agricultural workers

Diversity Lottery, 102, 105, 106

Dollar, Creflo, 120

Donovan, Jean, 75

DREAMers, 55. *See also* Latino populations
driver's education, 103, 104, 107
Drucker, Peter, 162
Duncan, Dave, 97–101, 111, 163–64
Duran, José, 60
Durkheim, Emile, 118
Dykstra, Robert R., 73

E. coli bacteria, 93, 182
economic depressions, xvii, 15, 74. *See also* farm crisis (1980s)
economic migrants, as term, xii, 225n2. *See also* migrant populations
Edith, 154, 157, 177
education: of agricultural workers, 91; in Columbus Junction, Iowa, 203–5; in Guatemala, 210; of Irish Catholic children, 15, 23–24; of Mexican migrant children, 28. *See also* teachers
Egert, Clifford A., 31–32, 34
egg production, 48
Eloida, 183
El Salvador. *See* Salvadoran refugees
emotional violence. *See* violence
employment visas, 47, 67, 213, 233n17
English language. *See* language
environmental impact of CAFOs, 48, 92–94, 136, 142
Environmental Working Group, 93
Eritrean refugees, xii. *See also* African refugees
Esmerelda, 95, 121–22
Est8 brand, 191. *See also* Iowa Premium Beef (IPB), Tama, Iowa
ethanol, 48, 93, 231n2
Ethiopian refugees, xii
"ethnic belonging," as term, 50–51. *See also* belonging
ethnic whites. *See* white Americans
evangelical Protestant Christianity, 6, 55, 97, 101, 110–12, 115, 217, 233n18. *See also* Christianity; paternalism
exsanguination, 167–68, 178

Faith at Work programs, 96–97, 109, 110–11, 113. *See also* workplace religion
family values rhetoric of corporations, 111, 112–13, 148. *See also* paternalism; servant leadership rhetoric of corporations; stewardship, language of
farm crisis (1980s), xvii, 23, 74, 149, 226n9. *See also* economic depressions
farming: by ethnic white families, 11, 17, 18, 22–23, 30–32, 35–37, 41, 130–34; 4-H program on, 41, 130, 161; impacts of, 48; monoculture of, 51; as self-employment system, 51. *See also* agricultural workers; beef production; corn production; hog production
farmworkers. *See* agricultural workers
feminist movement, 187
Fidencio, 122–25
Filipino Catholicism, 56–57
Fink, Deborah, 51–52, 67
food safety protocols and compliance, 150, 152, 177, 181–87, 193. *See also* disease; health and safety of agricultural workers
football, 204
Ford, Gerald, xiii
Ford, Ita, 75
forklift position, 144
4-H program, 41, 130, 161
Francis (pope), 89
French language, 97, 103, 115, 138, 152
frugality, 35–36
Fry, Hayden, 52
Furlong, Mike, 22, 26–30
fútbol, 119, 164, 200, 204
Future Farmers of America, 161

Gager, Mikel "Mike," 175, 180, 181, 182
gangs, xiii, 1, 55, 102, 151, 210, 240n17. *See also* violence
gardening, 24, 25, 38, 71, 130–31, 209, 210
Gary, 22, 29
GEAR UP (Gaining Early Awareness

and Readiness for Undergraduate Programs), 205
gender expectations. *See* women and girls
"general farm," as term, 17
Global Food Safety System, 181
Gordon, Colin, 144, 239n6
Gordon, Linda, 11
Grandin, Temple, 167, 168, 177, 178
Greeley, Colorado, 150–51, 240n17
Green, Emma, 109
Greenleaf, Robert, 162
Grem, Darren E., 162
groundwater pollution, 92–94, 136, 142
Grupo de Oraciones, 125–26
Guadalupana Society, 127
Guatemala, 209, 210
Guatemalan refugees, xii, 56, 123, 207, 209–14
Gunner, 153, 155–56
Guymon, Oklahoma, 215

H-2A visa system, 47, 67, 233n17. *See also* agricultural workers
H-2B visa system, 233n17
halal certified beef, 166–68, 241n26
Halal Food Authority, 167, 241n26
Halal Transactions of Omaha, 167
Hanson, Steve, 83, 162
Hargrafen family, 11–20, 24, 31–32, 40, 44. *See also* Mincks, Lois Hargrafen
Hayes, Ralph L., 32
head dropper position, 103–4. *See also* hog production
health and safety of agricultural workers: BSE and, 183–84; COVID-19 and, 4, 210, 214–17, 227n7; *E. coli* bacteria and, 93, 182; at IPB, 145, 153–55, 172–73, 186–89, 194; physical effects of meatpacking work, 98, 112, 124, 143, 171, 208; psychological effects of meatpacking work, 114–15, 117, 122; tuberculosis and, 127–29, 238n26; at Tyson,
4, 97, 124, 129–30, 216, 227n7. *See also* food safety protocols and compliance
health services, 4, 69, 85–86, 238n26. *See also* insurance; wages and benefits
Heartland (Smarsh), xiv
Heinz Company, 27–28
Heritage Foundation, 147
Hirschkind, Charles, 169
Ho, Karen, 169
hog production: CAFOs for, 48, 49, 92; description of Tyson plant, 97–101; environmental damage by, 92–94; integration system of, 94–95, 97; job descriptions in, 103–4, 122, 124; at Rath Packing Company, 33; smell of, 90, 96, 97; by white rural farmers, 130–34. *See also* meatpacking and processing
Holly Farms, 148
Honduran refugees, xii, 128
Hook, Bob, 34–37
Hook, Lorraine Gaunya, 34–37
Hoover, Brett, 53, 85, 236n7
Hoover, Bruce, 53
Hornick, Douglas, 128–29
hotel workers, 121, 150
hot side, 153, 154, 166, 175–86. *See also* meatpacking and processing
household chores, 12–13, 17, 18, 29, 31, 40–41
housing conditions of agricultural workers, 67, 68, 71. *See also* agricultural workers
humane killing. *See* animal welfare; slaughter of animals
Human Rights Watch, 233n15
hunger, 135, 136

ICE. *See* Immigration and Customs Enforcement (ICE)
Idaho, 174, 234n20
IEH Laboratory and Consulting Group, 182

Illinois: corn production in, 48, 231n1; farming in, 159; meatpacking plants of, 151; population groups in, 3–4, 225n1, 234n20

Immigration Act (1965), 54

Immigration and Customs Enforcement (ICE): migrant education on, 52, 53; raids by, 8, 56–58, 138, 150, 215

inclusivity, 61–67, 77, 80, 94. *See also* belonging

Indiana, 231n1; author's background in, 19, 141; corn production in, 48, 231n1; farming families of, 140, 158; meatpacking and processing in, 91, 101; population groups in, 234n20

insurance, 103, 146, 156–58, 164. *See also* health services; wages and benefits

Iowa, xiii–xv; ag-gag laws in, 174; environmental pollution in, 92–94; farming overview, 231n1, 232n8; hog production overview, 91–92, 94, 101; population overview, xii–xiii, 3–4, 8, 9–10, 225n1, 231n17. *See also* hog production; meatpacking and processing; *names of specific cities and churches*

Iowa Beef Packers, Denison, Iowa, 52, 76, 112, 141, 149. *See also* beef production; meatpacking and processing

Iowa City, Iowa, 80–82, 83, 104, 105–6

Iowa City Center for Worker Justice, 211–12

Iowan American Protective Association, 12

Iowa Policy Project, 144

Iowa Premium Beef (IPB), Tama, Iowa, 139; cold side description at, 189–94; environmental policies by, 94; Est8 brand, 191; focus on transparency of, 191–92; halal certified beef by, 166–68, 241n26; health and safety at, 145, 153–55, 172–73, 186–89, 194; hot side description at, 175–86; National Beef Packing purchase of, 239n3, 242n1;

new hire training of, 152, 153–56; PETA on, 241n31; as research site, xx, 172; values and service rhetoric of, 112, 148, 161–65; workers at, 137–38, 139–40. *See also* beef production; meatpacking and processing

Iowa Press-Citizen (publication), 80

Iowa Select (company), 93

Iowa Sends Help to Aid Refugees and End Starvation (SHARES) program, xiii

Iowa SHARES program, xiii

IPB. *See* Iowa Premium Beef (IPB), Tama, Iowa

Irish Catholic families: family life of, 15–17; farming by, 11, 17, *18*, 22–23, 30–32; migrant farm labor for, 27–29, 45; religious culture of, 12–15, 17–27, 195. *See also* Catholicism; white Americans

Islam, 165–67, 241n26. *See also* Muslims

James, 135–38, 142–43, 152, 165

Javier, 197, 198

JBS plant (formerly Swift), Marshalltown, Iowa, 143, 196, 197, 215

Jehovah's Witnesses, xx, 135, 138, 165, 239n1. *See also* Christianity

Jenny, 130–34

Jessica, 182–83

Jewish community, 56, 241n26

job satisfaction. *See* worker satisfaction

Joe, 143–44

Johnson, Jeffrey, 140, 141, 145, 162

Johnson-Reed Act (1924), 54

Jones, Christopher, 94

José, 8, 144–46, 196, 200–207

Josepha, 122

Juan (Esmerelda's husband), 95, 121–22

Juan (Rosa's husband), 1, 2

Juarez, Rudy, 52, 53, 80–81

Julie, 21, 36

Justin, 130, 131

JW Vittetoe Pork, Ltd., 131

Kaell, Hillary, 22

Kane, Paula, 14

Kansas, 3–4, 91, 149

Kansas State University, 181, 191

Kazel, Dorothy, 75

Kelsey, 181–82, 188–89

Kieswetter family, 158–61

killing of animals. See meatpacking and processing; slaughter of animals; violence

Kingdom Hall of Jehovah Witnesses. See Jehovah's Witnesses

KKK (Klu Klux Klan), 11–12

Knights of Columbus, 124, 125, 127

Labor Management Relations Act (1935), 147

language: of African refugees, 138, 143, 152, 239n1; bilingualism, 59–60, 61–62, 84, 152, 202; of Catholic mass, 14, 47–48, 59–64, 78–79, 133; driver's education and, 107; French, 97, 103, 115, 138, 152; meatpacking positions and, 97, 103, 104, 138, 152; monolingualism, 64, 229n14; of Reyna's family, 209–10, 211; school programs on, 83–84; staff training and, 152; workplace ministry and, 115. See also Spanish language

Larkin, Brian, 169

Latin language, 14

Latino populations: as agricultural workers, 27–29, 45, 47–51, 67–68; as caregivers and nursing assistants, 62, 228n14; Catholicism of, 1–3, 47, 50–51, 81, 233n18; in Columbus Junction, Iowa, 203, 204–5; fear of deportation and liminality of, 54–55; growth of, 65, 234n20; housing of, 67, 68, 71; in meatpacking jobs, 49, 51, 171; Spanish-language Catholic mass for, 47–48, 50–51, 59–65, 78–79, 133; statistics on, 55, 95, 235n28; voting activities of, 55–56; youth and employment, 60. See

also Catholic priests; migrant populations; migration stories; and names of specific nationalities and names of specific persons

League of United Latin American Citizens (LULAC), 28, 51, 55–56, 205

Lee, Isaac, 19

Lew, Thomas, 32

Lewis, C. S., 117

Liberian refugees, 138. See also African refugees

Lillis, Ann, 23–24

linguistic differences. See language

LOTO procedures, 187–88. See also health and safety of agricultural workers

Luís, 122

Lutherans, 12–13, 34. See also Christianity

mad cow disease, 183–84

malnutrition, 135, 136

Manfra, Jo Ann, 12

María. See Virgen de Guadalupe

Market Facilitation Program, xvii

Marshalltown, Iowa, xviii, 66, 143

Masour, Jess, 93

Matteo, 67

Maurice, 101–7, 113

Mazzuchelli, Samuel Charles, 33, 34

McDonald, Bill, 24

meatpacking and processing: ag-gag laws on, 174, 242n6; cold side, 153, 157, 181, 188, 189–94; corporatization of, 52; environmental pollutions from, 90, 92–94; Father Joseph's description of, 57–58; hot side, 153, 154, 166, 175–86; job descriptions at, 103–4, 111–12, 122, 124, 138, 142, 144, 153; physical effects of, 98, 112, 124, 143, 171, 208; prevalence of, 48–49; producer vs. processor distinctions, 52, 54, 115, 161; psychological effects of, 114–15, 117, 122;

meatpacking and processing (*continued*) smell of, 90, 96, 97, 186, 236n10; vertical integration system of, 94–95, 97, 148, 169; violence and death at, 56, 111–13, 114, 117–18, 154; as wage labor system, 51–52. *See also* agricultural workers; beef production; hog production; poultry production; slaughter of animals; *and names of specific companies*

Mein, Tricia, 53

melon harvesting, 68

Mendoza, Louis, 50

Meskwaki, 139, 144

Methodists, xx, 34, 35, 38, 55. *See also* African Methodist Episcopal Church (AME); Christianity

Mexican refugees and migrant workers: in Columbus Junction, Iowa, 200–208; ICE raid of, 56; migration stories of, 1–3; on small farms, 27–29; tuberculosis and, 128; Virgen de Guadalupe and, 1, 2, 47, 81, 125–27, 199, 206, 208. *See also* Latino populations; *and names of specific persons*

migrant populations: as agricultural workers, 67–70; Catholic priests as supporters of, 52–54; deportations of, 8, 54–58, 138, 209, 211, 233n15; federal policies on, xi–xii, 226n3; ICE raids on, 8, 56–58, 138, 150; inclusivity and social justice for, 61–67; interfaith coalition support for, 58–61; patterns of, 7–8, 49–50, 91–92, 149–50, 195–96; pro-immigration rallies for, 52, 53, 56; remittances by, 95, 111, 121, 145, 197; rural revitalization due to, 50, 92, 121; secondary paths of, 7–8, 202, 225n1; temporary farmworkers, 47, 68–69; term defined, 225n2; work visas for, 47, 67, 213, 233n17. *See also* agricultural workers; asylum-seekers/asylees; Latino populations; refugee populations; *and names of specific nationalities*

Migration Policy Institute, 7

migration stories: of Benita and Maurice, 101–3; of Brenda, 150–51; of Father Joseph Sia, 56–57; of James, 135–37; of Reyna and Alejandro, 209–11; of Rosa, 1–3; of secondary migrations, 7–8, 197, 202, 225n1; of temporary farmworkers, 47, 68–69. *See also* migrant populations

Miguel, 199–200

military service, 107–9, 114, 117–18, 156, 180

Miller, David W., 110, 113

Min, 143

Mincks, Lois Hargrafen, 17, 40–45

Mincks, Tim, 41, 42, 43, 44

mining, 73

Minnesota, 91, 231n1

missionaries, 33, 75. *See also* Catholicism

Missouri, 174

monoculture, 51. *See also* farming

monolingualism, 64, 229n14. *See also* language

Moore, Lawrence, 163

Mora, Jenny, 166

Mormons, 55

Mount Pleasant, Iowa, 8

Mugereke, Mugombekere. *See* James

Munhusen, Susan, 186–88

murals, 80–81, 133

murder. *See* violence

Muscatine Journal, 68

Muscatine Migrant Council, 28

Muslims: Christians relations, 43; halal certified beef for, 166–68, 241n26; meatpacking work by, 165–66; U.S. population growth of, 55

Myanmar. *See* Burmese refugees

Mycobacterium tuberculosis. See tuberculosis (TB)

Nabhan, Gary Paul, xix–xx

Nam, 143, 153

National Angus Association, 161

National Beef Packing (company), 239n3, 242n1
Native American agricultural workers, 139
Nebraska, 3–4, 91, 149, 231n1
New Jersey, 225n1
Nikuzi, Aziza, 152–53
No Closure (Seitz), 24
North American Meat Institute, 182
North Carolina, 91, 174
North Liberty, Iowa, 103, 104–5
Novak, Nicole, 8

Obama, Barack, xvii
O'Brien, Jean, 24
Occupational Safety and Health Administration (OSHA), 186, 193
O'Connor, Agnes, 19, 20, 22, 24–25
ofrenda, 206
Oglala Lakota, 30
Ohio, 91
O'Keefe, Gerald, 75, 76
Oklahoma, 215
Oregon, 102, 106, 234n20
OSHA, 186, 193
Ossian, Lisa Lynn, 17
O'Toole family, 11, 13, 19, 30, 36, 45
Ottumwa, Iowa, xviii, 66, 92

Pachirat, Timothy, 173
Pakistani refugees, xii
parish closures, 19–20, 24–25. *See also* Catholicism
Parnell, Iowa, 23–24
paternalism, 111, 112, 115–16, 146, 148, 163. *See also* family values rhetoric of corporations
Payne, Kate, 225n1
Pentecostals, 55, 57, 59, 213. *See also* Christianity
PETA (People for the Ethical Treatment of Animals), 241n31
physical effects of meatpacking work, 98, 112, 124, 143, 171, 208. *See also* health

and safety of agricultural workers; meatpacking and processing
physical violence. *See* violence
pigs. *See* hog production
pork. *See* hog production
Porterfield, Amanda, 162
posadas, 125–26
Postville, Iowa, 8, 56–57, 138, 145, 215
poultry production, 48, 49, 94, 110, 129, 148, 177. *See also* meatpacking and processing
Presbyterians, 34. *See also* Christianity
Prestage Foods, 94
priests. *See* Catholic priests
process monitoring position, 182–83
producers *vs.* processors of protein industry, 52, 54, 115, 161. *See also* meatpacking and processing
pro-immigration rallies, 52, 53, 56. *See also* migrant populations
pro-people rhetoric of corporations, 111, 112–13, 148
Protestants. *See* Christianity; evangelical Protestant Christianity
Prygoski, Alicia, 174
psychological effects of meatpacking work, 114–15, 117, 122. *See also* health and safety of agricultural workers; meatpacking and processing; physical effects of meatpacking work
Purcell, William, 19, 26

Q'anjob'al, 209–10
Quality Assurance department, 150, 152, 177, 191–93
Qur'an, 166–67, 241n26. *See also* Muslims

racism, xv–xvi, 7; angry white racist trope, xvi, 7, 229n14; against Black Americans, 11–12, 73–74; against immigrant populations, 54–55, 62–63, 203, 204–5. *See also* African American populations; white Americans; white privilege

rage, 228n14

railroad, 33

rape. *See* violence

Rath Packing Company, 33, 76. *See also* Iowa Beef Packers, Denison, Iowa; Tyson Foods, Inc.

Raúl, 154, 157, 177, 178–79

Ray, Robert, xiii, xvi

Reagan Republicanism, xvii

"Redneck Revival" festival, 70

Reformed Church, 34

Refugee Act (1980), xii, xiii

refugee camps, 135–37, 239n1

refugee populations: as CAFO laborers, 48–51; Catholic priests as supporters of, 52–54, 55, 56–58; deportations of, 8, 54–58, 138, 209, 211, 233n15; description of life in refugee camp, 135–37; federal policies on, xi–xiii, 225n2, 226n3; life in home countries of, xii–xiii; overview of Iowan, xvii–xxii; rural revitalization due to, 50, 92, 121; term defined, 225n1. *See also* asylum-seekers/asylees; migrant populations; *and names of specific persons*

religious faith, overview, xiv–xv, xx–xxi, xxi, 4–7, 169. *See also* Catholicism; Christianity; Islam; workplace religion

religious leaders: on inclusivity and social justice for Latino community, 61–67; interfaith coalition on migrant support, 58–61; sexual abuse by, 20, 81. *See also* Catholic priests; *and names of specific persons*

remittances, 95, 111, 121, 145, 197

Republican Party, xvi, xvii

research strategy, xix–xxi, 4, 49, 172, 174, 236n10

Reyna, 209–14, 218

Reza, Ernesto M., 28

right-to-work, 49, 67, 76, 92, 147–49, 215, 216. *See also* unionization

Rodriguez family, 47, 68–69

Romero, Oscar, 75

Rosa, 1–3

Rosaldo, Renato, 4

running, 200, 201, 202–3

Russian refugees, xii

safety. *See* food safety protocols and compliance; health and safety of agricultural workers

Salvadoran refugees, xii

schools. *See* education

Scott, 153, 156–57, 158

Seaboard Triumph, 94

secondary migration, 7–8, 197, 202, 225n1. *See also* migrant populations; migration stories; refugee populations

Seitz, John, 24

"Servant Leadership" (Greenleaf), 162

servant leadership rhetoric of corporations, 161–65. *See also* family values rhetoric of corporations; stewardship, language of

Sessions, Jeff, 55

Seven Habits of Highly Effective People (Covey), 162

76 Township, Iowa, 19–20, 22, 26, 195. *See also* St. Malachy parish, Ardon, Iowa

sexual violence. *See* violence

shaving hogs position, 124

Sia, Joseph, 49; friendships of, 119, 205–6; ministry work of, xx, 47, 52, 53, 56–61, 79; Tyson plant tour of, 96–97

Sinclair, Upton, 94, 97

Sinnwell, Emily, 212

Sioux City, Iowa, 20

Skaggs, Jimmy, 149

slaughterhouses. *See* meatpacking and processing

slaughter of animals: humane practices of, 167–68, 174, 177, 241n31; job descriptions of, 175–86; psychological effects of, 114–15, 117–18; sacralization of, xxi, 5, 87, 112, 118; smell of, 90, 96, 97, 186, 236n10; violence of, 56, 111–13, 114, 118, 154. *See also* animal welfare; beef production; hog production; meatpacking and processing; poultry production; violence

Smarsh, Sarah, xiv

smell, 90, 96, 97, 186, 236n10

Smithfield, 215

smoking, 181

soccer (*fútbol*), 119, 164, 200, 204

Social Responsibilities of the Businessman (Bowen), 162

soil contamination, 92–94, 142

Somalian refugees, xii, 165–66, 171. *See also* African refugees

South Africa, 101, 105

South African refugees, xx, 101–5, 137

South Dakota, 30, 48, 49, 91, 231n1

sow caregiver position, 122. *See also* hog production

soybean production, 48

Spanish language: Catholic mass in, 47–48, 59–60, 61–62, 78–79, 133; Father Bernie's experience with, 77; Father Greg's experience with, 82–83. *See also* bilingualism; language

Speed, Shannon, 3

sports: football, 204; running, 200, 201, 202–3; soccer (*fútbol*), 119, 164, 200, 204

St. Bridget's Church, Postville, Iowa, 56

Steckel, Greg, 52, 53, 82–87

stewardship, language of, 161, 168–69, 239n4. *See also* business values and service messaging

Stewart, John, 140

St. Joseph Catholic Church, Parnell, Iowa, 23–24

St. Joseph the Worker parish, Columbus Junction, Iowa, 126; immigrant groups of, 1–3, 50–51; priests of, 57, 59, 76–77;

rebuilding of, 31–33; Virgen de Guadalupe celebration at, 125–26; white families of, 20–21, 24–25, 38–40, 132–33

St. Malachy parish, Ardon, Iowa, 13–15, 17–27, 50, 195, 230n8

St. Malachy Preservation Society, 19, 21–22, 27, 195

St. Mary's parish, Wapello, Iowa, 20, 24–25

Stoller, Gail, 37–40

Storm Lake, Iowa, 66

St. Paul's United Methodist Church, Iowa, 225n1

Striffler, Steve, 147–48

Sudanese refugees, xii, 138; in meatpacking jobs, 139, 146, 165–66; workplace religion of, 113, 165–66. *See also* African refugees

Swift. *See* JBS plant (formerly Swift), Marshalltown, Iowa

Syrian refugees, xii

Taft-Hartley Act (1947), 147

Tai Dam. *See* Vietnamese refugees

Takenaka, Ayumi, 7

Tama, Iowa, xviii, 141. *See also* Iowa Premium Beef (IPB), Tama, Iowa

Tarahumara, 201

tariffs, xvii

Tarvin, Mike, 110

Taylor, Frederick Winslow, 100

TB (tuberculosis), 127–29, 238n26

TBI Capital, LLC, 140, 141

teachers, 15, 132, 135. *See also* education

temporary farmworkers, 47, 68–69. *See also* migrant populations

Tennessee, 225n1

Thai refugees, 215

Throne, Mildred, 232n8

Tongogara refugee camp, Zimbabwe, 135–37, 239n1. *See also* African refugees

torture. *See* violence

To Serve God and Wal-Mart (Moreton), 6, 162
trabajadores. See agricultural workers
translator position, 103, 104, 138, 142. *See also* language; meatpacking and processing
transportation, 69, 104, 105, 106, 146
Trump, Donald J.: administration policies of, 86, 215, 216–17, 226n3; election and rhetoric of, xvi–xvii, 56, 63
tuberculosis (TB), 127–29, 238n26
turkey. *See* poultry production
Turner, Victor, 118
Tyson family, 110, 148
Tyson Foods, Inc., 33, 76, 96; company success of, 110, 148; description of plant, 97–101, 109; health and safety policies of, 4, 97, 124, 129–30, 216, 227n7; hiring practices of, 58, 215; as research site, xx, 49; values and service rhetoric of, 111, 112–13, 148, 161–65; wages and benefits at, 103, 234n22; workplace religion at, 96–97, 109, 110–11. *See also* meatpacking and processing

Ukrainian refugees, xii
unionization, 52, 147–48, 215. *See also* right-to-work
United Packinghouse Workers of America, 215
USDA inspector, 190–91, 193
Utah, 174

Vatican II, 14, 75. *See also* Catholicism
Vega, Sujey, 51, 65, 232n7
Verariya, Nifasha, 225n1
Verhoesen, Roger, 190, 191–93
vertical integration system, 94–95, 97, 148, 169. *See also* meatpacking and processing
Vietnamese refugees, xiii, 128, 171, 228n14
vineyard, 27–29

violence: by Catholic priests, 20, 81; deportation and, 233n15; by gangs, xiii, 1, 55, 102, 151, 210, 240n17; ICE raids and, 8, 56–58, 138, 150; at meatpacking and processing plants, 56, 111–12, 114, 117–18, 154; migration and, 3, 55, 71, 101, 102, 105, 196, 233n15; in military service, 114, 117–18; in South Africa, 102, 105. *See also* slaughter of animals
Virgen de Guadalupe, 1, 2, 47, 81, 125–27, 199, 200, 206, 208. *See also* Catholicism
Vittetoe, Heidi, 131
voting campaigns, 55–56
vulnerability, xxi, 3, 4, 52, 67, 77, 117. *See also* asylum-seekers/asylees; citizenship; health and safety of agricultural workers; migrant populations; refugee populations

wages and benefits, 67, 95, 103, 146, 157–58, 234n22, 239n6. *See also* health services; insurance
wage theft, 144–45, 239n6
Wannamaker's Temple (Kirk), 6
water pollution, 92–94, 136, 142
Weaver, Janet, 28
Weir, Bernie, 52, 53–54, 73–80
West Liberty, Iowa, xiii, xviii, 66, 82–83, 85
white Americans: angry white racist trope about, xvi, 7, 229n14; family life of, 15–17; Mexican agricultural workers and, 27–29; overview of Iowan, xiv–xvi; racism of, xvi, 216–17; religious culture of, xiv–xv, xx–xxi, 4–7, 12–15, 17–27, 169, 195; response to demographic changes by, xv–xvi, 228n14, 229n18; small family farming by, 11, 17, 18, 22–23, 30–32, 35–37, 41, 130–34; support of immigrant persons by, 211–12. *See also* racism; *and names of specific persons*
white privilege: acceptance of recent *vs.*

earlier immigrants and, 71; author's positionality of, xix; Catholic parishes and, 64–65; family farms and, 18, 70; Father Bernie on, 77–78; Trump and, xvi–xvii, 63, 216–17. *See also* racism

Wirth, Danielle, 93

women and girls: Catholic culture on, 14–15, 39–40; homemaking role of, 12–13, 17, 18, 29, 31, 40–41, 74, 132; working lives of, 29, 39, 40, 74, 130–31, 132, 150–51, 187, 212, 213

worker satisfaction, 142–47, 169, 190. *See also* agricultural workers

workplace religion, xvii–xviii, 5–6, 96–97, 107–21, 165–70. *See also* religious faith, overview

work visas, 47, 67, 213, 233n17

World Health Organization, 128, 238n26

Wright, Robert, 163

Wuthnow, Robert, 4, 49, 51, 231n3

Wyoming, 174, 234n20, 242n6

Yolanda, 197–99

Zinkula, Thomas, 82